Getting Out

GETTING OUT

Life Stories of Women

Who Left Abusive Men

ANN GOETTING

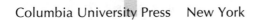

Columbia University Press   New York

COLUMBIA UNIVERSITY PRESS
Publishers Since 1893
New York Chichester, West Sussex
Copyright © 1999 Columbia University Press

Library of Congress
Cataloging-in-Publication Data
Goetting, Ann.
Getting out : life stories of women who
left abusive men / Ann Goetting.
p.   cm.
Includes bibliographical references.
ISBN 0–231–11648–9 (cloth : alk. paper).
ISBN 0–231–11649–7 (pbk. : alk. paper).
1. Abused women—United States—Psychology.
2. Family violence—United States.
3. Abusive men—United States—Psychology.
4. Battered woman syndrom—United States.
I. Title.
HV6626.2G65   1999
362.82'92'0973—dc21   99–21257

Printed in the United States of America
Design by Audrey Smith

c 10 9 8 7 6 5 4 3 2 1
p 10 9 8 7 6 5 4 3 2 1

This book is dedicated to

Louise Ann Bolinger
&
Kathleen Mary Goetting

Contents

PART III A TWO-TIMING BATTERER

Men batter the women in their lives differently. This section highlights that reality with the case of a man who concurrently battered his wife and his extramarital lover.

PART IV FAMILY AND FRIENDS TO THE RESCUE

Battered women can be liberated by family and friends who support and do not blame them.

PART V FACES OF SHELTER LIFE

Women's shelters are structured and work in different ways to assist escape.

PART VI WHEN THE SYSTEM WORKS
Sociopolitical structures other than shelters, informal as well as formal, can help battered women leave.

This is the tale of a Mormon woman abused by a professional athlete. The case and its jury trial drew national media attention. Colorado's mandatory reporting and arrest laws helped liberate her from abuse.

This woman's life demonstrates the intersection of class, race, homosexuality, and abuse. A shelter, in conjunction with food stamps, welfare, and transitional housing programs, allowed her and her children to escape their abuser.

This woman's story includes devastating losses: a mother's suicide and a young daughter's death by accident. Her tiny community mobilized an informal network of donated services to help her leave her abuser.

PART VII LEGACIES OF LOSS AND DEATH
These are stories of women who escaped battering, but at significant personal expense or with great loss.

This Puerto Rican–American woman relinquished custody of her children in order to escape her Vietnam veteran husband.

As a final gesture of control, the husband of this "preacher's kid" hanged himself where she was certain to discover his remains. She lives with that image of his death.

This is the story of a homeless African-American mother of five who contracted HIV from her abuser.

Acknowledgments

My deep appreciation goes to the sixteen women who told their life stories for this book so that others could profit from their experience. Several others generously contributed their talents, wisdom, and care to the benefit of this volume. My heartfelt thanks go to Chris Womendez for locating Freda and serving as a critical liaison during my work with her. My friend Micah Kleit offered superb council and continuous support throughout the preparation of this manuscript. The congenial staff of the offices of the Sociology Department at Western Kentucky University make my best work possible; thank you to Julie Raffaelli Ranger, Gina Raffaelli, Kim Edwards, Kim Brown, Jennifer Lee, Bridget Brown, and Susie Cunningham.

Getting Out

Thinking Through the Heart

This book is about battered women who safely and permanently leave their abusers. As scholarly research and media attention continue to inform us about woman abuse at the hands of male partners—its prevalence, its patterns, its dynamics—critical questions stubbornly persist among much of the general population. Probably the most common inquiries about woman abuse focus on the battered woman herself: What kind of woman gets into an abusive relationship? How does she connect with an abuser in the first place? Why does she stay after he hurts her? Why does she go back after she does get away? How does she finally get out for good? This book is designed to address these and other questions by probing into the life histories of a diverse collection of sixteen American women.

VIOLENCE AGAINST WOMEN BY MALE PARTNERS

For countless women intimacy with a man becomes a devastating encounter with betrayal, humiliation, shame, degradation, and fear. For some the abuse extends to include physical violence. Based on self-report information collected annually by the Federal Bureau of Investigation, the United States National Crime Victimization Survey estimates that in 1996 women suffered 837,899 violent crime victimizations at the hands of current or former boyfriends and husbands (Greenfield et al. 1998:3). Social scientists suspect that these self-report figures are dramatic underestimates—that many more women are not admitting their physical abuse to researchers and perhaps even to themselves. Documentation from a variety of sources attests to the critical nature of intimate violence against women and its consequences. James Mercy and Linda Saltzman (1989), researchers with the Centers for Disease Control and Prevention, have determined that the leading cause of injury to U.S. women is intimate partner violence. Jacqueline Campbell and Daniel Sheridan (1989) report that approximately 20–50 percent of all female medical emergency patients are battered women, and Murray Straus (1986) estimates that women make 1,453,437 medical visits per year for treatment of injuries resulting from an assault by a spouse.

Sometimes we hear reference to battered men or abusive wives. Conventional wisdom and some scholars would have us believe that men and women are comparably evil and violent in intimate relationships or even that women are more dangerous than men. There is talk that, for purposes of policy and prevention, we need show no favoritism toward women victims because they bring it on themselves. It is important to understand that spouse abuse is executed predominantly by men and that it is the man's brutality that underlies most intimate partner violence, even that perpetrated by women. The notion that there exists gender symmetry in partner violence is a myth supported by the underdeveloped interpretations of two distinct lines of evidence: survey results derived from the Conflict Tactics Scales (CTS) and homicide data (Dobash et al. 1992:74).

The CTS instrument was designed to accommodate two national United States surveys, conducted in 1975 and 1985, asking married and cohabiting persons about their behavior during arguments over the previous year. These National Family Violence Surveys were consistent in reporting the rate of partner assault by women to be commensurate with that of men. For example, the 1985 survey found 11.6 percent of men and 12.4 percent of women to have assaulted their spouses that year (Straus and Gelles 1990: 97). Based on these rather symmetrical figures, Murray Straus (1977–78:447–448), a principal investigator, concluded that "violence between husband and wife is far from a one-way street." At least thirty other surveys using the CTS in the United States and Canada have replicated the finding that women are about as violent as their male partners (Dobash et al. 1992:73; Straus 1993).

But the information yielded by the CTS can be misleading because that instrument conceptualizes partner violence in a way that favors men: a violent spouse is one who, over that study year, engaged in at least one of a list of behaviors including, but not limited to, pushing, slapping, shoving, throwing things, kicking, biting, choking, and threatening with a knife or gun. A person who threw a vase in self-defense, or threw it angrily in retaliation, missing the target, with neither partner considering that act to be an assault, is just as much counted a violent spouse by the CTS as one who punched a mate unconscious. The rates of intimate partner assault yielded by the CTS fail to consider context, consequence, and the motivations and interpretations of the men and women under study. Many more acts carried out by women than men that are counted as assaults by the CTS are not considered such by the men and women involved and do not cause injury. This is how results of studies based on the CTS perpetuate the myth of gender symmetry in partner violence.

Any argument that men and women contribute comparably to partner violence must either dismiss or ignore the preponderance of information to the contrary. Evidence from criminal and divorce courts, police, medical, and social service agencies, and surveys asking respondents to recall incidents that they considered to be violent (rather than employing the CTS) finds women far more likely than men to be victims of partner violence (Dobash et al. 1992:82). Consider, for example, the fact that the National Crime Victimization Survey (cited earlier) estimates that in 1996 there were about a million rapes, sexual assaults, robberies, aggravated assaults, and simple assaults perpetrated against current or former spouses, boyfriends, and girlfriends, and that more than 80 percent of these violent crimes involved a female victim (Greenfield et al. 1998:vii). From all information available we can fairly conclude that even though similar proportions of men and women may engage in at least one of the angry or defensive acts toward mates outlined by the CTS, when context, participant interpretation, and injury are considered, between 80 percent and 95 percent of offensive intimate partner violence is perpetrated by men (Dobash et al. 1992:74–75; Greenfield et al. 1998:vii).

The second line of evidence that has been invoked to support the claim that intimate partner violence is not gendered in any important way relates to lethal outcomes. During the two decades between 1976 and 1996, 31,269 women in the United States were killed by current or former husbands and boyfriends; 20,311 men in the United States were killed by current or former wives and girl-friends (Greenfield et al. 1998:6). Left to the devices of the unin-formed, these figures are interpreted as evidence that both men and women are fatally abusive but that men are just over one-and-a-half times more abusive than women. That is not true, however. Men typically kill women as an act of dominance and control, while women typically kill men while defending self, children, or both. Acts looked upon as similar by the United States Department of Jus-tice are not similar at all when meaning and context are considered.

BATTERING TAKES TWO: A MAN AND A PATRIARCHY

Beating is not synonymous with battering, though it can be a part of the battering experience. Battering is an obsessive campaign of coercion and intimidation designed by a man to dominate and con-trol a woman, which occurs in the personal context of intimacy and thrives in the sociopolitical climate of patriarchy. For the woman it is a terrifying process of progressive entrapment into an intimate relationship of subjection that is promoted and preserved by a social order steeped in gender hierarchy—where mainstream ide-ology and social institutions and organizations, including the crim-inal justice system, the church, social service and medical institu-tions, the family, and the community, recognize male privilege and accordingly relegate a secondary status to women.

Sometimes physical violence is incorporated into the battering agenda. When less risky intimidation strategies such as yelling, threatening, stalking, and harming the family pet fail, a man may have to resort to assaulting his mate—with all implied potential for serious injury or even death—in order to maintain control over her. In the face of defiance or even simple resistance on the part of the woman, he may feel forced to appeal to her most basic need for physical safety. That is what battering is all about: a man using male privilege derived from a patriarchal social structure to coerce a woman, sometimes through fear for her very life, into an exploitive intimate relationship that holds her hostage and in servitude to his personal needs and desires. With the weight of society behind him, a man is able to gain deference, and all that goes with it, from a woman.

A batterer may speak of killing "his woman" and sometimes in a violent rage bring her near to death. These near-fatal incidents are deliberate and desperate reminders to her of his ultimate power. The man does not really want the woman to die: she is his lifeline, after all. What he hopes to accomplish is to convince her of his power over her very life, in hopes that such a realization will keep her "in her place." Only infrequently does assault in the context of battering prove fatal, and that happens in three general contexts: (1) when an intended nonfatal attack on a woman goes awry; (2) when the batterer believes he is no longer able to control the woman in life—she has escaped him—so kills her as a gesture of ultimate control ("If I can't have you, no one else can"); and (3) when a battered woman, fearing for her life or those of her children, strikes back fatally.

It becomes clear that battering is control over women that thrives within the larger system of patriarchy; it reflects the patriarchal legacy of male ownership as it persists into romantic relationships, including marriage. Battering is the systematic abuse, by a man, of societally bestowed male privilege to exploit a wife or other female intimate companion. Using this definition there can be no battered men: men can be treated unfairly and even brutally by women, but they cannot be battered because to be battered requires a social order antagonistic to one's particular gender.

Men are able to intimidate and coerce women to their benefit because our world favors men and thwarts women at every turn (Acker 1989; Lorber 1994:298). It orchestrates women's emotional and economic dependence on men. Girls are taught to believe that in order to be whole they must please and be desired by men. The socialization of women emphasizes the primary value of being a good wife and mother at the expense of personal achievement in other realms of life. It is no surprise, then, that in 1995, United States women who were employed full-time earned, on the average, 75.5 percent of the amount earned by their male counterparts (U.S. Department of Labor 1996). Indeed, women are programmed to willfully play into a social order that minimizes their value and sense of self-worth and oppresses them.

Battering is comprehensive in that it includes both interpersonal and societal forms of gendered abuse. It represents the convergence of one man (the batterer), obsessed with controlling a particular woman and willing to abuse her to gain and maintain that control, with a social order that delivers that woman to him and helps hold her there as hostage (for analysis of battered women as hostage see Graham et al. 1988). Our patriarchal culture creates a generalized climate of risk where all men are allowed to, and particular men will, batter women. Battered women, then, constitute one of numerous categories of women (including victims of stalking, sexual harassment, incest, and rape) who fall prey to men's individual as well as collective oppression. Hypothetically, men could be battered, but only in a matriarchal society—if one were to exist. In the meantime we can only imagine such a state of affairs the likes of which is depicted by Gerd Brantenberg (1985) in her fictional account of a fishing village named Egalia. The ideal, of course, would be an equalitarian society, where no one could be battered.

THE DYNAMICS OF BATTERING

Reeling Her In

Battering is about the coercion and intimidation that men impose on women in order to control them. It has many faces and may progress gradually and subtly. Typically, a woman is seduced into a battering relationship by the charming and charismatic side of a man's dual personality. That man is wonderful to her all the time at first. He comes on strong, showering her with charm and adoration. He knows what she wants and he gives it to her. It is coercion and control even then: he is reeling her in. But to the unsuspecting woman it feels like fresh, innocent, young love. The woman is thrilled and feels fortunate to have found this desirable man who is so caring. No one has ever loved her like this. She feels great and wants to preserve that feeling. Reeling-in is the initial stage of battering.

Then something happens to shake this woman's sense of security: her vision of eternal happiness with this man is threatened. The incident introduces intimidation into the relationship and can be ever so subtle, such as a glance on his part suggesting that she has displeased him. She is terrified on the spot that his disappointment in her may lead to abandonment—that she may not be good enough for him and capable of keeping him after all. It is a fear of "paradise lost."

Intimidation and Fear

At this point in the battering trajectory, the initial stage of reeling the woman in gives way to intimidation. On her part, the energy base of the relationship transforms from ecstasy to fear. The relationship will remain based on intimidation and on fear of one thing or another until the battering stops. For now, the woman is afraid that she will be unable to keep her partner satisfied and in love with her.

It is here that her desperate struggle to hang on to that man—and with him, her happiness—begins.

For many women a twist of pity enters the battering equation early on. This man may present himself as sad and wounded by mistreatment: perhaps he was abused as a child or by another woman or at work. Whatever his source of pain and injury, it is the love of this woman alone, he says, that can deliver him from his tortured existence. He convinces her that he needs her unconditional love for his very survival. A woman may get hooked into this drama because it appeals to her salvation ethic (Ferraro and Johnson 1983), the typically feminine indoctrinated desire to rescue and to be of service to others. She sees an opportunity to compensate for all past injustices visited upon this man, a chance to rescue him and, in turn, earn from him a lifetime indenture. When pity becomes a factor in the battering, guilt emerges as a powerful retention force: How could she be so heartless as to compound his misfortune and pain with her abandonment, especially if there are children involved?

So now the woman is minding her p's and q's, busily attempting to avoid recurrences of this man's displeasure. She attends to details as she sanitizes his world; she prepares his favorite meals, makes certain that the children are clean and well behaved, and even intervenes on his behalf at work—whatever it takes to keep him happy and the love coming.

But he continues to find fault in her. It is always something: the meals, the children's grades, her appearance. Why can't she just get it right! She scrambles around in her efforts to please, but senses quicksand underfoot. She used to be perfect; he had told her so. And he had loved her for it. Now she is not measuring up and he is loving her less. She lies awake nights contemplating ways to be better and to cushion his world. She yearns to get things back on track—to the way he used to make her feel.

Throughout all this the batterer knows what he is doing and that it is wrong. He is abusing this woman by orchestrating a climate of intimidation, self-doubt, blame, humiliation, and fear to progressively entrap her in a relationship of servitude to him. She fails to recognize the grand plan and, therefore, falls prey to it. All she sees is what he intends for her to see—a wonderful man and a wonderful relationship souring due to her inadequacies. She is frustrated but remains determined to renew the relationship by improving along those dimensions where he has found fault. She erroneously believes him when he tells her that she has control over the situation, that all it will take is change on her part to recover the happiness they once had together.

A battering relationship can remain indefinitely static at this point, with the abuser enjoying the benefits of his mate's servitude as she continues in her struggle to correct his endless list of constructed faults in order to recapture an illusionary romantic utopia. But in many relationships the battering progresses in severity. Some women rear up at least now and then in defiance of male privilege. For example, a woman may announce that she has no time to press his shirt or that against his wishes she intends to return to college or visit her sister. When that occurs, he must decide either to escalate his battering campaign in order to "keep her in her place" or to suffer the loss of control and its associated benefits.

Techniques of Escalated Battering

If the batterer opts to escalate his battering campaign, several forms of abuse are available to him. He can employ them in seemingly unlimited form and combination and continue escalation as he deems necessary to maintain control. The techniques of escalated battering described below are not mutually exclusive.

Intimidation is the primary tactic of battering once the reeling-in is completed. In the beginning intimidation typically assumes the form of harsh looks and gestures, but escalated battering can evolve into more severe manifestations. The batterer may smash things, destroy the woman's property, abuse her pets, and display weapons. Intimidation can extend to include direct threats—to leave her, to injure her, to commit suicide, to report her to welfare authorities—and ultimately to include physical assault. Often it is the physical assault component of battering that most readily identifies and draws attention to a battered woman. In other words, often it is the beating that causes a woman or someone around her to realize that she is battered and consequently prompts a woman to get out of a battering relationship.

While all forms of battering have a psychological component, the term *psychological abuse* is reserved for the kind of abuse that is designed to manipulate the psyche in order to gain an edge in control (Dutton 1992:4, 6). Common forms include putting the woman down verbally and making her feel bad about herself through name-calling (typically names are sexually charged, such as "whore," "bitch," "slut") and both private and public humiliation. Making her feel guilty about her constructed flaws is another common form. These are ploys to convince a woman that she could not survive alone and that no one else would have her. Some abusers are masters of psychological manipulation and are able to create doubts in their partners' minds about their very sanity. For example, a man might rearrange furniture, then claim that she must have done it. The movie *Sleeping with the Enemy* artistically demonstrates the extremes of psychological abuse in the context of battering. To women entering the arena of escalated battering, psychological abuse is no stranger. The reeling-in process served as their introduction to psychic manipulation.

Minimization and denial are common to battering. Typically, a batterer will minimize the abuse and injury. He convinces his partner that their problems are not serious and that she is overreacting. When he does admit to his brutality, he denies culpability: it is not his fault. It is the fault of the woman, he says, for her inadequacies and provocations or the fault of external forces beyond his control, such as work pressures, legal problems, or alcoholism. She believes him.

Isolation and surveillance are typically drawn into the battering agenda. The abuser may discourage and even attempt to sever his partner's relationships with family and friends. These people have her interests at heart and would support her efforts to escape him, should they ever learn of the abuse. These connections to the outside world could neutralize his psychological manipulation by providing to the woman "reality tests" of her sanity. Friends and family are a competing force not to be taken lightly. In fact, any outsider is a potential threat to the battering agenda. Batterers commonly monitor what a woman does, whom she sees and talks to, what she reads, and where she goes. They are known to further isolate women by leaving them at home without a car, forbidding them to attend school or work outside the home, and removing the telephone from the home in the batterer's absence. Batterers impose much of this isolation in the name of jealousy: she should be flattered with his attempt to keep her from other men.

Additional techniques may or may not be included in a particular battering equation. One is the use of children to help keep the woman in subjection. A man can threaten to hurt the children or to take them away, and he can make his partner feel guilty about her mothering practices. Another "optional" battering technique is economic abuse, which involves the use of money to terrorize and oppress the woman, and includes blocking her access to knowledge of the family economy, preventing her from working for pay, taking her money, forcing her to manage the household on an inadequate allowance, and making her ask for money. Finally, sexual abuse is a technique of escalated battering that constitutes any form of coerced or forced sexual behavior. It includes not only oral, anal, and genital intercourse but also penetration with a foreign object, sex with a third party, including prostitution, and forced exhibitionism.

The Cycle of Battering

About two decades ago Lenore Walker (1979) recognized that battering can occur in a continuous cycle of three distinct stages: tension building, explosion, and loving contrition. She referred to it as the cycle of violence, but the model can be generalized to apply to battering that does not include physical violence. Once a woman has been reeled in and the battering is escalated, the cycle kicks in.

During the tension-building stage the man may draw liberally and creatively from the menu of escalated battering tactics to let the woman know that he is not getting the "respect" from her that he wants. He may intimidate her with glances, criticize her incessantly, call her names, mope, freeze her out and maybe leave home for days, slam things around the house, speed with her in the car, hit her. To the extent that she fails to figure out what he wants and give it to him, or simply refuses to give it to him, the battering intensifies. She "walks on eggshells" during this stage, smoothing things over, sometimes withdrawing, always trying to placate him. She rationalizes his brutality, denies her own anger, and blames herself. Out of humiliation and fear she tells no one of the abuse and covers for him and defends his actions if necessary. Her commitment to religious ideals of serving the husband and conventional ideals of romance or the nuclear family help overshadow the mundane reality of abuse and diminish her ability to take advantage of practical options, including alternative housing and income.

If the man is unable to find relief, the tension will culminate in an explosion. It is a seemingly out-of control tirade, yet if the police pull up, he stops. He devastates her with words and perhaps physical violence. This stage is the shortest, lasting from an hour or two to perhaps two days. It is during this stage that the woman may release her anger and fight back. Or she may fight back out of fear in self-defense. This episode of rage is a desperate attempt on the part of the batterer to humiliate and coerce that woman into subjection—to show her "who is boss." Intensity varies of course, and can range from a verbal outburst to a fatal beating.

The loving contrition stage completes that particular revolution of the cycle. The man knows he has gone too far, and now he must make it up to his partner lest he lose her. He apologizes, begs forgiveness, pledges his eternal love, and promises never again to resort to such extreme behavior. Turning on that old charm and transforming into that wonderful man with whom she fell in love in the beginning, he reels her back in. He may offer her gifts, invite her to romantic dinners and vacations, promise her anything—whatever it takes to keep her with him under his control. She believes him; they reconcile. Eventually this stage passes, and the couple slides once more into tension building and begins the cycle all over again.

Many abused women refer to their batterer's dual personality in terms of "Dr. Jekyll and Mr. Hyde." Abusive men flip between extreme and incongruous temperaments to keep their mates confused and controlled. The two distinct personality types work in different ways to entrap the woman. The Mr. Hyde part of the batterer's personality holds a woman in servitude to him out of fear that he will leave her, humiliate her, or in some other way cause her pain. The Dr. Jekyll personality, on the other hand, also holds the woman hostage to her batterer, but this strategy is much different: Dr. Jekyll flashes before her glimpses of the kind and loving man he was in the early stages of their relationship—and could be again if only she were to shape up. The appearance of Dr. Jekyll incites hope and struggle for recovery. That hope becomes another powerful tool of entrapment: she will not leave as long as she sees hope. It becomes clear, then, that two separate forces in a batterer's strategy operate in combination to hold the battered woman in captivity: hope and fear. Dr. Jekyll holds her with hope, while Mr. Hyde holds her with fear. Dr. Jekyll and Mr. Hyde alternate at will during the tension-building stage. The woman never knows which will show up at her door. The explosion that follows is a pure blast of Mr. Hyde, and the loving contrition stage is Dr. Jekyll at his best.

The length of any particular revolution within the cycle of battering is unpredictable for any given relationship, and the stages vary in length and intensity. A couple can remain in the tension-building stage for years. The loving contrition stage is altogether absent from some relationships and may decline or disappear in others. Some men get by without subjecting themselves to that ritual of humiliation. If the woman continually responds to accelerated abuse by accelerating her resistance in turn, the cycle spirals upward in intensity accordingly. It is important to keep in mind that battering is a lot of trouble for a man, and he will devote only that degree of effort required to keep his partner where he wants her. In that sense, the intensity of abuse is determined by what he perceives to be the needed amount of adjustment in her behavior. When he believes she is way out of line, he must respond with especially harsh punishment.

GETTING OUT

Safely escaping a battering relationship can be a long arduous journey. The rationalizing, minimizing, denying, and hoping for change must give way to a redefinition of self as victim rather than devoted and long-suffering mate. In fact, the woman must redefine her partner and her entire situation and, in the process, admit betrayal and defeat both personally and publicly. The person she loved the most and trusted to protect her has been brutalizing her, and her devotion to him is not enough to make him stop.

Love and hope wane with the progression of abuse and of unfulfilled promises of change and are replaced with loneliness and pessimism. Endless ridicule and condescension have deflated the battered woman's confidence. All this while she has bought into her partner's campaign to convince her that she is incompetent, stupid, ugly, unworthy of love, and incapable of surviving without him. Eventually she faces emotional bankruptcy, surviving each day in a state of dull depression. While some battered women eke out a lifetime of this kind of numbed existence, others are spurred by resources that serve as catalysts for the redefinition and evaluation necessary to begin the exit process (Ferraro and Johnson 1983). Some such catalysts spring from within the woman or relationship themselves, while others are external to them. There must be an internal awakening before that outside support can come into play.

One catalyst for redefining abuse is an escalation in that abuse beyond acceptability. A woman may one day be jolted into realizing that she cannot tolerate this treatment. A particularly devastating incident or an unexpectedly severe explosion (stage two) serves as a "wake-up call" that a woman's emotional, psychological, and perhaps physical safety are in jeopardy. Perhaps her very life is in danger. A related catalyst is the extension of the abuse to include victimization of the children. Many women who leave batterers recall an incident involving the children as the point of no return.

They simply will not tolerate the children either witnessing the abuse of their mother or being abused themselves.

A third catalyst is a change in the relationship. Sometimes after a number of explosions (stage two), a man may realize that his partner will not retaliate or escape and thus he may feel no need to continue expressing remorse and contrition (stage three). But it may have been the loving contrition and its associated hope for change that held the woman hostage to the battering. If so, extended periods devoid of kindness may alter her feelings toward him, perhaps to the point of despair, triggering a redefinition of herself as a victim.

Change in the visibility of abuse is a fourth catalyst. Rationalization, minimization, and denial are accomplished more easily if no outsiders are present to question their validity. The extension of woman abuse from the private to the public domain may prompt reinterpretation: battering in private is humiliating, but in public that humiliation assumes a whole new dimension. A fifth internal catalyst is change in self-concept. Even entrapped in a web of battering, a woman may experience a boost in self-esteem that causes her to redefine her entire situation. A battered woman may discover, for example, that she is an excellent mother. Clearly her baby loves her and is happy and thriving, while at the same time her abuser is calling her an incompetent mother. She knows she is right and, therefore, he must be wrong. That single inconsistency calls into question his general credibility and consequently his ability to continue battering her.

External catalysts include a change in resources and external definitions of the relationship. Laws may change, as may law enforcement policy, allowing the woman to define herself as a victim and ultimately to use those changes as tools of escape. These and other resources, including an inheritance or a promotion at work, could tip the power balance in the relationship in favor of the battered woman. External definitions can be potent catalysts. If people outside the battering relationship discover the abuse and respond with unqualified support of the victim and condemnation of her abuser, their definition of the situation may incite the woman to reconsider hers. Friends and relatives who show genuine concern for a woman's well-being may spark an awareness of danger contradictory to that woman's current mindset.

After numerous revolutions in the cycle of battering—much suffering, countless reconciliations, scores of empty promises—and spurred by catalysts to total despair or perhaps mortal fear, many battered women embark on a painful and complex process of reinterpretation as they begin to see themselves as victims and then choose a course of escape. The best information we have suggests that between 43 percent (Okun 1988) and 70.5 percent (Strube and Barbour 1984) of physically abused battered women who seek refuge at shelters or professional counseling eventually leave those violent relationships permanently.

It is important to understand that a woman leaving a batterer is in some ways similar to anyone leaving a love relationship and in critical ways similar to any woman leaving a man. When there are ambivalences stemming from dimensions of the partner and of the relationship that she continues to value, she must prepare to absorb those losses. Uncoupling almost never occurs without painful costs (Salts 1979; Wiseman 1975). Sometimes when a woman gets out and faces loneliness and a patriarchal society that opposes her at every turn—lower pay, weak child-support enforcement, lack of affordable quality health care and child day care, deplorable government support for single mothers and their children—that still available unsatisfactory love relationship looks better. So she may return to try the relationship again, only to be quickly reminded of why she left in the first place. Next she regroups and begins preparation for a better-informed exit.

Having tested the waters, the woman now knows what to expect. She evaluates the shortcomings of her first exit, corrects them, strategizes anew, gathers her resources, and then, when the time is right, strikes out on her own again. This time she fares better: perhaps she has more education, more money, better job skills, a friend or two standing by, more determination. But still that may not be enough. The exit process may need further refining, so the fits, starts, and reversals continue until finally she is able to get out and stay out.

Adding the element of battering intensifies the getting-out process manyfold (Kurz 1996). Now, in addition to the agonies of uncoupling in the context of patriarchal oppression, the woman must work around a man who is obsessed with keeping her under his thumb. If he even suspects her intention to flee, his battering agenda will intensify. He may vow to find her should she slip away, and both know that, like other components of our nation's helping system, the criminal justice megasystem implicitly collaborates with violent men by supporting traditional family roles and treating battered women as though they are the problem. Leaving a batterer does not necessarily make a woman safe; women increase their risk of sublethal and lethal violence at the hands of their male partner when they leave (Davies et al. 1998:25–26; Straton 1994:80; Wilson and Daly 1993). Intimate partner violence against women separated from their husbands is twenty-five times higher than that against married women (Bachman and Saltzman 1995:4).

While abuse typically does intensify with a woman's threat to escape, most exits do not erupt into fatal or even life-threatening conclusions. Most men's aggression stops short of that depicted in those extreme cases seen in the news and entertainment media. Men eventually give up and perhaps find another woman to batter. Some never resort to threats at all; their tactics to keep or bring a woman home remain limited to expressions of remorse, pleas for forgiveness, and promises to reform. Typically, women get out more or less safely and, with time, cut their losses and reconstruct their lives.

Two points are important in closing this section. First, the reasons that a woman stays and returns change over the course of the battering relationship. In the very beginning, as she is initially reeled in, she stays because she, of course, is unsuspecting of her own abuse. Her partner is totally wonderful and she is ecstatic, after all. Or he is pitiful and she is certain that she can fix him. Then later, when the relationship begins to hurt, she fears losing him and stays because she believes the problems are her fault and that she has the power to restore their mutual love by changing her behavior. By the time she has come to define herself as a victim, which is usually much later, she stays or returns for different reasons. Sometimes there are practical considerations, including children's financial and educational needs, and always by now her self-esteem is deflated. Commonly, she reasonably fears reprisal for attempting to leave or for not returning.

Finally, I want to emphasize that getting out of a battering relationship, like all uncoupling, is a process rather than an event. It may involve one exit or several. Either way, that process extends back to the decision point to leave and includes the evolution of strategy refinement. Research suggests that women leave their abusive partners an average of five times before getting out permanently (Okun 1986) and that the getting-out process takes an average of eight years (Horton and Johnson 1993). If representatives of the criminal justice system and medical practitioners were to appreciate the processal nature of uncoupling for battered women, the journeys to liberation for these women would be easier and safer. As it stands, these professionals lose patience with women's repeated requests for services and so blame them for their victimization. They need to understand that the woman is on a journey out and that the more support rather than blame she encounters along the way, the sooner and more intact she will be when she reaches that finish line.

OVERVIEW OF THE BOOK

This collection of life stories is designed for women and men who, for either personal or professional reasons, wish to truly understand battering relationships. The personal accounts assembled in this book, when considered as a whole, testify to the fact that every kind of woman can be battered: there is no single profile of a battered woman. And the stories speak to the complex pattern of dynamics that progressively entrap a vital woman into a life of fear, false hope, self-doubt, humiliation, guilt, depression, and ultimately poor health, and then later release her. The biographies presented here breathe life into the principles and patterns of the battering process, from inception through exit. They invite you to slip into the skins of these women and to witness, through their eyes, their tempestuous journeys to hell and back.

THE PROJECT IN DEVELOPMENT

This book is the product of an idea long in incubation, with antecedents reaching back into my youth. My father's unpredictable episodes of rage followed by fits of hollow kindness, in the daily context of condescension, trepidation, and humiliation, introduced me to battering before it had a name. No one in the household was spared my father's wrath, which continues to affect every member of my family today. The hardest part, as I see it now, was my inability to understand what it was all about. It was that ignorance that victimized me and rendered me powerless all those years. Later, as a family studies scholar and criminologist, I was drawn to the notion of studying and teaching about family violence. The knowledge and insights gained by that work provided the framework necessary to free me, to a great extent at least, from that childhood legacy of battering. It is that sense of liberation that inspired this book. Battering thrives on ignorance and is snuffed out by understanding. I want everyone to understand battering because I want it to stop.

The project called for biographical accounts of American women that described the battering process from inception through exit.

Diversity in terms of ethnicity, age, social class, religion, geographical region, sexual orientation, and general experience was a critical consideration. There was no intention to create a representative sample, because the goal was to demonstrate patterns and provide instructive cases rather than to generalize. Armed with this vision, I set out to find the women.

A nationwide call for participants to abuse shelters and other organizations and agencies sympathetic to battered women elicited a substantial response. Additionally, a personal search concentrating on my university and community yielded several participants. I first gathered basic background information from each woman and then shifted my attention to her battering and exit processes. My work was theory driven, always focused on the patriarchy and established patterns of battering and getting out (as I have already described). The texts I have created to tell women's stories combine information supplied by them—from autobiographical essays, diaries, newspaper and magazine articles, letters, and interviews—with my own interpretations. Their stories are filtered through me. I met with all except two of the participants, Lucretia and Raquelle, and in all cases I was invited into their homes. I wrote a story only when I was certain that I "knew" the woman well enough.

Early on, as I approached the third or fourth essay, the original concept of the project underwent dramatic revision. It was when I was preparing Colette's story that I knew for certain that I could not sterilize women's biographies by excluding critical dimensions that may at first blush seem unrelated to the subject at hand—battering.

I had read and heard Colette's heartrending account of her treacherous childhood that culminated in the blood-drenched suicide of her clinically depressed mother. My image of Colette in the telling is frozen in time: visiting her on a summer afternoon in her cool, shaded, open sunroom, her clear-eyed candor and her serene style. A small, framed black-and-white photo of her fashionably suited mother as a young French woman rested on a shelf nearby. Then, as Colette concluded the story of her own battering, I heard the tale of the death by car accident of Colette's only child at age six—with whom Colette had endured and escaped years of abuse. There were more framed photos on display to relay the significance of Michelle's life and death. Here was a woman's life story whose integrity should not be violated in the name of research on battering (Riessman 1993:4). It is only in the context of Colette's story of her youth that her account of her battering rings true.

At that point the book in progress became a collection of *life stories* of women who had endured and safely left abusive men— *not just stories of abuse and escape.* The stories are more honest this way. They are stories packed full of women's issues and human issues: contextual knowledge at its best. The thematic link is the abuse and the getting out. I revised the biographies completed before Colette's, then went on to construct the rest contextually. So now the book teaches about childhood, good and bad alike; eating disorders; homelessness; clinical depression culminating in suicide; alcoholism; sibling relationships; baby smuggling; drug trafficking; public school desegregation; homosexuality; motherhood; and adult child-parent issues. And it provides glimpses into Puerto Rico; Israel; Star Lake, New York; Wind River Indian Reservation; professional baseball; a Michigan outlaw militia; and the dreadful personal toll exacted by the United States involvement in the Vietnam War. When placed in context, issues surrounding battering seem neutralized and perhaps even dwarfed by the other life processes and events experienced by some of these women.

The construction of the biographies progressed at a brisk and even pace and without a hitch for one year beginning in February 1995. Each essay was a joint endeavor for me and the storyteller. I sent her my first draft, and from there we revised and refined together until we were both satisfied with the product. The women were allowed choice in revealing or suppressing first names and other identifying features. Some participated in the project as a gesture of liberation—a "coming out" of sorts. Their disclosure of their identity symbolizes their pride in having escaped a life of fear and oppression. Other women chose pseudonyms and withheld other specifics in order to protect family members. Using first names only, and leaving the real undifferentiated from the contrived, was my decision.

The stories are uneven. Some are eloquently expressed and nuanced exposés, while others are stilted by comparison. The variation in tone and texture reflects the uniqueness of the teller. Some women found comfort and even elation in the reflection process from their now safe spot, while others could barely tolerate remembering. Additionally, some women were basically more verbally expressive, articulate, and uninhibited than others. These variations produced detectable differences in the biographies, making an important contribution to understanding women's diversity. That women's lives cannot be packaged in some standard way is clearly evidenced by this collection. Nevertheless, every story is worth the telling, and each makes a unique contribution to the product of our combined efforts: a better understanding of battering and getting out and their consequences.

Ethnic diversity is an important part of this collection of life stories of battered women. A small but telling research literature apprises us of the enhanced problems that battered women of color face because of their minority status (Hendrickson 1996; Mousseau and Artichoker 1993; Bachman 1992; White 1995; Zambrano 1985, 1994; Moss et al. 1997). Six women in this book—Sharon, Lucretia, Freda, Rebecca, Annette, and Blanca—are women of color, and their life experiences, when compared with those of White women, reflect reported differences between minority and White battered women. Themes of racism as well as sexism permeate the stories of these six women in predictable ways.

I have no war stories related to the production of this book; without exception, the women were generous, gracious, and patient teachers. This feminist project has made my journey to feminism well worth the trouble (see my autobiographical essay: Goetting 1996).

THE TRUTH ABOUT BIOGRAPHY

Concerns with accuracy have surrounded the literary form of narrative or lifetelling, including biography, for a couple of decades (Goetting 1995). Do people tell the truth about their lives? The answer to that question is succinctly articulated by the legendary Cree hunter who traveled to Montreal to offer court testimony regarding the effect of the new James Bay hydroelectric scheme on his hunting lands. He would describe the way of life of his people. But when administered the oath he hesitated: "I'm not sure I can tell the truth. . . . I can tell only what I know" (Clifford 1986:8). We tell the truth pretty much as we know it, but that may not be someone else's "truth."

Some scholars of narrative speak of lifetelling as fiction. They claim that memory is faulty and leaves but a quiver of recognition of times past, which we then adjust into story. In that sense biography is "something made," "something fashioned"—the original meaning of *fiction*. The claim is not that life stories are false but rather that they are interpretations constructed around a string of imperfect recollections. These scholars point out additionally that lived experience is mediated by language, which is also imperfect. Often there are not words to accurately describe what has happened to us. Lived experience is further mediated by the context in which it is told. The version offered by Colette that day in her sunroom may be different in tone and texture from the version she told her current husband during their courtship years earlier. Biography, as a special form of narrative, further "distorts" the lived experience by adding the biographer's layer of interpretation to those of the storyteller. The perspective of the biographer can add a critical dimension to a story. My biography of Colette is surely different than would be, for example, O. J. Simpson's version of that same life. In sum, biography is not simply a "true" representation of an objective "reality"; instead, memory, language, the context of the telling, and the interpretations of both storyteller and biographer combine to create a particular view of reality.

The counterpoint to lifetelling as fiction rather than truth is that it is truth if truth is properly defined. It is argued that in spite of inherent distortions, lifetelling does reveal truths. These truths do not disclose the past "as it actually was" by some arbitrary standard of objectivity; instead, they are reconstructed and, therefore, superior truths. We continue through our lifetime to interpret old events from new positions. Each time, we tell the story differently, and with each telling the story matures and gains depth. My story, as a ten-year-old, of my father's rages was different than the story I tell today of the same times and incidents. From this perspective on truth, biography is better than having been there, because it adds the element of seasoned consciousness to the original experience. In the words of Georges Gusdorf (1980):

In the immediate moment, the agitation of things ordinarily surrounds me too much for me to be able to see it in its entirety. Memory gives me a certain remove and allows me to take into consideration all the ins and outs of the matter, its context in time and space. As an aerial view sometimes reveals to an archaeologist the direction of a road or a fortification or a map of a city invisible to someone on the ground, so the reconstruction in spirit of my destiny bares the major lines that I have failed to notice, the demands of the deepest values I hold that, without my being clearly aware or it, have determined my most decisive choices. (38)

Our real concern with biography is not whether it is "truth" or "fiction" but what it can teach us about human feelings, motives, and thought processes. For example, in this book we are far less interested in knowing who hit or slapped whom how often than we are with knowing how a woman feels about being hurt by her partner, how she reacts and why. Biography does not supply us with verifiable truths; rather, it offers a special kind of impassioned knowing.

A final note on truth as it applies specifically to these biographies: certainly a curiosity about "his side of the story" is reasonable. Would these women's abusers tell the same stories about the relationship? Would they minimize or deny what they are accused of in these pages? First, it must be emphasized that we live in a gendered universe, where men and women are considered to be two distinct types of people and are treated accordingly. In that sense men and women occupy two different worlds and, in so doing, define and understand little, if anything, similarly (Tannen 1990; Szinovacz 1983). It is no surprise, therefore, that when researchers separate couples and inquire about shared activities and the dynamics of their relationship, those couples seem to describe two different relationships altogether (Szinovacz 1983). It is that phenomenon that inspired sociologist Jessie Bernard (1972) to title her now classic essay of American marriage "Marriage: Hers and His." Battering is no exception to the rule. Two sound studies of couples in relationships where the woman is physically abused (one, from the United States [Szinovacz 1983]; the other, Scottish [Dobash et al. 1998]) inform us that women report more types of violent victimization and in greater frequency than their male partners admit to. Furthermore, more women than men report injuries from the abuse and, again, women report higher frequencies. All in all, women perceive more violence in these relationships and tend to judge it as more serious. I suspect that the abusers of the women in this collection would tell very different stories and that they would minimize and deny the abuse of which they are accused.

WINNING WITH BIOGRAPHY

Biography enjoys popularity among readers of every stripe. It offers privileged access to understandings of the human condition in all of its complexity. The life of the emotions, the life of the mind, the physical life, and the social life are told in context to produce a comprehensive whole. It is all there within easy grasp: the obscurities, the reasonings, the motivations, the passions. German sociologist Wilhelm Dilthey touts biography as the highest and most instructive form of knowledge about humanity (translated by Kohli

1981:126). From that perspective the best way to truly understand a category of human experience, such as escape from battering, would be through examination of a diverse assemblage of biographies focusing on that experience—in this case life stories of battered women who got out.

In addition to providing a superior method of understanding the human experience, reading biography helps us make sense of our own lives by connecting us with others. It activates us to construct a benchmark against which to compare our own existence, thereby prompting us to rethink that existence. We continually test our own realities against such stories and modify our perceptions accordingly. In that way biography transforms us. In the process of this personal transformation, this reconceptualization of our life, we typically are comforted and sometimes elated by the newfound connections that inspired the journey. Finding people in situations comparable to ours who have discovered similar truths fortifies us with consensus and affirmation. We are no longer alone and vulnerable. Jane Tompkins (1989) tells it best:

I love writers who write about their own experience. I feel I'm being nourished by them, and that I'm being allowed to enter into a personal relationship with them, that I can match my own experiences with theirs, feel cousin to them, and say, yes, that's how it is. (170)

By delivering sensitive insight and inspiring a reinterpretation of life through human connectedness, reading biography can forge informed life change. The sociologist C. Wright Mills's promise of "the sociological imagination" (1959) instructs us that insights into social context can supply the resources necessary not only to understand one's own life but to at least partially control its outcomes. Similarly, social theorist Max Weber insists that humans can succeed only if "each finds . . . the demon who holds the fibers of his very life" (Gerth and Mills 1946, 156).

It becomes apparent that reading biography can be personally rewarding and a joy to experience. It has the potential to nourish and fortify us and to propel us into a constructive path of personal renewal. Biography represents reason informed by passion, arguably the most powerful form of knowledge production. Robbie Pfeufer Kahn (1995) refers to that process as "thinking through the heart." The women whose stories grace these pages have generously and bravely embraced this process to one point of completion, many specifically in hopes that their stories would find, inform, soothe, and intelligently activate battered women. This book personifies "thinking through the heart."

IN CLOSING

The biographies are loosely organized into seven parts. Yet I ask readers to make their own connections among them. Part I, "The Privileged Are Not Exempt. . . ," presents two accounts of women from privileged backgrounds. Their stories attest to the fact that, while battering is overrepresented in the lower classes, even the educated, moneyed, and politically powerful can fall prey to its agonies. Part II, ". . . Nor Are Children," extends this notion that battering can happen to anyone by focusing on the experiences of two adolescent girls. Part III, "A Two-Timing Batterer," depicts the case of a man who concurrently battered his wife and extramarital girlfriend. When we compare notes, it becomes clear that he battered them quite differently. Part IV, "Family and Friends to the Rescue," illuminates two variations of the unqualified support of family and friends that can liberate battered women. In Part V, "Faces of Shelter Life," two women demonstrate how battered women's shelters operate to accommodate a diversity of needs. In Part VI, "When the System Works," three stories attest to the fact that in a patriarchy, known to be unresponsive at best and often hostile to battered women, there exist informal as well as formal helping systems other than shelters that work. Part VII, "Legacies of Loss and Death," stands in hideous reminder that escape is not necessarily synonymous with happy ending. These three women had the hardest jobs of all in telling their stories. The book closes with a message to battered women about safety.

It should be noted that these stories are emotionally intense and often disturbing. They are not intended to be read in a single sitting or in any particular order. Rather they should be consumed and absorbed in a way that optimally cradles and informs each reader uniquely.

This book is a celebration of women's tenacity, determination, and resourcefulness under the most formidable conditions of patriarchal bondage. The stories herein assume their place in a long tradition of captivity narrative by American women (Castiglia 1996). They are intended for use by women and men alike, to enhance our understanding of battered women and to aid each of us in our personal struggle toward a better informed and more humane and activist lifestyle.

Part I

THE PRIVILEGED
ARE NOT EXEMPT

CHAPTER ONE

Jan

Jan and I attended graduate school together in Michigan and have remained friends over the two decades since then and across the thousands of miles that separate us. We have always enjoyed sitting around cups of tea or vegetable omlettes, chatting over the day's events and sharing stories from our pasts. Without doubt some of my best memories capture Jan and me amusing ourselves with unconventional projects (for example, designing and sewing matching cheery green with pink-rose-patterned and gaily ruffled Carmen Miranda taffeta dresses suitable to wear nowhere) and benign mischief (for example, as students, breaking into our departmental office in the middle of the night to use typewriters and eat leftover doughnuts). Sometimes we notice a pair of eccentric little old ladies wearing hats tottering along the city streets together and comment that someday that will be us. Because Jan and I have always loved to tell tales, it should come as no surprise that when I decided to collect women's stories for this book, I would call on Jan. She had escaped an abusive husband whom I had witnessed taking pleasure in humiliating her. Jan accepted my offer to tell her side.

Jan's life story brings to this collection the element of battering without physical violence in the context of a man's unbridled ambition to rise from the depths of poverty and child abuse to the heights of success in the financial district of San Francisco (and wife abuse!). Hers is a story of a pretty, personable, artistically gifted and highly educated young woman in search of security and comfortable lifestyle via marriage, colliding with a man in search of a woman to control for his personal gain. It would have worked indefinitely had he not gone too far.

Today Jan is in her middle forties, struggling once again for financial security, this time in the aftermath of a brutal divorce. Residing in the pleasant surroundings of San Francisco, she aspires to the flexible and lucrative lifestyle of a successful novelist and focuses her current energies on the publication of her first book.

Jan surmises that her mother was pregnant with her when her parents, then graduate students and left-wing atheists at the University of Michigan, married. Her mother was an only child and the product of an educated, culturally enlightened, and affluent family, whose fortune in Michigan farm real estate had been lost to the Great Depression. In her post-Depression upbringing, she was doted on as the family darling and groomed for success. Her marriage to Jan's defiant and exploitive father outraged the family, causing her parents to temporarily disown her and her wealthy uncle to disinherit her. Jan's mother became a teacher, then a high school counselor until retirement. Her father, on the other hand, worked in middle-level sales and marketing, started two unsuccessful companies, and taught high school and college English.

Jan was brought up in a middle-class suburb of Detroit. By the age of six, two siblings had joined the family: a sister and then a brother. Jan attributes the excessive permissiveness of their upbringing to her mother's compensatory reaction to her own strict rearing and to the diminishment of parental supervision once both parents worked full time. Jan's mother tried to be a good mother and in many ways succeeded. Energetic, devoted, and positive, she possessed a particularly easygoing personality. She channeled her children, especially the girls, into numerous activities: Girl Scouts, ballet, art and language classes, summer camps, swimming and riding lessons. She proved an inept disciplinarian, however, eventually resorting to the "You just wait till your father gets home" routine. Jan remembers her mother working to the point of exhaustion as she juggled the responsibilities of family and career. In the meantime, Jan's father took to spending less and less time at home: working late, staying out drinking with friends. Eventually he became an alcoholic.

The words *precocious* and *incorrigible* were sometimes used to describe Jan as a child. Reflecting back, she views herself as having been self-absorbed, popular, and diversely talented. As the eldest child she benefited more than her siblings did from her mother's time and energy. Her mother devoted many long hours to accelerate Jan's reading comprehension and to ensure her academic success. Additionally, Jan's mother urged physical and social development. As a result Jan's pursuits and accomplishments were wide-ranging: honor student, eight years of ballet, ten years of swimming, a sash full of Girl Scout achievement badges. In high school, where Jan was among the most popular students, she was a cheerleader and belonged to the Pep Club, the French Club, and the National Honor Society. Her graduating year she was on the Homecoming Court and was voted the most attractive girl of the senior class.

Over her childhood years Jan's father became progressively abusive. He evolved into a man of extremes: as likely to fill a room with warmth and charisma as he was to inflict a sense of white-knuckled terror into his family. Jan recalls her father in these terms:

He could be infectiously witty and entertaining—fun to be around— but this pleasant side of him diminished as his professional disappointments mounted and his alcohol consumption increased. By the time I attended college, he had become overwhelmingly surly and negative. He had a professorial style and a tendency to pontificate. His sharp wit and cruel tongue were used to belittle others, increasingly his wife and children. My mother suffered the brunt of his verbal abuse. He ranted and raved that she was stupid, disorganized, and incapable of doing anything right. Ignoring his condescending remarks, she strove to coax him out of his tirades.

An example of Jan's father's cruelty occurred when she returned home after completing her doctoral degree in education at age twenty-four. He laughed off this accomplishment, referring to her Ed.D. as a "Mickey Mouse degree." Years earlier he had failed to complete his doctoral program in Russian literature at the University of Michigan. This condescending remark did not crush Jan. By this time in her life she saw him for what he was and regarded him with disdain and disgust. Her mother and siblings, "who never reached that level of awareness," remained targets of his abuse.

Jan recalls an unusual incident with her father when she was about ten years old. Her best friend Sandi was spending the night, asleep with Jan in her twin bed. They were awakened during the wee hours when Jan's father, totally naked, climbed into bed with them and promptly fell asleep. Jan ran to wake her mother, who then escorted Jan's father to his own bed. Apparently he had awakened to use the bathroom, then accidentally wound up in the wrong bed. The situation proved embarrassing. Sandi's mother phoned Jan's mother to discuss the event, and Sandi was never again allowed to spend the night with Jan. To this day Sandi believes this incident to be an indication of sexual abuse. Jan recalls no such abuse. At her house the matter was never mentioned after that night.

During her college and graduate school career, Jan distanced herself from her family. It was only much later, after her father's death and after her divorce from her abusive husband, that Jan and her mother established a closer relationship.

Jan's interest in boys kicked in just prior to her teen years. The interest was platonic and fickle: "hanging out" with boys her age—talking, riding bicycles, swimming with them. Small groups of boys would visit her, laughing and chatting on the front porch of her home while her parents were inside. During adolescence having a boyfriend was not paramount to Jan's well-being, though she was seldom without one. She did not chase boys; rather, she became involved with those who more or less "fell into her lap."

The summer before her sophomore year of high school, Jan became involved with her first steady boyfriend, the senior class president. That relationship lasted until his graduation, when she broke it off. During her junior year she again dated a senior, this time an athlete. Again the relationship ended when he graduated. Her senior-year boyfriend was captain of the school football and basketball teams. He was extremely popular, an all-around nice guy from an "Ozzie and Harriet"–type home. That relationship marked Jan's introduction to sexual intercourse and continued, mostly long distance, for a decade after their graduation.

THE ABUSIVE RELATIONSHIP

Jan was thirty when she met Tom, the man who was to become her husband of nearly ten years; he was thirty-one. She had moved to San Francisco at the age of twenty-five and had been working on the faculty at San Francisco State University since shortly after her arrival. After four years, Jan tired of academia and did not have the security of tenure to dissuade her from searching out other professional opportunities. This was a high point in her life. She felt optimistic and attractive, excited about making a career change. She began networking outside the "ivory tower," informational interviewing in the business world. Life changed quickly. Friendships with academicians waned, and she began dating a wealthy stockbroker. It was while this broker was vacationing for a month on Cape Cod without her that Jan met and began dating Tom.

Tom was a partner in a start-up venture capital firm in San Francisco. Jan met him when she made a drop-in call at the firm in an effort to secure an informational interview with Tom's senior partner. When Tom noticed Jan speaking with the receptionist, he told the receptionist that he would take care of Jan, that there was no need to bother the senior partner. Jan describes that first meeting with Tom:

He then introduced himself and invited me to lunch. He came on very strong, fawning over me, probing into my background and life. I admired his intelligence and ambition. He was charismatic, attractive, and extremely successful.

From a dirt-poor background, Tom grew up in Arkansas, only a few miles from the home of President Bill Clinton. He attained a perfect grade-point average in his Masters of Business Administration (MBA) program at Memphis State University and rose in his career to compete with a crowd made up almost exclusively of Harvard and Stanford MBAs. Jan failed to recognize the significance of his family dynamics: both of his parents had been married three times, and there was emotional and physical abuse in the homes. Tom's father once broke Tom's mother's arm, and on another occasion he burned down the home he shared with his second wife. Tom had been shuffled back and forth between divorcing parents. Some of this Jan did not learn until later in the marriage. Some of it she ignored. After all, she quips, her own family was no paragon of virtue.

Tom's pursuit of Jan was dogged from the moment she began dating him. When Jan's stockbroker boyfriend returned from the Cape, she resumed dating him as well. Jan remembers what happened next and the beginning of her courtship with Tom:

Tom, whose job required extensive travel, went ballistic. He would call me several times daily from around the country, pleading with me for a commitment. He used logic, emotion, tears—whatever worked. Eventually, I concluded that he must love me very much and decided that settling down would be a positive move in my life. I felt ready to make a commitment; my stockbroker friend remained adamantly non-committal. Numerous outside observers perceived Tom as a "very eligible bachelor" and "an excellent catch." He seemed totally devoted and very much in love with me.

Jan agreed to move into Tom's apartment for six months, after which they would marry. This six-month period was pleasant. Their togetherness eased the stress of his demanding career and her professional adjustment as she entered an MBA program full-time. Peaceful domesticity exploded two weeks before the wedding, when Tom presented Jan with a prenuptial agreement designed to block her legal entitlement to any and all community property. Jan refused to sign. They fought. The wedding was postponed. A month later she signed a revised prenuptial agreement that was to become null and void after five years of marriage, and Jan and Tom were married.

In retrospect, Jan admits that she was never head over heels in love with Tom. Instead, her perspective was pragmatic: she respected him, believed he loved her, and believed they could build an enduring and successful life together. From the outset, Jan viewed this marriage to Tom as an investment of sorts. Later, when the relationship became difficult, she would refer to it as her "job."

Jan and Tom's lifestyle changed dramatically after the marriage. In concert with the booming venture capital business of the 1980s, Tom's income doubled annually for six consecutive years. Every two years during the marriage, they moved to a nicer home. They took increasingly expensive and exotic vacations: New Year's Eve in Paris, skiing in Vail, a sailing trip to Turkey. On the surface Jan and Tom appeared to be a couple with everything: youth, beauty, health, friends, beautiful home, plenty of money, infinite opportunity. The quite different reality, glaringly apparent to Jan, became increasingly discernible to the people close to them.

Tom grew increasingly volatile and vicious during the marriage. For years Jan attributed this behavior to the enormous pressure of his work, and she made excuses for him. Jan elaborates:

[Tom] was exceedingly confrontational, constantly lashing out at subordinates and service people (waiters and maitre d's, taxi drivers, contractors, etc.). Increasingly, these attacks were directed at me and those close to us. (Insulted and fed up, friends fell by the wayside.) I erroneously assumed that the attacks would subside when he quit work and had a chance to relax, but the attacks only intensified. He told me he planned to take off six to twelve months before transitioning into another career. I believed him. The six months turned into two years, much of which we spent traveling around the world, and still there was no sign of him returning to work. His anger and volatility escalated. At times he drank heavily.

He became obsessed with appearance, hiring a personal trainer and working out three hours a day; dieting obsessively. He lost forty pounds and seemed to fixate on his virility. Our sex life had never been active and did not change during this period. I sensed he was looking around for an affair. Aside from his preoccupation with his physical state, nothing made him happy or put him at ease. Ultimately, he directed his fury entirely at me, as though I were the sole source of his discontent.

It was much later, after the separation, that Jan surmised the truth about Tom's departure from his firm: it had not been voluntary as he had claimed; rather, it had been forced. Although the partnership had proven successful enough to provide all three partners with several million dollars in income, Tom's personal contribution had been negligible. An unsuccessful track record lowered his chances for finding an opportunity with comparable earning potential and prestige to nil. He was a "has been," and he knew it.

Meanwhile, Jan's career went sideways and downhill. A year into the marriage she completed her MBA and did some fairly lucrative consulting. Tom encouraged her to pursue a risky entrepreneurial venture, and Jan welcomed the challenge. The venture, a small publishing company, performed at twice the industry average during its first year of operation. At the end of the second year, however, Tom insisted that it be shut down because of a lack of profitability. As the major funding source for the company, Tom owned most of the stock, so the decision was his. Jan interprets this business debacle as notable for two reasons. First, it marks the point at which she began working for Tom, a pattern that endured for the remainder of the marriage. Second, it proved an excruciating career failure that shattered her confidence.

Tom argued that unless Jan could make at least a half million dollars a year, it made better sense for her to spend her time supporting his highly lucrative career than for her to develop her own. Following the publishing company's demise, he pressed her to pursue real estate sales and investment. She did so reluctantly. This detested career was cut short when Tom "retired" (was fired) and decided that they should travel. Throughout the marriage Jan also served as general contractor and decorator for their three homes, as well as personal secretary to Tom.

Jan's financial dependence on Tom escalated during the marriage. After the expiration of their five-year prenuptial agreement, at which point all earnings during the marriage were to convert to community property, Tom still refused to permit joint accounts. When Jan worked as general contractor on their properties, she was required to pay for all services and materials from her personal account, then submit requests for reimbursement to Tom. During periods when Jan did not work outside the home, Tom provided her with a modest monthly allowance of $2,000 for food, clothing, and household expenses, despite his base income of $50,000 per month.

Early in Jan and Tom's relationship, Tom began denigrating Jan. Initially, it was subtle. During their first year of marriage he warned her that she was getting too old to pursue a successful business career. She was thirty-three and had just completed her MBA. A year or two later, he criticized her as being stupid, fat, and unattractive. She weighed 105 pounds and was five foot three inches tall. Increasingly, he made these claims publicly. In the fourth year, Tom described Jan to guests at a dinner party as "certainly not as smart and attractive as she thinks she is." Drunk, he slammed his fist through a closet door as soon as the guests departed. The next day he phoned Jan half a dozen times from work, apologizing by voice mail, begging her not to leave him and promising that he would never behave violently again. By this time Jan was clearly fearful of Tom.

During the final three years of the marriage, while Tom was unemployed, Jan lived her life "walking on eggshells," unable to do anything right in her husband's eyes. Verbally attacking her "advanced" age, he claimed that any man of his means should not get stuck with such an "old" woman. He yelled at her constantly, degrading her in one way or another and complaining that she had no life independent of him. Jan says, "Whatever I supposedly lacked became desirable to Tom. He continually commented on other women's nicely shaped hips, slim thighs, interesting careers, inherited wealth." Toward the end, when Tom frequently went out alone, Jan received hang-up phone calls—presumably from other women.

Tom also denigrated Jan's friends and family. He claimed that her mother, who lived in the Midwest, was rude to him over the phone. He forbade her to visit them. Actually, Jan's mother was and remains shy and reserved and in no way rude or imposing. She phoned infrequently and visited Jan only once during the marriage. (Jan's father, who died four years after her marriage, never met or spoke with Tom.) Tom's rejection of Jan's family was not a crushing blow because Jan had remained alienated from them since late adolescence. So she tolerated his insistence. The rejection of her friends was a more difficult matter, however. Over time Tom seemed to disapprove of everyone who befriended Jan; he squelched even those relationships initiated by him.

Tom's terrorization of Jan intensified over time. One particularly frightening incident stands out in her mind:

One year after the prenuptial expired, I discovered that he took out a $600,000 life insurance policy on me. The life policy on him totaled $100,000. His reasoning for the high policy on my life was: If I (husband) die, you get everything (meaning that he considered community property to be his). But if you (wife) die, I get nothing (again because all community property was already his; the life insurance would at least give him some financial compensation).

Now Jan was fearing for her life. A bit later she learned that in their first year of marriage Tom had told his friend that he had gotten Jan to sign a prenuptial agreement and planned to get her to do all of the grunt work in their lives before leaving her penniless. The friend's wife relayed this incident to Jan in confidence. Near the end of the marriage, while on a pleasure trip to Israel and in a seething rage, Tom kicked Jan so hard that she fell out of bed onto the floor. This introduction of physical violence to the abuse intensified Jan's terror.

Jan's family knew nothing of her unhappiness until after the separation. Several friends recognized her situation and tried for years to coax her out of the marriage. Some believed that Tom was physically abusing her all along. One friend from several years before the marriage noted, "Every year you stay in that marriage, I watch you grow more and more miserable."

GETTING OUT

Leaving Tom first occurred to Jan about three years into the marriage. The overall tone of the relationship had become negative, spiraling downward with no sign of improvement. With Tom's criticism and condescension, Jan began to hate him; she cowered and cringed at the sight of him. During those early years Tom traveled about 70 percent of the time. Relief washed over Jan every time he left on a business trip; she faced his return with knotted stomach and frazzled nerves. Increasingly, her thoughts turned to escape. Privately, she vowed to leave as soon as she could gain financial security.

But that security eluded her. She was working for Tom, which brought her only a meager allowance. Her promising entrepreneurial effort, the publishing company, had been aborted—never given sufficient opportunity to succeed. Other less significant initiatives were similarly interrupted when Tom insisted that she focus her energies elsewhere. Tom allowed no joint accounts, so Jan was blocked from millions of dollars in assets, all of which had been accumulated during the marriage. Tom dissuaded Jan from working at a regular job that could have provided her with financial independence and a sense of personal identity. He argued persuasively that any income that she might contribute to the joint enterprise would be rendered as taxes. Technically, Tom was correct. And Jan admits that she enjoyed the freedom that not having a regular job gave her to pursue entrepreneurial ventures, travel and social opportunities.

Ultimately, Jan realized that she had to get out—with or without the illusive financial security. Her life was hell. Often now, she was awakened in the morning to the sound of Tom yelling at her—berating her as pathetic, disgusting, and overcome by inertia. The abuse pattern appeared to be a downward cycle in terms of intensity and danger. It was becoming more vicious and public. Also, it had gravitated toward the physical: from a fist through a door to throwing dishes to kicking her. Jan exclaims: "I felt like a beaten dog—every bit as stupid, ugly, incompetent, and worthless as he claimed me to be." She truly feared for her life at the end. Unable to eat, she lost fifteen pounds (weighing in at ninety-eight pounds) and felt like a zombie. Concerned friends inquired about her health.

Jan began preparations to leave Tom about a year before the separation took place. She describes the incident that incited her to act:

Tom arrived home one day and announced that he was going on a two-week trip to Europe without me. I was crushed, but I knew my marriage was over. The minute he left town I scheduled one-hour appointments with three divorce attorneys for advice. I was instructed to make copies of all financial documents and to keep an eye on the accounts for unusual activity. He kept these documents in a locked file cabinet to which I had no access. Fortunately, I found the cabinet key hidden in the back of his desk and I made a duplicate. I copied hundreds of pages of financial statements, leaving the files looking undisturbed. (He had been claiming that we were nearly out of money, but the documents reflected over a million dollars in liquid assets.) He called me several times while on the trip and returned home several days early without forewarning. The trip had been yet another disappointment. He was glad to be home. He did not detect my tampering with his files. For a while things seemed to calm down. I maintained updated copies of the financial documents while he was away from the house.

Ten months later Jan and Tom took a lengthy trip to Asia. A month after their return, Tom announced that he felt under a lot of pressure and needed "space." This was puzzling in light of the fact that he had not worked in two-and-a-half years and that the two of them occupied a spacious four-bedroom home overlooking San Francisco. He informed Jan that he had rented an apartment across town, where he intended to spend two to three nights a week, but that their lives should continue as usual. He would be home about five nights a week and they would spend all weekends together. Everything would be fine. Nothing would change. When Tom left the house, Jan immediately scheduled an appointment with a divorce attorney, who was able to see her two days later. In the meantime Tom behaved cordially, acted as though nothing had happened, and spent most of his time at the house. He asked Jan what she would like to do over the weekend; she remained calm but told him that she did not want to see him. Two days after the appointment with the divorce attorney, Jan had Tom served with divorce papers. Shortly afterward, on the advice of her attorney, she changed the door locks on the house. They were now formally separated, with her living in the house and him living in his apartment.

Tom begged Jan to talk to him. He swore that people were lying to her about him—that he never had been deceitful or adulterous. It was about that time that Jan discovered by tracing calls on his cellular phone bill that, prior to Tom's securing his apartment, he had been running relationship ads in a local newspaper. She never confronted him with this discovery. One such ad read:

Are you a wonderful person in a marriage that isn't everything it once was or could be? Despite spouse, friends and family, do you sometimes find yourself a little dissatisfied or even lonely? That's the case for me. Until I work it out, I would love the company of a special lady, one who understands such a situation. My friends describe me as humorous, sensitive, empathetic, a good communicator and someone who is fun to be with. I'm 40, a nonsmoker, fit and active and have many interests. I'm very successful and only work for fun. My female counterpart is probably married and in her thirties or early forties. She is intelligent, beautiful, educated, sophisticated and discreet. If you seek a unique friendship, please contact me.

Jan began hanging up when she heard Tom's voice on the phone. His mother called Jan, urging her to reconcile with Tom. She insisted that Tom was simply going through a stage that would blow over in a couple years. She recommended that Jan weather the storm.

Tom pleaded with Jan not to involve attorneys, claiming that attorneys would simply bleed them dry. Although Jan recognized the vulturous nature of some attorneys, she also knew that Tom had lied to her for years and realized that he was not going to be truthful or honorable with her at the divorce stage. He had never been generous or fair. He would not start now.

Jan remained terrified of Tom. She had her attorney demand that the $600,000 insurance policy on her life be canceled. His attorneys replied that he refused to cancel the policy, claiming that he would need the proceeds to pay Jan's share of the mortgage in the event of her death. In reality, Jan had never made a mortgage payment. It was only after Jan agreed to a settlement that Tom agreed to cancel the policy.

Tom and Jan spent two years and more than $200,000 battling through attorneys without getting to court. He outspent her five times over. He threatened to spend an equal amount and take another two years if she took the case to court. If she were to win in court, he promised to appeal and to take another two years and spend another $200,000. Jan settled without her share of the community property. She left the house and moved into a comfortable but modest apartment. Tom moved into the house.

A NOTE ON MARITAL SEX

Although Tom was an attractive man, Jan's attraction to him was intellectual, not sexual. Early in their courtship he liked to "talk dirty" to her during intercourse, which she found to be a real turnoff. When she failed to respond to this talk, it subsided and their sex life limped along at a rate of approximately once a week until the argument over the prenuptial agreement. An emotional and sexual barrier shot up between them. By the end of their third year of marriage, they were averaging a sexual frequency of five to ten times a year. Bear in mind that Tom was traveling 70 percent of the time and they were both exhausted by work. But then, as Jan points out, this is an excuse rather than a reason.

Jan believes that she latched on to sex as the only factor in the relationship over which she had control—power to negotiate. She felt as though she were living in a concentration camp, overcome by hair-trigger fear and a total lack of warmth and security. By the time Tom left his job five years into the marriage, they were having sex four or five times a year. There were brief periods when Jan tried to reverse the situation—times when she did not want the marriage to end and felt it slipping away—but Tom was not responsive. When Jan and Tom finally separated, he claimed that she had been the best friend he had ever had but complained that there was no passion between them. He suggested that it might help if she were to have an affair. Instead, she filed for divorce.

REFLECTIONS

When asked what it was that propelled her into this relationship with Tom, and where did love come into play, Jan offers an elegant and profound analysis:

Right from the beginning, the warning signs flashed like neon: Beware . . . Proceed with caution . . . Enter at your own risk. What made me avert my gaze and pretend not to see them? Why did I dismiss what I intuited and plunge into a destructive relationship? Good question.

It's been said that the stimuli for all human behavior can be distilled down to greed and fear. People either respond to get more of what they want (behave greedily), or they respond to avoid aversive situations (behave fearfully). What about love? one might ask. Didn't love play a role in propelling me into my marriage? That depends on definitions and perspective. Behaviorists, after all, might rationalize love as a complex set of responses an individual engages in to "hang on to" a source of positive reinforcement. When I reflect back over what it was that I was hanging on to, it bears a far greater resemblance to greed and fear than to love.

So what were my objects of greed and fear? In terms of greed, I wanted to feel loved and desired; he was obsessed with me. In terms of fear, I was tired of fending for myself; he offered security. My error lay in the discrepancies between appearances and reality. I created an image of the better life I would have with this man—a perfect panacea designed to escape some of my own problems, while oblivious to his shortcomings. I was so wedded to this illusion of a better life that I ignored the early warning signals. Only when alarms blared nonstop did I confront the fact that I had a hundred-and-eighty pound problem who was hell-bent on destroying me.

In retrospect, Jan sees much of her father in Tom. Both expressed their own unhappiness by intimidating, dominating, and lashing out at others. She realizes that she may have adopted her mother's "ostrich" posture by refusing to acknowledge what was happening to her in her marriage—by shielding her agony with denial. Though friends had been urging her to leave for years, by Tom's design she was alienated from those friends. An emotional and mental wreck, she refused to impose on them. She felt she had no place to go. Family was out of the question. While going home might have been a logistical option, it was a psychological impossibility. Jan remains humiliated that for nearly a decade she allowed herself to be drawn into a web of isolation, fear, self-blame, and humiliation. She sees her life as better now in all ways except financially.

CHAPTER TWO

Netiva

Netiva was visiting my university from her home in Chicago when I met her. We were attending a women's studies conference on campus. While dining together in a group one evening, the subject of my *Getting Out* project came up and prompted Netiva to volunteer snippets of her personal experience with battering. I seized the moment to invite her participation. In short order Netiva enthusiastically crafted a generously detailed and lengthy autobiography, cleared for accuracy through written correspondence with her mother in Israel.

Netiva's youth is set in Israel and, to a lesser extent, Paris. Through her story we learn from a young girl's perspective a wealth of Israeli history and custom, including kibbutz life, and also gain a glimpse of Parisian anti-Semitism in the mid-1960s. Netiva's abuse occurred in the context of her being a newly transplanted young woman of Mediterranean descent attempting to make a home in Chicago. Her isolation from everything familiar was a batterer's dream.

Now in her middle forties, Netiva lives in Chicago with her husband and three daughters and teaches computer science at the university level. Five years ago she began a career of painting and sculpting and exhibits her work at every opportunity. Children, as well as "adults with children's hearts," especially love her style and technique. Recently Netiva wrote and illustrated a book for children, and she is currently composing her first novel. Her Israeli condominium anchors her to her native land.

Born in Israel in 1949, a year after that country won its independence, Netiva is the product of a Sephardic Jewish (of Spanish descent) marriage. Her mother's family left Salonica, Greece, for Palestine in 1932, when her mother was four, probably in conjunction with the Zionist movement. While Netiva's maternal grandfather had prospered with his vegetable and fruit market in Salonica, he never succeeded financially in Israel, which necessitated Netiva's mother toiling her youth away ironing clothes with coal irons and, as a result, being denied a conventional formal education. She compensated by completing two years of high school at night and then continuing her education on her own through readings, free lectures at the university, and work-training programs. Netiva respects her mother as a wise, hardworking, and learned woman—even a poet.

Netiva's father is from a third-generation Israeli (then Palestinian) family that originated in Turkey. His paternal grandfather was a rabbi, and his own father, a printer by trade, was what was referred to as "a wise man," one who knew the Bible by heart. Netiva's father was the first of his family to be born outside Jerusalem, "the holy city," near Tel Aviv, "the modern city." His mother suffered an accidental death when he was twelve, leaving behind four children. He recalls her as a saint, sending him every Friday evening, just before the break of Sabbath, with a bowl of food to deposit at the door of a poor neighborhood family. He was instructed to knock on the door, then run. Such anonymous giving was one of the highest levels of tzedaka (charity).

Netiva's father did not get along with his older brothers; at sixteen he left home to join the Palmach and later the Haganah, both underground armies created to defend Jewish settlements from the Arabs and create an independent Jewish state. At nineteen he joined the Jewish brigade of the British army (Israel was then under British mandate) and two years later fought the Nazis in northern Africa and Europe. Still a member of that brigade, he spent a year in Holland after World War II, rebuilding bridges.

Netiva's parents met at a Tel Aviv wedding when she was fourteen and he nineteen. They became romantically involved on the spot and maintained the relationship throughout his travels.

After his return to Palestine in 1946, they served in the same military unit during the War of Independence, then married in

1948, two months after Israel became an independent nation. She was twenty and he twenty-five; both were soldiers. Four months into her pregnancy, Netiva's mother was honorably discharged from the army and delivered Netiva a year after the wedding. Netiva means "path." She was named after the battle her parents' brigade had fought to free the road to the Negev desert.

During the first year of her life, Netiva and her parents lived with her maternal grandparents in a modest fourth-floor central Tel Aviv apartment with a community outhouse. Conditions were cramped, but those were good days. Netiva has been told that both grandparents cried when she and her parents left. During that time Netiva's father was transferred to the mounted police of the army, then on to a desk job with the Ministry of Defense.

The family purchased their first house in the outskirts of Tel Aviv. It was a two-bedroom duplex with no living room but a large patio—typical for a middle-class family in those days. Economic depression had set in, so food was scarce and people depended on the black market. Netiva's father would bring milk from the city, only to find that with the sizzling climate and long bus ride it had spoiled before reaching the icebox. At first there was no electricity. Netiva recalls the highs and lows of everyday life in that first house:

Early childhood was fine. I only remember two episodes of being physically abused by my mother when I was around three years old (can't remember exactly how she hit me or where). The first was because I couldn't tie my shoelaces. The second was after I chewed on a pound bill out of nervousness of being expected to go shopping by myself. The salesman at the counter refused to take the chewed-on bill. It is not unusual to see kids buying chewing gum or the like in a kiosk near their house. I also remember an episode that happened at two years old when our neighbors [lifted] me out of the window as I was crying for my parents who were out. I remember the dew under my feet as I was running to our neighbors' door and sleeping on a mattress watching the moon through their open window. My parents explained later that in those days no one could afford baby-sitting and one would just ask one's neighbors to listen for one's child.

My father claims he never hit us, but I remember once in Tel Aviv him slapping me on my naked butt (only once). I believe there were other times, but no recollection of specifics. I remember having had to eat a too-oily soup that my mom made and crying about it. I remember I always had to apologize to my father when I did something bad. He would not talk to me otherwise. My mom always begged me to apologize, something I did not like to do.

Happier times included walking and being carried by my parents, a few miles on Saturdays from our house, through a river, to visit my mom's sister and their two daughters. We would pretend I was the queen of England. Other times I was walking on pillows pretending to walk on clouds . . . I also remember folk dancing on the hill behind our first house. I have pleasant memories from those days.

During the first three or four years of marriage, Netiva's mother tended house while sending her to various childcare centers—wanting only the best for her daughter. Then she, like Netiva's father, took a position with the Ministry of Defense, where she remained, except for a couple brief diversions, until her recent retirement. By this time Netiva's father was heavily entrenched in becoming a painter. He had taken an art course in Holland and was in pursuit of a four-year degree at the prestigious art academy at Avni. In his spare time he was to become a prominent artist, as evidenced by his appointment at midlife to the teaching faculty at Avni. Some of Netiva's favorite early memories of her father capture him and his artist friends painting in the sunny hills behind that first house. Later, when she was nine, he held his first gallery exhibit, a point of exhilaration for the entire family.

When Netiva was five, the family relocated to a better neighborhood, designed for honorably discharged officers. Soon thereafter her father entered a teacher education night program while continuing his job at the Ministry of Defense and his artistic endeavors. It was about this time that Netiva's parents' marriage began showing real signs of stress. Her mother disliked staying home alone in the evenings; Netiva's father was threatening to leave her mother if she complained. There was much heartache on the horizon.

Netiva has fond memories of being an only child in that second house. Every Saturday her father took her to art galleries and museums. Netiva's parents decided not to send her to the nearby school, but rather to one more distant that was of better quality. That, coupled with her shy nature, made it difficult to find neighborhood friends. She preferred to read after school and exchanged books at the local library almost daily. There were no telephones or cars then, so play arrangements were difficult. But on Friday evenings her classmates would come looking for her to go folk dancing in the park. She happily readied herself for those outings with the help of her father, who prepared her weekly bath (water was scarce).

Netiva's brother, Nir, was born when she was nearly eight. With the addition of the baby, the house was enlarged to include a dining room and studio. Netiva happily shared her room with Nir, while her parents continued to use the hide-a-bed sofa in the living room. Netiva describes the welcoming of Nir:

I wanted that brother very much and so did my father. My mother got convinced of the necessity of a sibling once I turned six and became rather spoiled. I was very proud of my brother and took him for walks in his stroller. My friends would take turns as well . . . [the] whole class . . . made a book for me with drawings of baby and wishes.

There was a downside to the era of Netiva's childhood that commenced with the arrival of Nir. Her parents had ugly fights, mostly over the children, her father's absence and perhaps other women, and financial hardship. Much of her father's income went to his interests and habits, leaving her mother to pay for everything else. That pattern would persist throughout the marriage. Netiva's mother was bitter. Today she explains that bitterness to Netiva as a consequence of Netiva's father's daily threats of leaving her if she spoke harshly to him. She lived in continual fear and could never speak her piece.

Netiva's mother was and remains compulsive about her domestic duties. When she would get tired of working, she would scream at the others for not lifting a finger. Her father, on the other hand, was and is mostly calm and respected by his wide community of friends and, later, students. To the consternation of Netiva's mother, he helped very little around the house. Netiva's mother was totally devoted to the family, whereas her father was devoted first to his art and then to the family. Her mother gave off conflicting messages about Netiva's father: he was selfish but at the same time her only real friend. Netiva recalls always admiring her father and being ashamed of her mother—because of her excess weight.

When Netiva was twelve, she, her mother, and Nir left Tel Aviv to live in a kibbutz for two years while her father moved to Paris to study at the Beaux Arts de Paris, where he earned a certificate commensurate with a master's degree. Netiva's mother believed that the family could not survive financially in Paris so chose to stay behind; she did not want to live alone in the city with the children so opted for the communal life of the Israeli kibbutzim.

This kibbutz was secular rather than religious, accommodating three hundred people, all families committed to community ownership and cooperative living. All work and benefits were shared; no money was exchanged. In this particular kibbutz the children stayed with their parents rather than in the children's house, except for breakfast and lunch. At dinnertime parents and children came together in the big dining room. Houses were small duplex apartment units, all basically alike. Netiva and Nir shared a room and their mother had the living room. There was a kitchen area for making hot drinks only and a small bathroom. Netiva recalls trying to watch her entire body changing through the small (four-by-six-inch) mirror that her mother hung above the sink.

Both Netiva and Nir had difficulties the first year adjusting to kibbutz life. Netiva was one of only four seventh graders, so her class was combined with the sixth grade for some subjects. The younger boys teased her about her unusual pronunciations and even her developing breasts. Nir, who was only four, suffered more from the transition. He was close to their father and blamed their mother for the separation. During the first week he was found on the main road, running away from the kibbutz in search of his father. Nir hid many times, worrying their mother, until she explained that he might be caught by the Arabs—Lebanon was over the hills only four kilometers away. The second year in the kibbutz was much better for everyone. Netiva, Nir, and their mother became true kibbutzniks and thrived in the wholesome community atmosphere. Netiva recalls this slice of kibbutzim life from those days:

I enjoyed Sabbath at the kibbutz. All adults and children (300 of us) gathered in the big dining room for dinner, candle lighting, and singing. Some of us kids were reading different parts of prayer or appropriate poetry for the event. Later at night we would folk dance or watch a movie on a big screen (or wall). My father came to visit us only once during those two years, upon my bat-mitzvah celebration at age thirteen, which was a party for the four of us of the same age.

At the end of that second year, when Netiva was fourteen, her parents decided that the three of them should join her father in Paris. They stayed in Paris five years. That transition was hard too; everyone had to learn French. It was a particularly difficult adjustment for Netiva's mother because, within a few days of her arrival, Netiva's father told her of his mistress, whom he could not live without. To that, Netiva's mother responded quite decisively: he was to leave the apartment and take the children with him while she moved in with a Jewish family as their maid. She asked to meet Monele and instructed her on the care of the two children. Netiva, Nir, and their father relocated to Monele's efficiency apartment, which had no shower. That lasted less than two weeks; Netiva's parents reconciled, perhaps at least partly because of her mother's suicide attempt, and the entire family returned to their original apartment.

The marital drama intensified. Fights grew outrageous and focused on the scarcity of money for food. Netiva recalls the screams and her father's attempts to calm her mother as she threatened to leave or kill herself. Six months after their arrival in Paris, Netiva's mother obtained security clearance from Israel, so she was able to quit her job at a nearby laundromat to assume a secretarial position at the Israeli consulate, where Netiva's father was employed. That increase in steady income relaxed the tension somewhat. But Netiva's mother remained unhappy a while longer—not knowing the language and having no close friends. There were one or two more suicide attempts before she settled into a stable and productive lifestyle.

In the beginning Netiva faced anti-Semitism in the Parisian schools and for that reason was forced to attend a school for workband rather than college-bound girls. The others excluded her on the pretense that she was not fluent in French. Under her father's tutelage she was able to overcome the language barrier and earn straight As. After two trimesters Netiva's parents were financially able to enroll her in a proper private school. She was still wearing white socks while her classmates wore stockings and makeup. But this did not bother her, and eventually her mother bought stockings for her.

It was in Paris that Netiva blossomed romantically and sexually. She claimed her first boyfriend at sixteen, then at seventeen became involved with her classmate Patrice. After four months of courtship she allowed him to kiss her when he received the highest mathematics grade. The relationship progressed from there, but ended after a year when she announced she would not continue having sex with him because a friend had persuaded her that good girls don't do that. A few days later he told her that he could not live without sex and so would be looking for another girl. Patrice did replace her, and consequently Netiva's senior year was miserable. There were plenty of boyfriends to come, however.

Netiva spent that last summer in Europe, before her return to Israel for military duty, camping through Spain with her family. Summer camping had become a family tradition and family relationships were at their best then. Nir was a great navigator, and Netiva helped with the tent and dishwashing. Netiva had a wonderful love affair that summer. Then in November 1968, at nineteen, she was drafted into the Israeli army—by request after a year's delay so she could finish high school.

Netiva was happy to return to her homeland and thrilled to serve her country. All eighteen-year-olds to this day are drafted into the military unless they have some religious excuse or are maried. Men serve thirty-six months and women twenty. After the war of 1967 (the Six-Day War), Netiva was energized with patriotism. Coming from a four-generation Israeli officer family and having spent recent years away in France, Netiva was ready to make her military contribution. In fact, in 1967 she had pledged to bear five sons to fight and die for Israel.

Netiva found her military stint challenging and satisfying. She began as a private, teaching mathematics and physics to younger recruits, then progressed to officer school. Her family returned to Israel in time to attend the closing ceremony of her basic training, so were there for her when she had weekends off. Upon discharge, Netiva returned to live with them and shortly thereafter enrolled at Tel Aviv University to study mathematics and French. At about this time her father was appointed to a professorship at the art academy where he had attended night school, and Nir was designated a gifted child and allowed at thirteen to study in part at the university. By now the family had a car and a private phone line.

THE ABUSIVE RELATIONSHIP

Even before completing her military obligation, Netiva sensed from her parents and uncles a pressure to marry soon. And she was anxious to begin a family of her own. She had dated extensively, so by now was a veteran in the ways of love. Yoav was by all counts her best "catch." Netiva stayed with him a year and a half and discussed the possibility of marriage, but he was determined to complete his military and university work before accepting that responsibility. Five years seemed an eternity to Netiva back then and unacceptable to her spontaneous nature.

So at the commencement of summer vacation, when Sidney, a handsome American tourist with a master's degree, appeared on the scene, Netiva was quick to seduce him, but found herself seduced as well. He was two years her senior and an elementary special education teacher in inner-city Chicago. Netiva was able to speak English with him, a language learned in school since the sixth grade and used occasionally with tourists and during her two-month summer stay in London at seventeen. Sid was impressed with Netiva's trilingual skills.

Netiva and Sid met through a mutual friend, and the three spent a wonderful day at the beach. That evening Netiva and Sid went off alone to a movie and talked late into the night. Netiva was spell-bound. The next day Sid took a previously scheduled tour of Jerusalem, then the following day the two again met for a long walk and talk in the park. Netiva recalls what happened next:

He proposed to me that evening after our first kiss and I accepted. His only condition was that I keep kosher (basically keep meat and dairy food separate). Little did I know it was much harder to keep kosher in America than in Israel, where everything in the stores was always kosher. In America one needs to read the label and make sure there are no animal products in shortening, or even in soap.

The next day Sid accompanied Netiva to the wedding of a class-mate at her old kibbutz. Netiva's father wanted Sid's formal request for her hand in marriage, and Netiva promised that this would hap-pen on their return from the wedding. So on the fourth day of the relationship, Sid approached Netiva's father. The meeting was somewhat of an interrogation ritual as Netiva's father queried Sid regarding his finances and his life plan. Upon completion of the inquisition and leaving the house, Sid flew into a rage and at one point threatened to call off the marriage. Netiva attributed the out-burst to the particular situation and proceeded to calm him and per-suade him to marry her.

Wedding preparations commenced, and within three weeks of having met, Netiva and Sid were married in Tel Aviv. After a week-long uneventful honeymoon, Sid returned to Chicago on schedule to begin his academic year, leaving Netiva to negotiate the paper-work required for her to join him as a legal alien. During those two months she remained excited at the prospect of a new life in a for-eign land, though Europe would have been preferable to the United States (Netiva surmises that she had been influenced negatively about the United States by a combination of anti-American French sentiments and the unsightliness of "mostly fat American tourists in long shorts"). As a parting gesture Netiva's mother hand wrote a cookbook for her with some extra instructions on how to do laun-dry and be a good wife. Netiva did not mind leaving family and friends. She was fairly close to her family but wanted independence from them.

Netiva arrived in Chicago in October 1972 at the age of twenty-three. Sid's apartment was nicer than anticipated and his family was loving. She needed another year of college to complete her baccalaureate degree, but because the next session would not begin until the following January, she took a bookkeeping job until then.

It took only a week for the marriage to turn to disaster. Netiva recalls:

I can't remember what the first fight was all about, but I didn't control it as well as I did in Israel. Sid was more assured in his own surroundings and expected me to become an instant American. . . . Sid wanted to control me entirely by forbidding me, for example, from talking to men at my job. Although he was not around, I obeyed him. I guess this terrorism at home started to have an effect on me. I was brainwashed. It took me many months before I dared talk to any man again. Somehow, by my saying, Sid found out that I had [had sex with] more than one man, exactly three to his knowledge. . . . He had only one woman before me, and the thought that I had more than him had enraged him. He mentally tortured me about this issue. He kept asking me why I had slept with other men and how I could do such an immoral thing. I ended up believing that I was wrong having had lovers and that I would raise my daughters-to-be to remain virgin till they marry. I can't remember many details of my first year in the U.S. except that it was very cold even with my huge sheepskin coat that I brought with me. I lost weight and was very unhappy. It was the worst of times. I cannot think of any pleasant time with Sid that year.

In the midst of Sid's terrorism, Netiva enrolled at the University of Illinois, Chicago.

As Sid's control agenda intensified over that first year of marriage, Netiva remained isolated in her misery. Alone in a foreign land, limited in her use of its language, she languished on the turf of the enemy. Older than her classmates and culturally different, in a commuter climate without dorms where students rushed about among home, school, and work, she was unable to strike up even one collegial friendship. She got along with Sid's family but was forbidden to discuss the marriage with them. Once a week for the Sabbath dinner, Netiva and Sid joined his brothers and sister-in-law at his parents' home. These visits nourished Netiva, gave her some sense of family.

Though Sid made much more money than he and Netiva spent, she was not allowed to have a car or even to drive Sid's. She had an Israeli driver's license and was a good driver but failed her first Illinois driving test because Sid screamed at her in route to the exam, leaving her too upset to concentrate. Netiva resorted to public transportation, which can be brutal in Chicago in the winter, especially for the novice. Cigarette smoking was another focus of Sid's control. At first Netiva was allowed to smoke everywhere except the bedroom, then only in the living room. Eventually she was limited to the porch.

Sid was training to become a Transactional Analysis (TA) therapist, and therein lay yet another tool of oppression. According to the TA perspective, only four emotions—anger, sadness, happiness, and fear—should be expressed, and that should be done properly. Netiva describes her ordeal with TA:

I used to cry in anger. That was not the right way to express it, according to him. I could not express any other feeling that was not on the list of four. I had to turn to TA methodology myself in order to cope with his growing demands and start defending myself an as individual. Parent-Adult-Child were the only states that we were in. It was best to be in the Adult state, according to Sid. I was spontaneous, going from one state to another. Sid would catch me every time I would wander outside of the Adult state of being. It was mental torture. I worked hard at it, and after a lot of training I succeeded. For example, I couldn't say "pass the butter, please" because "please" would put me in a Child state. "Will you pass the butter" was the only way acceptable. I couldn't tell him to do certain things or pass judgment, as then I would be in a Parent state. I couldn't cry, as it was childish, etc. After a while I became expert at not crying, I who used to shed tears very easily. I built a thick wall around me so that Sid's tortures would not hurt me as much. At first, I had to deal with that piercing pain in the throat when wanting to cry. Then, I just became cold as stone.

At last Netiva had been molded into Sid's perfect TA robot.

Netiva and Sid spent their first summer together camping out West. Those months proved to be the best time in their marriage; with Sid removed from his natural habitat, the two were quite compatible. Sid drove while Netiva navigated. Each evening, upon arrival at a new campground, chores were divided: he cooked while she erected the tent then later did dishes.

But even that trip was critically marred near its conclusion by an episode, one that introduced physical abuse into the relationship. Spilled soup and a hostile verbal exchange culminated in Sid grabbing Netiva by the arm, dragging her to the car (out of public view), and hitting her. In disbelief, anger, and sadness, Netiva left the scene, heading down the road leading away from camp to the unknown. What followed was a gesture that intensified Sid's control of Netiva—one regretted by her to this day: she came back. She knows now that she should have walked longer, giving Sid a chance to apologize and her to renegotiate the balance of power in her favor. Instead, it went the other way. She had demonstrated that he could humiliate and now even beat her into submission. As it turned out, he went on to do just that.

The second year of the marriage was characterized by regular physical abuse. Sid would hit Netiva if she were to argue any issue. The more she protested or fought back, the more enraged he became. Eventually she learned not to defend herself. Always he was careful to limit injuries to bruises covered by clothing. Periods of hitting would be followed by a few weeks of calm. Sid always blamed Netiva for the beatings, insisting that she drove him to it with her defiance. Netiva reflects:

After every beating episode, he would ask forgiveness and promise not to repeat. I refound then in him the Sid that I loved when I first met him in Israel. He appeared always very sincere and loving. I wanted to believe him.

When "Dr. Jekyll" surfaced, Netiva became determined to become a better wife so they could together reclaim that love of her dreams.

There were several reasons Netiva stayed with Sid. She wanted to believe his tearful promises that he would change. She believed him when he said his rages were her fault; if she were to just stop challenging him, she could recover the Sid she once knew. She thought she had control. Also, she did not believe divorce was the appropriate response to marital problems; she saw it as an irresponsible out. It was taboo in her family at the time. There was also the hope that Sid's therapy group (attended as part of his TA training agenda) would induce change in him.

Finally, and perhaps most importantly, Netiva stayed because there was no acceptable alternative. She had no support; no one knew of her troubles; she was too ashamed to disclose her entrapment in a life that she associated with uneducated, poor, and drunken families. Her only recourse, as she saw it, was to return to Israel, carrying the shame of having been discarded. That would be worse than the abuse.

GETTING OUT

Immediately following that first summer with its tragic conclusion, Netiva took a self-defense class for women as part of her physical education requirement for graduation; she thought it might also help her at home. That is where she met her first American friend, Ronnie. It would be a year or two before she would confide her horrible secret, but still it was good to have a friend. It was Netiva's small first step to getting out—although she did not recognize it as such at the time.

In December 1973 Netiva graduated from college with honors, then continued directly into the graduate program in mathematics. She was awarded a teaching assistantship, and with that came a communal office where she and other assistants worked, fraternized, and received students. Though Sid's terrorism continued, Netiva now had a respite. That office was significant in that it represented another small, and again as yet unrecognized, step in dismantling the isolation that held her captive to Sid's abuse.

The tyranny continued. Netiva recalls running away from home after Sid, in his rage, ripped up her parents' letter before she could read it. She remembers roaming the streets wanting not to go back, yet hoping Sid would find her, which he did. Another time she narrowly escaped a severe belt whipping by crawling under the bed covers; it did not hurt as much. Once Sid threatened Netiva with a knife; she played down her fear, giving him no incentive to repeat. It was then that she began to fantasize killing him in self-defense; but she did not know how, so she simply wished him dead.

When Netiva and Sid were at home in Chicago, he would never hit her in public, for fear of being recognized. Near New Orleans on a camping trip, he struck her outdoors in broad daylight; Netiva's surprise came when no passersby helped her. Later, after two years of marriage, when they were visiting her parents and he attempted an assault on the streets of Tel Aviv, an old man yelled at Sid. That same day Sid ripped a page from Netiva's passport, leaving her terrified that she would not be allowed to return to the States. The missing page went unnoticed by authorities.

Around this same time, in fall 1974, Netiva struck up a friendship with a mathematics professor, not one of her own, in her department. They would take the subway together home from school. Brayton was handsome, warm, cheerful, and nine years Netiva's senior. A romance evolved, but because Brayton already had a woman in his life, Netiva was destined to remain secondary. They met mostly in his apartment, and it was in that context that Netiva first revealed Sid's abuse and first heard another's sentiments that she should leave him. Although Brayton offered his home to Netiva in the event of an emergency, he never encouraged her to move in. Without that invitation of permanence, she was not secure enough to leave Sid.

Once she had opened up to Brayton, it was easier to do so with Ronnie. Then Netiva confided in her new friend Judy, whom she met at a social gathering at the home of Sid's friend. As had Brayton, Judy offered her home as temporary refuge from Sid; but Netiva needed more than something temporary. She made another friend, Lois, then went on to have a short-lived affair with another graduate student in her department.

Netiva's newfound friendship network enhanced her self-esteem and confidence—not unnoticed by Sid, who then redoubled his campaign to control her. She explains:

Sid, noticing my grown confidence, was taking away my green card (immigrant visa) every beating episode, threatening [to throw] me out of the country if I dared leave him. This was the last thing I wanted. He knew my weak point. I did not want to return to Israel empty-handed and ashamed. I never questioned the validity of Sid's threats. I guess I was too scared and ignorant and just did not know where to find out the truth about him being able to throw me out of the country.

The emotional and psychological support provided by her friends was working to free Netiva, but now there was an added impediment to her escape: fear of Sid's retaliation. But at least she was on the right track: she knew she wanted to leave; she just didn't have a way.

With the onset of a new romance, Netiva was finally able to get out. Her passion to be with Dick, coupled with the encouragement and assistance of Brayton, Judy, Ronnie, and Lois, propelled her to action. Dick was her former professor and dean of the graduate college. Twenty-five years her senior, he too was seeking relief from a marriage. In the beginning they played racquetball together at the university; next they met at restaurants, then ultimately for short out-of-town trips and at his apartment. Dick proposed marriage and offered to join the Jewish faith. Life with him was spiritually and intellectually enriched, and he offered security, Netiva's long-awaited treasure. Netiva adored Dick and continues to view him as the one true love of her life. Now it was possible to leave Sid.

The first step was to tell Sid of her intention to leave (but not about Dick). Fearing that she might suffer a severe beating on that designated night, Netiva arranged for Judy to phone her at 10:00 P.M. to check on her safety. At 8:00 P.M. she broke the news to Sid. He remained calm until after Judy's call; then he stormed in for the kill. Knowing that the landlords with a dog were home downstairs, Netiva screamed for help. The dog barked wildly, but there was no human response.

Netiva believes that it is a miracle she survived that episode. She was able to calm Sid with the suggestion that she transfer her savings of $2,500 to his account of $25,000, money saved from his salary by living frugally over Netiva's "three-and-a-half years of hell." Sid insisted on weekly marriage counseling during the separation. With that agreement, Netiva located an affordable apartment with two roommates and contracted to move in one month later. She slept in their tiny guest bedroom for two weeks, then moved in with Dick for the second two weeks—a few of her belongings were stored at a friend's house to reinforce the story that Netiva was there rather than with Dick.

With the use of Dick's vehicle and the help of Judy and Brayton, Netiva moved her few belongings from Sid's apartment to her tiny new bedroom. It was there over the weeks that followed that she produced her first artistic paintings: their creation brought her peace and solace. Fifteen years later, under the influence of a visit from her father, she would return to and develop her art.

The relationship with Dick withered during those two weeks that Netiva lived with him. She remembers:

Living with him for two weeks was different. It brought me back to reality. Sex was not as exciting. His toilet habits turned me off. I still loved him and cherished his endless care for me. He prepared delicious meals for me, beautiful cocktails, and wanted me to pamper myself, a concept I never knew about.

The thrill was gone! And Netiva's father's outrage over Dick's advanced age dissuaded her. She continued seeing Dick a while longer, then they drifted apart.

At Netiva and Sid's tenth weekly therapy session, Sid finally agreed to divorce (he had found a girlfriend). It was important to Netiva that she have a religious as well as a civil divorce. Only the Jewish divorce would be recognized in Israel, and she could not contract another Jewish marriage without it. Because Jewish divorces are controlled by men (a woman cannot divorce against her husband's will), Netiva was at the mercy of Sid. He agreed to grant a religious divorce only after the civil divorce was final, with Netiva having requested no money from him and having claimed no physical abuse. Netiva capitulated. Both divorces were processed without a hitch in February 1977. As for the communal savings from the marriage: they disappeared at about the time Sid grew new hair on his bald spot.

REFLECTIONS

When asked to reflect on her abusive marriage and getting out, Netiva speaks only of fear. She has no memory of happiness or even comfort with Sid once the abuse began a week after her arrival in the United States. She hated the beatings, but more than that, she feared being without a man and being viewed as a failure in the eyes of her family and the world at large. She had learned early on that a woman needs to acquire and keep a man at any cost—a woman standing alone is not whole. So she stayed with Sid. It was her collection of friends who ultimately neutralized that fear of failure associated with getting out, who convinced her the abuse was not her fault and that she deserved better.

Part II

. . . NOR
ARE CHILDREN

CHAPTER THREE

Kimberly

Kimberly responded to one of the posted announcements that I had distributed around my community. Her little girl accompanied her to my office for our initial meeting. As Kimberly and I discussed the "Getting Out" project, Ann amused herself with the bottle of Mr. Bubbles that stays on my desk in case children visit or something good happens to me. Always beaming, Kimberly popped into my office periodically during those weeks that she was composing her autobiographical sketch; clearly lifetelling was doing her a world of good. Perhaps the most interesting thing that I recall about working with Kimberly is an incident in her apartment while I was there to go over one of my drafts of her story with her. She wanted to take me through her photo album so that I could see her family at various spots in the progression of her story. I could see how her children had grown and how greatly her weight, the bane of her existence, fluctuates. Then she flipped to a page reflecting a single large Olen Mills–type portrait of her and her former husband, posed as a loving couple sometime during their abusive marriage. Proudly Kimberly exclaimed, "Isn't he just gorgeous!" She could think that, after all he had done to her and after working through it all in sculpting her life story. At that moment, now frozen in time, Kimberly taught me just how very long the getting-out process can be; even now she was not totally free.

Kimberly's story is one of loneliness and despair rooted in parental substance abuse and child neglect and confounded by obesity. It demonstrates how a small girl's desperation for love can leave her vulnerable to eating disorders and to sexual predators in childhood and beyond.

Though still young, Kimberly has come a long way. At age twenty-five, she is aggressively confronting the demons of her childhood and of her abusive relationships with men. Recipients of AFDC and food stamps, she and her two young children live in public housing in Bowling Green, Kentucky, where she is enrolled at the university. In these times of social services cutback rhetoric, Kimberly's story opens our eyes to the reconstructive ability of welfare. Temporary financial support is allowing Kimberly to transform three lives otherwise destined for dependence into lives radiating health, well-being, and productivity.

Kimberly was a late entry to a troubled and rather large family. She was the fourth and last child born to a working-class couple in Richardsville, Kentucky, just outside Bowling Green, whose marriage would dissolve two years later. Her mother had married at age fifteen with an eighth-grade education, and her father at age nineteen. At the time of her parents' divorce, Kimberly's oldest sister had left home to marry her high school sweetheart. Her brother, a disc jockey with a local radio station, was ready for a change, so packed up and moved to Omaha, Nebraska. That left Kimberly's older sister Lannette to care for her while their mother, then thirty-four and a bit overwhelmed with her newfound freedom, tried to find whatever it was she was looking for. Lannette became a lifelong mainstay to Kimberly, and they remain close today.

When Kimberly was about four, her mother married a man whom Kimberly describes as "ugly as homemade sin, but a very good provider." At that time her mother worked in a factory, and their combined incomes supported a comfortable lifestyle. The money also gave the couple access to copious supplies of liquor. Soon into the marriage, this new stepfather demonstrated a "Dr. Jekyll/Mr. Hyde" personality: while he was sometimes generous and charming, he began hitting Kimberly's mother, beating her sister, and "raging at the world most of the night." Kimberly recalls that though her mother seemed happy during those days and this man took the family nice places, "the bottle and rage always came along for the ride." Before it was over, Kimberly's mother suffered much at the hands of her second husband: twelve stitches on the

back of her head, seven over her brow, and her "pink
ground into an ice crusher. She married and divorced
twice. Kimberly was seven or eight when that was all over,
nette had left home, to be shuffled from relative to rela
within a year Kimberly's mother connected with another a
a man who would share their lives for the next eight years.
favored this boyfriend over the former stepfather: his wea
not his fist but a sharp, condescending tongue. Anything w
than watching her mother be beaten.

Through all of this, Kimberly's father remained in her life. He
was a hardworking railroad foreman and her "weekend daddy." He
was also an alcoholic. When Kimberly was five, he remarried. That
step-relationship was difficult: wife and daughter rivaled each other
for the man's affection. Neither got much.

After the divorce of Kimberly's mother and stepfather, her
mother retained her factory job, and the two of them shared a
mobile home. Kimberly has fond memories of growing up with her
mother. Her favorite times were trips to the grocery. They would
make a game of it. Together they would make out the list. Then in
the store they would mentally compute the bill as they placed each
item into the cart. At the end they would guess the total bill. Kimberly was around nine at that time.

But her bitter memories overpower the happy ones. While she
witnessed much physical abuse as a child, personally she endured
emotional abuse and neglect rather than physical violence. As a
child Kimberly was placed in charge of housekeeping. She would
anxiously await her mother's return from work for recognition of a
job well done. The recognition came, but always with criticism: "I
see you got the dishes done, but why didn't you vacuum? Your
room looks like a pigsty; why don't you start on it next." Kimberly
notes that things have not changed between her and her mother:
"Mom, I got an eighty-nine on my term paper." "Well, that doesn't
sound good; can you do extra credit?" But, she adds, she no longer
hopes for water from a dry well. That makes life easier.

Weekends were particularly difficult for Kimberly during those
childhood days spent with her mother in the mobile home. She
explains:

My mother always spent her weekends with her boyfriend and their
bottle. You see, my mother was a beauty to look at. Her clothes were
always fresh and clean. She always wore matching eye shadow, and
every hair was right in place. To see her drunk every weekend, slurring

er words and ignoring me like the plague was hard for me and never got easier. By the time I was twelve I wanted to stay at home by myself instead of making weekend trips with Mom. I was beginning to fight with her about her drinking and driving; it scared me to ride with her. My pleas to stop were denied, and I was told to shut up.

At this point Lannette had married, and the two sisters spent time together whenever possible. Kimberly's favorite place to be was with Lannette.

In 1984, when Kimberly was a high school sophomore, her mother broke up with the boyfriend. About that time she became injured on the job and as a result acquired an addiction to pre-scription drugs—in addition to her alcoholism. Soon she found another man, a neighborhood widower, and married him. That marriage persists today, with a major role reversal for Kimberly's mother, who now dominates an apparently willing subject.

Kimberly's father was a less influential force than her mother; she continued seeing him on alternate weekends. Typically, during these visits, Kimberly, her father, and stepmother would go out to eat at one of the finer restaurants. She and her stepmother would dress up, then dread the hours ahead. Her father would begin drinking at home around four-thirty in the afternoon. When seven o'clock rolled around, they would head to dinner. He would begin behaving rudely at the door and continue by flirting with the waitresses. Kim-berly felt her stepmother's embarrassment as well as enduring her own. She provides a glimpse into those dreaded weekend visits:

[My father] liked to have me order whatever I wanted on the menu, then ridicule me for being a pig. I was heavyset from the time I was six; my weight fluctuated from then on out. I remember once my dad offered me one hundred dollars to lose fifty pounds. When I failed to do that in a year's time, he laughed at me and said, "I knew you would never lose it, so I wasn't worried about losing my hundred." I cried myself to sleep for weeks after that, and the words still ring in my head when I set goals for myself.

Kimberly's father was physically abusive, but mostly with his wives, both of whom have confided such in her. She recalls only two incidents where he hit her: a belt spanking and, years later, a shove across the coffee table.

Kimberly first experienced sex at age twelve with a sixteen-year-old neighborhood boy, Rob, whom she thought "hung the moon."

He ignored her in the presence of others, but when they were alone she felt as though she were the prettiest girl in the world; she even felt thin. Though her mother had noticed Rob hanging around and sternly warned Kimberly to stay away from him, that did not deter her. Kimberly was apprehensive about sex with Rob at first. Her mother had told her nothing and her grade school girlfriends knew nothing. She was left totally in the dark and believed all that Rob told her.

One day Kimberly's mother departed for the day, leaving behind a list of domestic chores and strict orders not to go around Rob. By coincidence, Rob knocked on the door during the admonition. Instead of telling him to leave, Kimberly's mother simply glared at her. Kimberly was angry with her mother for demanding that she avoid the only person who paid any attention to her. With her mother away that day, it happened. Kimberly remembers the coercion, the force, the screams, the pain, the vomiting when it was over. She had been raped but did not define it in those terms. She told no one except Lannette. Lannette cried. Kimberly was seriously confused with bittersweet sensations. She thought that now Rob would love her forever.

Kimberly and Rob continued to have sex whenever he wanted over the next four years, until Kimberly was sixteen. He would sneak in her window or walk her to the barns behind the trailer park. She was not to tell anyone. He denied coming to her house and ignored her around friends. He once accused her of having not been a virgin when they met. With that she ran home and cried for hours. Kimberly thought that because Rob always returned for sex, he loved her. But that ended when he punched her in the mouth for calling him a "son of a bitch." The exploitive nature of the relationship had become clear and unbearable. Kimberly's sexual encounters continued, however, now with many partners: she had sex with any man who demonstrated an interest in her. Her mother remained unaware and Lannette her sole confidante.

At seventeen, while a senior in high school and working part-time as a waitress at Pizza Hut, Kimberly entered her first serious relationship with a man. Like Rob and those who followed, Lance was much older—by a decade. He was divorced with a son, had a steady lucrative factory job, and owned his own home. Kimberly thinks she loved Lance at least partly for his wit. Certain that he would deliver her from the pain of no one loving her, she counted on their marrying after graduation. About six months into the relationship, she learned of Lance's intravenous drug use. Devastated, she severed the relationship immediately and, as a result of her grief, missed work and barely ate for three months. She was delighted with the resultant weight loss—forty pounds—but believes that this incident marked the beginning of her serious food addiction, which persists today, abated by a twelve-step program designed to control her obsession. Traumatized by the split with Lance and chronic disharmony with her mother, Kimberly relocated to live with her father and stepmother.

THE ABUSIVE MARRIAGE

Kimberly met Grant late that senior year of high school. A girlfriend arranged the introduction. Grant was Kimberly's age and had attended her school until two years earlier, when he was committed to a group home for boys. Now he was back at school. As a form of introduction, Grant phoned Kimberly and stated: "I heard you wanted to go out with me." She agreed to meet him early the next day at school. Approaching the designated spot, her eyes scanned the area for the short scrawny kid she vaguely remembered. She describes what happened next:

He was absolutely gorgeous! My heart was pounding, and I began to wonder if maybe he wouldn't like me. I was still overweight and paranoid about it. I asked him if he wanted a ride home from school that afternoon, and he agreed. After school we met at my car and I drove him home. He was the most smart-aleck, egotistical ass I had ever met, but like I said, he was gorgeous.

All in all, the first date went well, and from then on Kimberly and Grant were together nearly everyday. Sex kicked in two weeks later and was the focus of their relationship. She liked artistic endeavors, especially drawing, he liked pool; she liked romance, he liked yelling; she liked making love, he liked forceful raw sex. For Kimberly, sex was not good, but it was a point of common ground. It was her key to keeping Grant. Kimberly was encouraged with her quickly won approval from Grant's very religious parents. And he bought her a T-shirt that said "Grant loves Kim," which she wore faithfully. Kimberly continued to view Grant as an "ass," but by now he was her very own "ass," her identity, and he represented hope of escape from the loneliness, fear, and sadness she had known.

Unlike Grant's parents, Kimberly's father was wary of the relationship. He allowed her to see Grant but was harsh and judgmental—throwing up to her the fact that she and Grant were using her car and her money. He became angry when he caught Kimberly initiating the phone calls. Kimberly's mother received Grant with open arms, which Kimberly viewed as a manipulative strategy to bring Kimberly back home to her.

Three weeks prior to graduation, Kimberly was accepted to the art school of her choice. About that time, under her protest, Grant dropped out of school. But now she was no longer interested in furthering her education; she had Grant, and that was where her priority lay. After graduation she took a local waitressing job, and, for the most part, Grant remained unemployed.

Just before Grant turned eighteen, he had a serious argument with his parents and was required to leave home. Kimberly's mother offered to rent Kimberly's former bedroom to him. It seemed the perfect solution for Kimberly, her mother, and Grant. At that point Kimberly moved back in with her mother and essentially began cohabiting with Grant. Within a month that living arrangement failed bitterly, forcing the young couple to seek housing elsewhere. Kimberly found refuge in the home of one of her work friends and her parents. During those two or three months Grant lived in Kimberly's car, and she snuck food to him from the restaurant where she worked. Kimberly recalls those days and their relevance in her life trajectory:

Even though things were terrible, we always found time for sex. In the car, at [my friend's] parents' house, it really made no difference as long as it happened. During this time in our lives, I liked having sex as much as he did, and all this activity paid off. I got pregnant. Here we were: no money, no home, one job, and a baby on the way. Grant was so excited; I was so scared.

Under the pressure of the pregnancy, Grant found work erecting fences and later washing trucks. His mother helped them settle into an efficiency apartment, and life was good for a while. Then Kimberly became ill with borderline toxemia; her blood pressure went haywire, and she swelled up like a balloon. She was forced to quit work. Before this affliction, she was self-conscious about her weight problem; now she was terrified of losing Grant to another woman. Then it all began: Grant began staying out late without explanation. His brother would provide him with an alibi, then confide to Kimberly that Grant had been with other women. Kimberly chose to believe Grant rather than his brother.

Kimberly and Grant were married when she was six months pregnant. Only five guests attended the ceremony. They had isolated themselves from all but a few family members; there were no friends. All of Kimberly's energies and resources were invested in hanging on to Grant.

Before the baby came, the couple moved in with Grant's parents. Grant again switched jobs; he was now working the graveyard shift as cook at the Waffle House, which was to become his pivotal source of income. Kimberly describes the Waffle House as "home of the swinging doors—meaning you can walk out, spit at your boss, yell at the customers, but you can always work here again." Grant and Kimberly were able to save money and to borrow what else they needed from Grant's parents to rent a two-bedroom trailer that was out in the middle of nowhere and without a phone. Kimberly was excited about having their own home but afraid to stay there alone at night when Grant was working. So she typically spent nights with her mother. Life was good again. She fixed up the trailer and prepared for the baby. She sensed a whole new beginning. But all of that changed just two weeks before the baby was due.

As usual, Grant worked the late shift and on this evening had taken Kimberly to her mother's. They arrived there early, so settled in to watch some television. Grant left the room to make a phone call; when queried, he told Kimberly that he was speaking with his boss. That made no sense to her; she was gripped with that old familiar fear. When she awoke the next morning at eight-thirty, Grant had not arrived to take her home. A series of telephone inquiries determined that he had never arrived at work, he was not hospitalized, and his parents were unaware of his whereabouts.

Kimberly's stepfather rushed her to the trailer, where she found their car, her and the baby's personal belongings strewn over the yard, and a locked door. At nine months pregnant and 265 pounds, Kimberly climbed through a trailer window into a triangular scene of immense proportions. Kimberly describes the aftermath of that incident:

To make a long story short, I took him back that very night. We continued to live in that same trailer for about four months. When I had first went back into the trailer after knowing they had been in my bed together, I took the whole set of sheets and threw them in the dumpster. After doing this, I looked around the room for a while and saw that our marriage license was hanging right over the bed. What balls he had! There is a story behind the license, you see. When we went to get it, we only had twenty-four dollars in our pocket. Grant wanted to buy a dog, and the dog he wanted would have cost just that. I told him it was a dog or me, and after we got married he always used to joke and say he wanted the dog instead of getting married, but he got the dog anyway. It may have seemed funny at the time, but looking back, I really don't think he was joking.

When Nathan was born, things improved—that is, until Grant began gambling and the family was forced to move. They shifted back and forth between Kimberly's and Grant's parents during most of the seven-year marriage. Until Kimberly reentered the labor force, they could have a place of their own only when Grant was willing to work.

In spite of Grant's resistance, Kimberly enrolled in a nurse's aide program soon after Nathan's birth. She completed the course, was hired for eight months at the nursing home where she had done her internship, and ultimately took a position at nearby Greenview Hospital in Bowling Green. She loved that job; it provided her with a sense of accomplishment and self-worth. Grant quit the Waffle House only to return less than a year later. His employment was problematic in that it left Kimberly without childcare.

Kimberly worried when Grant was caring for Nathan. He was an irresponsible father, leaving the child in dirty diapers until Kimberly returned home from her eight-hour shift. She left Grant in charge of Nathan and handling the bills; Nathan came up with unexplainable bruises, and the bills went unpaid even though Kimberly handed her paycheck over to Grant. In December of 1989, fifteen months after the arrival of Nathan, the couple's daughter, Ann, was born. Kimberly was nineteen and Grant had just turned twenty.

Finances were tight, and during that second pregnancy Kimberly sustained herself on chicken broth and crackers from the hospital where she worked. Eventually the car was repossessed, and as a result, after just one year Kimberly lost her much-loved job. So the family once again was uprooted and returned to Grant's parents for "catch-up" until they could afford another place of their own. Kimberly stayed home with the children for more than a year. The bills stayed paid longer than ever before, even though the income source was from four or five different jobs, always leading back to the Waffle House.

At this point the emotional abuse had been constant. Now a new dimension was introduced: sexual abuse. Grant became interested in pornography, obsessed with movies and girlie magazines. He wanted

Kimberly to watch and read them too; and he began trying different things in bed, many of which bothered her. He wanted her to masturbate in his presence. Next it was verbally fantasizing different partners during sex. Then, after two or three months of relentless badgering, Kimberly agreed to a threesome. But when finally they were in a position to carry through, the third was another man and someone interested in Kimberly. Grant agreed to the arrangement as long as another woman joined in. But when the woman failed to materialize at the designated time and place, Grant flew into a rage, telling Kimberly that she was disgusting, he was not going through with this, and he would leave her if she even thought about it again.

That night, while Kimberly lay in bed crying, Grant approached her sexually and reassured her that he loved her and could never leave her and the children. Kimberly continues the story and shares the pain inherent in her battering relationship:

I rolled over with tears in my eyes and allowed him to crawl on top of me and bang himself until he was through. He never once cared if I was crying or not, as long as he finished what he was doing. Many times this happened; it sort of became a ritual with him. He would criticize, yell, start fights, ignore me. Yet when he became aroused, he would use my body to accommodate whatever it was he wanted for the night. I really can't explain why I could never get up or force him to stop. It was [as] if while he were laying on top of me, I could wish myself out of my body and not feel the emotional pain. I can say that at those times, if you could have watched me, it would have been like looking into the bottom of a well, dark and empty.

Grant and Kimberly were together a total of seven years; he went through a series of jobs and affairs during that time. Kimberly could not leave because of what she now recognizes as an irrational fear of being without him. She addresses the question of why she stayed and offers some details of the abuse:

I stayed with him for reasons unknown and some reasons I do know. For instance, at the age of nineteen you have two children and no skills to get a decent job, and you have lived with abusive parents who never loved you the way you needed. So what [difference did it make] if you had to endure it now? At least you could say you were a part of something.

The abuse ranged from being told on a regular basis that you are a fat, ugly bitch and no one will ever want you, to being pounded in the ribs till you lost your breath for breaking a coffee cup [or] yelling at him. It always seemed that we worked it out. The apologies were usually mine because he would eventually convince me that the whole argument was my fault. He was a master manipulator. I could cook and clean and wait on him hand and foot, yet never thought I could survive on my own. I had to have him, even when he repulsed me.

GETTING OUT

In Kimberly's mind, Grant's worst offense against her was abandoning her and the children. He joined the army in 1991 at age twenty-two. Kimberly and the children followed him to New York. She was so proud and optimistic. Perhaps this change in direction, coupled with the new location, would breathe life into the marriage. At first things went well. Soon they began socializing with a couple who had children the same ages as theirs. Kimberly suspected a connection between Grant and Mary. When she confronted him, he became defensive and used the opportunity to accuse her of being involved with the neighbors' thirteen-year-old son. The argument followed the usual pattern: he transferred the focus from him to her; she apologized; he froze her out; he won.

Six months into the military stint, Grant was deployed to Florida to clean up after Hurricane Andrew. He failed to come home the night before he left; Kimberly was certain that he had been with Mary. When he arrived home in the morning with a weak excuse, Kimberly flew into a rage, the gist of which was her inability to exist in the marriage and the necessity of her getting out. Grant begged her to stay with him, claiming that he loved her, that it was the deployment causing him problems, and that things would improve. They had sex. She withdrew her threat. At this point Kimberly felt hopelessly trapped into dependency, ravaged by a sense of worthlessness. If Grant ever did leave her, she would merely exist on this earth, not live.

Soon after Grant left New York for Florida, Kimberly returned to Kentucky to be with her mother until his release from the Florida mission two months later. Upon his return to New York, he phoned Kimberly to inform her that she could not return there, that he wanted a divorce. Then two weeks later he phoned again, this time from the hospital to tell her that he had attempted suicide out of despondence over all his mistakes. Swearing that Mary was out of his life and promising to seek marriage counseling, he cried and begged her to rejoin him in New York. Also, he used the children, insisting that they deserved to be with their father. Kimberly gathered the children and returned to New York.

Once again things seemed better in the beginning. Grant was good to Kimberly and the children; he seemed genuinely remorseful. Then, after a week, they had sex. No one could describe what happened and the sentiments it stirs now in the telling better than Kimberly herself:

Lo and behold, here comes the real Grant; he wanted anal intercourse and to stick popsicles inside me. What a warm way of reconciling. I had hoped for romance and candles; I got crude illicit sex, no two ways about it. You must understand, I don't think the word "no" was in my vocabulary when it came to him, and whatever he wanted he got. My emotions throughout this whole time in my life were numb. I did not know what I felt or thought—only that this was the way it was supposed to be for me. He could do whatever he wanted to me physically and emotionally, and I would stay faithful and submissive. This was sound religious advice from my mother-in-law, who knew God like no one else. So I knew it must be what God wanted.

When Grant learned his projected date of discharge from the military, he sent Kimberly and the children ahead of him to Kentucky in search of housing. This was early in December 1992. He was to follow in two weeks. When a month had passed, Kimberly learned through hearsay that Grant had run off to Ohio with Mary, so she declared the family abandoned and secured AFDC and public housing in Madisonville, Kentucky, to be near her mother. Four months tardy, Grant appeared "with apologies in hand and a letter of the finest sugar you have ever read." Apprehensively, Kimberly let him in "for the kids' sake." But it was the same old thing all over again—as though it had never stopped. Instead of attempting to talk things over and decide how to proceed, Grant wanted to have sex, and it was the kind she hated—the kind that humiliated and objectified her. She began to sob uncontrollably and asked why it was that if he really loved her, he was doing this to her. His response was simply: "Shhh, you are the only one for me; you are my wife."

Kimberly gave it one more shot, but her heart was no longer in it. She told Grant to return to Bowling Green to live with his parents until he could secure a job, save money, and ultimately afford housing for the family. Grant agreed. He once again found work at the Waffle House. After four months Kimberly and the children joined him, but there was no house, so they again moved in with his parents. One Sunday about two weeks later, Kimberly answered a phone call for Grant—from a woman identifying herself as Buffy. At the conclusion of a long private conversation, Grant offered no acceptable explanation for the call. His nervous waffling was all too familiar. Shortly thereafter Kimberly sat down with Grant to announce that she and the children were leaving. She returned her wedding ring to him. Grant responded with all the appropriate protests, but this time she was determined. She had survived on her own for seven months now, and that sense of independence had fortified her. With no particular destination but out, Kimberly left with the children and has never looked back.

Shortly before Kimberly had relocated from Madisonville to Bowling Green, her mother had done the same. Now her mother welcomed the three of them into her home, but that arrangement was quickly aborted. There was a heated debate about Nathan: Kimberly believed that her mother was encroaching on Kimberly's maternal role—that she was trying to take over. The argument culminated in Kimberly's mother slapping her. Once again, Kimberly packed up the family and moved on—this time to the Salvation Army. Lannette provided transportation and some encouraging words.

The threesome remained at the Salvation Army for two days, the maximum stay allowed. They were required to be out of the building by five-thirty each morning, so roamed the streets until lunchtime. Kimberly recalls being incoherent during that small window of time—being a zombie—as though she were on drugs. She remembers falling and cutting her knee, crying irrationally and repeatedly, "I am so sorry." Today that scar reminds her of how far she has come.

On the second day a worried Lannette arrived at the Salvation Army to bring Kimberly and the children home with her and her family until they could find housing. Kimberly views those days with Lannette as the true beginning of her healing process. Within a month and with Lannette's help, Kimberly was furnishing her new government-subsidized apartment, and things were falling into place. She sensed her inner strength intensify by the day. Her mother offered assistance, but Kimberly declined and remained distant.

Then came a turning point. The housing authority newsletter advertised a self-esteem course that offered a free haircut and facial in addition to a one-hundred-dollar gift certificate. Kimberly signed up. Within eight weeks she was transformed. She had filed for divorce, decided to attend college, and sharpened her parenting skills. The course alerted her to her parents' hand in her life decisions, life chances, and quality of life. She realized that drastic change was required if she were to break the intergenerational cycle. She wanted to avoid passing on to her children this legacy of pain.

REFLECTIONS

Kimberly believes that things happen for a reason and that some good can spring from every bad situation. She is religious and understands God's place in her destiny. The self-esteem course and its teacher, Elizabeth Lyons, were her God-sent salvation. Through them He breathed new life into the shell left by her parents and Grant. Kimberly aspires to work with Ms. Lyons, inspiring other women to discover their potential for liberation and self-respect. In retrospect Kimberly interprets her relationships with Grant and the men before him as refuges of desperation—as following in the footsteps of her mother. She views her mother as vulnerable yet manipulative and no longer seeks her approval.

Regarding her chronic obesity, Kimberly traces that to her grandmother, who also was heavy and loved to feed anyone who would eat. Today she acknowledges that as a child she used food to indulge her emotions because she was not allowed to experience them. And then, throughout her marriage, food became her best friend. Now Kimberly confronts her emotions, no matter how painful. "My feelings are something I own," she says. "I can choose to stuff them or feel them. In order to live a better, richer, and non-self-abusing life, I take one day at a time and allow myself to feel."

Kimberly actively wrestles to gain control over her demons. She has taken them all on simultaneously: her relationships with her parents, with her children, and with men; her obesity. She nurtures her intellectual life and emotional well-being.

CHAPTER FOUR

Jessica

Jessica is "the girl next door." At twenty-two she radiates all that is good about traditional American femininity: genuineness, a caring nature, and a general sweetness often lost with maturity. Everything about her appearance and demeanor suggests that she has been valued and cherished. So when she approached me in my office after our Introduction to Sociology class one day, I was not expecting her to inquire about the possibility of being included in the *Getting Out* collection. Jessica's story is a lesson in the unexpected. Her White, middle-class, highly traditional, small-town Kentucky background, coupled with the tight family, community, and friendship ties that she has always known, announce to the unsuspecting that there can be no abuse here. Who could guess that the high school's most envied couple, the prom queen and star athlete/honor student/"Best-Looking of the Senior Class" were in a battering relationship.

Today Jessica is completing her college degree in public relations and marketing. Her part-time employment as marketing assistant for a Nashville, Tennessee, advertising firm will become full-time in a few months. She optimistically and realistically anticipates a charmed life, both personally and professionally—a life free of abuse in all of its dimensions.

Jessica was born and reared in a tiny rural Kentucky town. She loves her family dearly. Her parents have been married for thirty-two years and get along famously. Her only sibling and sister, Tonya, seven years her senior, teaches high school and is one of Jessica's best friends. Jessica's extended family is huge; her father has seven siblings and her mother four, the latter all younger sisters and all married. That generation produced twenty-two cousins for Jessica.

Jessica describes her middle-class family as loving and supportive; she knows of no abuse there other than her own. Her parents are good Christian Baptist people who took their daughters to church whenever the doors opened. In elementary school, Jessica was active in Girls in Action, then graduated to Acteens, both clubs for Baptist girls. Also, Jessica participated in Bible drills, Bible school, and the church choir. Her best friend, Kate, was a member of her church, so they spent a lot of time together with their youth group, including the much-enjoyed church trips. Jessica never felt pressured to be anything she wasn't and was always encouraged to do her best.

Being the younger of two daughters, Jessica was a bit spoiled—at least in the eyes of Tonya. She was a pretty and sociable child, always surrounded by friends and invited to birthday parties. When she was small, she liked softball, Barbie dolls, kickball, playing house, and riding bikes, and spent most of her time with cousins and neighbors. Jessica has always been friendly and has gotten along with most everyone.

When Jessica was in kindergarten, her mom took a position as a bank teller, where she remains today. Her father has worked for a factory since Tonya was a baby. Both jobs allowed plenty of time for the family. Jessica recalls a slice of family life from early childhood:

I loved to "help" my dad work in the garden. While he did most of the work, I would run barefoot through the cool dirt or drop seeds for him. One year for my birthday, my dad built me a playhouse right beside the garden, so my friends and I enjoyed it for years. I also liked to help my mom wash the dishes, and she taught me how to bake a cake in my first little Betty Crocker oven.

Jessica and Tonya shared a room until Tonya left for college. The girls bickered a lot; the main reason, Jessica explains, is that Tonya was older and Jessica annoying. Tonya had to take her everywhere, and Jessica always tattled. She was the brat who brought out embarrassing photos of Tonya to show boyfriends. Not until Tonya's first year away from home did the two become friends.

Tonya would bring little gifts on her weekend visits, and Jessica began to look up to her.

Jessica liked school and made good grades. Her favorite subjects were reading, writing, and vocabulary; she disliked science. She was placed in the Gifted and Talented program in the first grade through middle school and loved it. For five years, beginning in the fourth grade, her class competed at "Olympics of the Mind," a state and national competition of youth in the Gifted and Talented program. In the sixth grade they won the state competition and were sent to the national finals in Washington, D.C. This program also exposed Jessica to facets of American life that were otherwise out of reach in her hometown: attendance at ballets, operas, plays, and museums were an integral part of it.

Jessica showed an early interest in boys. Her first crush was on Mark in the first grade; she "fell in love" with him at a Halloween party. He remained her boyfriend for a few weeks, but he lost interest because she was a year younger than he. Basically, from then on Jessica always had a boyfriend.

Her first kiss occurred in the fifth grade, when she and her then boyfriend were practicing on school grounds for a cross-country race. They broke away from running with another couple and clumsily kissed behind a pine tree. A schoolmate spotted them, told the teacher, and they were confronted. All four children were required to write letters describing the incident to their parents. Jessica recalls the humiliation and fear. Fortunately, the letters were never mailed. Sweating it out was considered punishment enough.

After a few months Jessica broke up with that boyfriend and moved on to someone else. She surmises that boys liked her because she was not afraid to approach and talk with them. She was known as a flirt; in reality, her friendliness was sometimes misinterpreted. Around this time Jessica met Tim, who was to remain a compelling figure in her life over the next decade. For her, it was "love at first sight."

Not long ago Jessica was revisiting her sixth-grade diary. One day Tim had approached her at her locker and all the girls were jealous. Her narrative elaborated about how cute he was and detailed every word spoken. Even when one of Tim's best friends was her boyfriend, Jessica wanted Tim. That boyfriend, Jared, broke up with her because Tim had come to sit with them at a ballgame and Jared could tell she liked Tim. Tim always flirted with Jessica, but that was the extent of it. He too was In the Gifted and Talented program but was in the class ahead of her. On Gifted and Talented trips, he would sometimes sit next to her on the bus, which always afforded Jessica fodder for contemplation and hope.

At the conclusion of Jessica's sixth grade, Tim and his family moved away. She remembers vividly the day he returned; she was in the eighth grade and he was a freshman. He stopped her on her way to class to inquire about her friend Molly. Jessica was devastated. For a while she got over her crush. Then, within a few months, Tim left again; his parents' on-again, off-again marriage kept him in perpetual motion.

Throughout her middle school years, Jessica attended dances and occasionally invited boys to her house. She moved from boyfriend to boyfriend, with Kate and Molly aiding her cause along the way. Molly introduced Jessica to the wilder side of life. From Molly, Jessica learned to smoke cigarettes, and occasionally they would steal a beer or wine cooler from her refrigerator without her parents noticing. Kate was boy-crazy, Jessica thinks, perhaps even worse than she! The two spent their time together hanging out at "the complex," a community-supported recreation center where baseball and softball were played and motorcross races and tractor pulls were held. They found new boyfriends every time. Jessica was a year ahead of Kate in school, so when she moved on to high school, they temporarily grew apart.

Jessica's freshman year was wonderful. She was voted class president and class favorite and joined every club possible. She belonged to the pep club and Future Business Leaders of America and was a student council senator. Her boyfriend Jason, with whom she had spent much time the preceding summer, was a senior. Because Jessica was not yet allowed to date, he became a bit restless and they broke up.

A friend introduced Jessica to Kyle, a junior, and they began to talk a lot. Kyle represents Jessica's introduction to abuse. Because of his arrest for driving under the influence of alcohol, his driver's license was suspended. Jessica was willing to be his girlfriend because his inability to drive was of no consequence to her—she could not date anyway. Her mother would provide transportation to his house, and his brother would bring Kyle to hers on weekends. Until it was over, Jessica failed to realize how she had been used. Jessica describes her first battering relationship:

He was really aggressive with me: grabbing my arm, pushing me down, calling me names [primarily "stupid" and "ignorant"]. I hated it. When I would tell him that he was hurting me, he would just laugh and say something like, "Oh, I'm not; you need to toughen up a little." Well, I stand only 5'3" and at that time weighed about 105 pounds. Kyle was a football player who weighed about 180. His dad would see how he treated me and would just laugh too. Of course, he treated his wife about the same way.

After about three months, I found out that whenever I wasn't around, or he wasn't at my house, he was going out with other girls. A few friends even mentioned that they heard the only reason he wanted me as a girlfriend was because he couldn't drive. He was just biding time until he got his license back. I decided I deserved better, so I severed the relationship.

That summer, Jessica was finally allowed to date, and she initiated that ritual with Jared, her sixth-grade boyfriend. They went out on a few casual dates because Kate was dating his friend Andy and Jessica enjoyed being with the group. Jessica and Jared attended a picnic for football players a few weeks before she entered her sophomore year. Then Tim reappeared on the scene.

THE ABUSIVE RELATIONSHIP

The moment Jessica saw Tim it all came rushing back. She reflects on that moment: "He was gorgeous: great body, big green eyes, nice smile. When he said hi, I just melted. I still remember how excited I was." Days later she clarified to Jared the platonic nature of their relationship, then proceeded to pursue Tim by asking Andy to somehow get her together with him without being obvious. Andy tried a few times to no avail. Then, a couple weeks after the picnic, Jessica and Kate visited Andy at home and met Tim there by chance. Jessica was nervous; she wanted Tim to like her. Eventually the two ended up sitting on the couch together and doing a lot of kissing. Jessica knew she was in love.

Jessica and Tim began dating seriously and two months later, in October, had sex for the first time. They had discussed it and were simply awaiting the opportunity. So one night when Jessica's parents were away from home, she invited Tim over. He arrived to a darkened house and candlelit bedroom. She wanted everything to be perfect, and it was. Tim loved her, and he made her feel special.

For the next few months all was well. Tim had a temper but never directed it toward Jessica. She learned to just stay out of his way through football season if the team lost. He would punch things: walls, cars, other guys. In time he became upset when she stopped to talk to friends in the hallway. At first she thought nothing of it—just learned to live with his moods. While some of Jessica's friends thought he was a jerk, most liked him. They all tolerated him for her sake.

Tim had always been popular. He had many friends and had dated a lot of girls. Teachers and school administrators loved him; he was an outstanding student. In retrospect, however, Jessica suspects that many of them saw his dark side but chose to ignore his cockiness and temper. He was a star football and baseball player and a power-lifter. And because the town was small, most people in the school system knew of his troubled home life. Tim's parents separated several times during his adolescence. He witnessed his father hitting his mother, and he in turn beat up his father. Jessica pitied Tim:

It made me feel sorry for Tim. I mean, I had such a wonderful family, and his childhood must have been the pits. Anyone who, in eighth grade, would pick up a kerosene heater and throw it at his father must be unhappy.

Jessica and Tim ate lunch together daily, then sat on the wall in front of school—unless, of course, he was angry with her for something. In that case he would bring her to tears with his yelling or just walk off, leaving her hurt and humiliated. In fact, Tim made sport of hurting and humiliating Jessica. He insulted her intelligence, made her feel fat, and accused her of having no sense of style. Once he refused to speak to her the entire day because she would not honor his request to skip class and go home to change the sandals that he found offensive.

About seven months into the relationship, Jessica discovered that Tim had been calling another girl, a cute freshman cheerleader. She became upset, confronted him, and he broke up with Jessica, claiming that she was being stupid because he "hadn't kissed her or anything." He seemed unable to understand Jessica's pain. This is when Jessica began feeling insecure and afraid of losing Tim. She became obsessed with Alicia. Her self-esteem plunged when she saw the two speaking in the hall. She recalls comparing herself in every way to Alicia. Finally, Tim called and wanted Jessica back because he thought Alicia was stupid. Jessica was delighted. The next few months were without incident, perhaps because, out of fear of losing Tim, Jessica just put up with more. She recalls little that her friends tell her of those days because she was consumed with placating Tim and trying to make his life better and just hanging on to him.

In May Jessica and Tim attended his prom and had a good time for the first few minutes. Then, when photographs were taken, she told him that she thought she had accidentally looked away. Tim was furious, so for the rest of the night he barely spoke to Jessica. A couple of weeks later, on her sixteenth birthday, he broke up with her because the prom pictures had arrived and she had indeed looked away. He thought it would have been a great picture because he looked so good—but she had messed it up. Jessica was devastated, but that afternoon Tim sent her roses and they got back together.

Because she could drive now, Jessica's parents wanted her to work the summer after her sophomore year, so she took a job as a deli waitress. Tim worked too, so they were spending less time together. The first part of July he announced that he wanted to break up, contending that both would be happier if they went out with others. The next day she saw him driving around with Dawn, another cheerleader, and Dawn was leaning way over against him; clearly the relationship was not platonic. Jessica was angry, suspecting something had been going on between them for a while.

The next night Jessica cruised town with some friends and once again saw Dawn and Tim together, this time hanging out in a group at a gas station. Jessica's friends attempted to raise her spirits, assuring her that he would regret his loss, but it hurt nonetheless. As they continued cruising, they spotted a good-looking guy sitting alone in a Pathfinder in the funeral home parking lot. After passing by him a few times, Jessica's friends dared her to get out and talk to him. Nervously, she finally took the dare and approached his window. Introductions were made, and soon Jessica's friends pulled off and left her there in the parking lot. So Robbie invited Jessica to sit in his truck and explained that he was waiting to meet an uncle who was expected to arrive in town momentarily.

Robbie was from Illinois, but his family had a lake house nearby where they spent much of their summers and some weekends throughout the year. He didn't know a soul in town, including Tim. That encouraged Jessica, because local guys avoided her out of fear of retribution by Tim. Robbie and Jessica talked, and eventually he asked her out. They were exchanging phone numbers just as her friends pulled back into the parking lot. Jessica and her friends were anxious to show Tim how it felt to see Jessica going out with someone else.

Jessica and Robbie dated for a few weeks. Her family loved him and he treated her wonderfully. Jessica could not have asked for more from Robbie. They spent much time on the lake, and he told her she was beautiful and assured her of his heartfelt devotion. With time, Jessica realized the depth of Robbie's feelings. She became frightened when, their having known one another only a month, he told her he loved her; she was not ready for that.

Then Tim reentered the scene, claiming boredom with Dawn and the realization of his perpetual love for Jessica. So Jessica and Tim reconciled, but secretly at first because Tim wanted to let Dawn down slowly. They continued to see Dawn and Robbie for a while, then ultimately broke off those relationships to resume their exclusivity. In retrospect Jessica views her sacrificing Robbie for Tim as the biggest mistake of her life. Robbie was deeply wounded, especially in light of the fact that he had treated Jessica so well and all she had ever told him about Tim was his lack of consideration and even brutality.

Over the course of Jessica's junior year, things worsened with Tim. There had been shoving, but now it had become public. Jessica elaborates:

One night at my friend Brooke's, a group of us were making signs for a pep rally. Tim got mad at something and pushed me so hard that I fell down on all of the signs. I couldn't believe that he did it, not because he had never done this before, but because everyone was around. He left the room and I ran after him. I wanted to see what was wrong and apologize if I did something to make him mad. Eventually, I went back downstairs alone and made excuses for him, but my friends were very upset.

This was the year that their football team entered into state competition—fall 1989. Tim was the starting quarterback, and Jessica never missed a game. Their team remained undefeated in regular-season play. But there were still those games where Tim believed he could have done better. After he left the field he might or might not speak to Jessica as they walked to the locker room. Sometimes it was her fault: she had put him in a bad mood before the game, or when he had glanced into the stands, she had been talking to a guy.

Near season's end, Jessica sensed that something was awry. She suspected that Tim was fooling around with Dawn and asked her friends to keep their eyes peeled. Then, one night after a game, she and Tim attended a small gathering at Brooke's house. Dawn was there and so was Alicia. Jessica and Alicia had set aside their differences from the year before and become friends over the summer. During the course of the evening Jessica turned to Alicia for support regarding Tim. They retreated to a back room where Jessica confided her fears about Tim and Dawn. Alicia reassured Jessica of Tim's devotion and loyalty and suggested that she might be overreacting a bit.

Jessica's spirits improved for a few days, until her friend Susan stirred doubts again. Susan had spotted a note in Tim's locker that was not in Jessica's handwriting. As Jessica walked the corridor, she sensed that some cheerleaders were gossiping about her. Later she approached one of them to declare that she was well aware of what was going on and refused to take it any longer. The bluff worked. This cheerleader apologized profusely, saying that she had wanted to tell Jessica all along. It was Alicia again. Jessica felt betrayed by them both and was too angry to even cry. She set out to find Tim.

Tim was sitting with a group on the back of a truck by the weight room. Obviously upset, Jessica approached him directly and asked him to step aside and speak with her. All conversations within earshot came to a halt. Tim said that whatever she had to say could be said right there. He knew Jessica had found out about Alicia and wanted her to humiliate herself in public. And she proceeded to do just that. She told him what she had learned and how hurt and embarrassed she was that he was going out on her and that everyone knew except her. Tim laughed as Jessica cried. She told him she never wanted to look at him or speak to him again. He just smirked and replied that that was fine—he could do better. Etched in Jessica's memory are the faces of those bystanders: ". . . a couple of cheerleaders laughing; some of the guys looked away while others just smiled at Tim."

A few days later Jessica attended the state football championship in Louisville with her sister Tonya; they stayed in the same hotel as the football team. Tonya knew of the situation with Tim and of Jessica's humiliation and depression and encouraged her to just hang out and have a good time. While fraternizing around the indoor pool and talking with one of her football player friends about the breakup, Jessica heard Tim call her name. She ignored him. Most of the guys on the team knew how Tim treated Jessica and had seen him at his worst. Some of them told her to go talk to him lest he cause a scene. She didn't listen. Jessica describes what happened next:

The next thing I knew, Tim had grabbed me and yanked me from my seat. The whole time he was calling me a bitch and told me to quit "whoring" around. A couple of the guys jumped to my defense and calmed him down. He apologized to me and tried to get me to come up to his room to talk, but I wouldn't. . . . Tim begged me to go with him to where his dad and his girlfriend were staying. I reluctantly agreed. Once we got there, his dad asked me to give Tim another chance and let him sort things out with me. He told me that he thought we should go to his room and talk. Of course I gave in and decided to hear him out.

Once we got in the room, he told me how much he loved me and that he wouldn't talk to Alicia again—I was the one he wanted. He said he couldn't stand to see me talk to other guys and accused me of flaunting my body by wearing a swimsuit. I was still so angry, I just kept telling him that it was over, that I didn't want to put up with it anymore. He didn't believe me. Then he said he wanted to show me how much he cared by "making love" to me. I kept telling him no. I was crying, but he raped me. I had never felt so miserable. I cried the whole time, with him telling me how he would make everything better. Before we left the room, he insisted that I assure him that everything would be fine between us. I capitulated. Once again we were back together.

Life progressed as usual during the winter months of Jessica's junior year: more punched holes in Tim's bedroom walls, a busted windshield because he thought she was cheating on him. He threw her against her closet door, knocking it off the track; she told her mother that she had accidentally fallen into it. Tim cheated on her again while she was out of town on a school trip. He denied it, and she just let it go, hoping her friends were exaggerating.

With the arrival of spring, Tim mellowed out a bit. The two got along well for a while. At the prom Jessica was crowned queen. She felt wonderful, as though she had everything. Tim was an honor graduate, the star quarterback, and voted Best-Looking of the Senior Class—what more could she want? He was awarded a four-year tuition-paid academic scholarship to Western Kentucky University. Jessica was delighted because she had always wanted to go to Western but had been afraid Tim would attend school elsewhere.

The night before his graduation, Tim had to practice the ceremony at the gymnasium, so Jessica passed the time by riding around town with Molly. Spotting Tim and some friends in front of the school, they stopped to visit. A heated argument ensued between Jessica and Tim, seemingly out of nowhere. Tim's friends tried to calm him, and Molly pulled Jessica into her truck and drove off. Tim followed. He tried to run them off the road several times while yelling out the window. Finally Jessica convinced Molly to pull over.

When Jessica got out of the truck, Tim raced at her, demanding that she stop riding around with her "slutty" friends. Jessica slapped Tim when he called Tonya a slut. It was the first time she had hit anyone. With that, Tim threw her against a concrete bench, down onto the pavement, with Molly screaming the entire time. Then he left.

Tim apologized the next day, saying that he hadn't meant any of it—that he had simply been angry. He explained that he disapproved of Jessica riding through town with Molly because he didn't trust Molly, or any of Jessica's friends for that matter. Jessica assured him that they had not spoken to any other guys. And she forgave him.

Summer passed quickly. Jessica and Tim saw little of each other because their work schedules were staggered. She developed a routine of taking food to him every day during his break. All seemed well. When it came time for him to leave for the university, he informed her that he wished to see other girls while he was away. Jessica was crushed but did not let on. She believed Tim would soon come to his senses.

Tim came home nearly every weekend and continued to behave as though the relationship were exclusive. One Friday night he met Jessica in a nearby town to watch her school football game. He brought two friends, a girl and a guy; Jessica incorrectly assumed the two were an established couple. As it turned out, the girl was sleeping with Tim. Jessica learned later that Tim saw humor in his ability to get away with bringing a girlfriend to sit next to her at the game. Recently, Jessica happened upon this woman, who apologized, explaining that she had not known Jessica was a serious girlfriend of Tim. He had spoken of her as an occasional sex partner.

Tim had slept with several other girls before Jessica figured it all out in November. At that point she began dating Joe, five years her senior. They went out only a few times; basically, they were just buddies. When Tim found out, he showed up at Jessica's house, screaming obscenities, then leaving in a rage. She complained that it was unfair for him to be allowed to date while she was not. That night Jessica went to a party where Tim and Joe were both in attendance. Tim continued his rage and ultimately threw a beer bottle at Jessica. It missed. Joe and his friend asked Tim to leave Jessica alone, but he continued. The argument evolved into a fistfight, which Joe won. Even then, Tim followed Jessica to her car, screaming and cursing, calling her "slut, bitch, whore." Susan and Kate whisked her inside to safety, while he called them the same names. The next day Tim called, then came by to collect the senior ring,

T-shirts, and photographs that he had given Jessica, and they said goodbye. Jessica reflects on the aftermath of her loss:

For the next three months, during the winter of my senior year, I was totally without Tim, and resultantly suffered low self-esteem and depression. I dated Joe and Robbie a bit, but was totally unmotivated. I felt unattractive and found myself crying often. I kept my feelings to myself most of the time, and tried my best to keep my parents from noticing my depression. I stayed in my room a lot, but attributed it to homework. My friends Kate and Susan were the only ones who really knew how depressed I was. Susan has told me since that during that time I would sit on my bed and rock back and forth, she thought I had gone crazy. She and Kate were both very supportive through these months, but they couldn't understand why I acted as though I had nothing to live for—even I couldn't.

Jessica thought of nothing but Tim. Nothing made her happy. Tim had occupied her mind since elementary school and her life since the beginning of her sophomore year. She could not let go. She needed him to release her. His passion nourished hers and held her hostage. She would be able to slip away only when he no longer wanted her, when his passion had expired. So, seeking even the slightest suggestion of familiar passion but expecting a painful release, Jessica phoned Tim in February.

Tim wanted to talk, thereby prolonging Jessica's captivity. They spoke on the phone periodically over those next few weeks. Jessica could tell no one. By now, Kate and Susan despised Tim, and, since the fight between him and Joe, they (superficially) threatened to sever their friendships with Jessica if she were to go back with him. When Jessica decided to reenter the relationship in March, she had to tell them; they were upset but stayed to see her through it.

Tim visited Jessica infrequently because he had few friends left in town. Susan and Kate refused to speak to him on his rare visits. So Jessica traveled to Western or met him at Tonya's in Indiana. The relationship was still full of grief, but Jessica was happy again because she had Tim back.

GETTING OUT

Tim refused to attend Jessica's high school graduation; instead, he went out drinking with friends. That was a turning point. Jessica explains:

I took my sister with me that night to Project Graduation, an all-night lock-in for the graduates and their guests. We played games and had a great time. I realized that I wouldn't have been talking with most of the people I was with that night if Tim had come there. I began to realize that this very painful relationship was preventing me from enjoying my real friends.

Tim remained at the university that summer after Jessica's graduation, so they were able to get together only infrequently. Jessica took summer waitress work in the state park, where she met Malerie, who quickly became her confidante. Malerie actively supported Jessica in her effort to escape the confining and destructive relationship with Tim. She arranged a blind date and they double-dated. They went dancing, which Jessica loved; Tim had never been willing to dance with her. Jessica's date was polite and treated her as though he was genuinely interested in what she had to say. Soon after, Kate fixed Jessica up with Chris, whom Jessica also liked. At this point she and Tim spoke on the phone infrequently, and she saw him as little as possible.

Jessica had agreed to visit Tim for a weekend at the university shortly after meeting Chris. As the time approached, she resisted going alone, so convinced a friend from work to come along. She wanted to break up with Tim that weekend but was afraid. What if it was the wrong decision? Tim had told her he loved her, and they had been together for nearly three years. And she knew he would be angry—he had told her in February that if he gave her a second chance, she had better not make a fool of him. He could physically hurt her; many times he had come close, then someone or something had intervened. She knew what set him off, and this certainly would. She just could not risk facing him emotionally or physically, so she faked her way through the weekend. Tim never suspected that it was all but over. At home Jessica continued seeing Chris, who finally convinced her to make the break. It was just a matter of time, after all, before Tim would hear about the two of them.

Jessica mustered up the courage to break up with Tim by phone. She describes the incident:

He begged me not to leave him. He cried, promising that he would change and when I got to the university everything would be different. I couldn't take the chance, so I didn't see Tim again until I got to Western in mid-August. He never caused a scene.

Over the nearly five years since then, Jessica has seen Tim occasionally, and they have talked. He has apologized for his treatment of her, and sometimes she still catches herself feeling sorry for him, wanting to do something for him—then she remembers the humiliation and pain he caused her. He was forced to quit college when his drug abuse interfered with his studies, and he lost his scholarship.

REFLECTIONS

In retrospect Jessica sees the patterns that characterized her abusive relationship. She explains:

I realize that the abuse began as emotional and escalated to physical violence, including rape. At first, Tim tried to control me by dictating my friendships and what I could wear. Never did he slap or punch me, but he did a lot of pushing, grabbing, and throwing me into things. On a few different occasions, he forced me to have sex with him. Until I read on the subject last year, I never understood forced sex to be rape.

Jessica identifies Malerie as the single most influential factor contributing to her exit from abuse. Malerie was from an enlightened intellectual community and recognized the situation for what it was. Unlike everyone else in Jessica's social network, she did not see Tim as the superstar, but rather as the abuser. She was smart, compassionate, and skilled at abuse intervention.

Part III

A TWO-TIMING
BATTERER

CHAPTER FIVE

Rebecca (Singing Water)

Kentucky was never home to Rebecca, though she had lived here for a couple of years when we met. Her abusive husband had uprooted her and their two children from their familiar world of Native American Indian culture in the western states to find refuge with his parents. Rebecca sought me out in the context of my work with battered women. Upon first seeing her, I was struck by the beauty of her distinct Indian features and style and also by her sadness. Later I became impressed by her artistic beadwork, once displayed in a local gallery. Rebecca and I remained friends throughout the bitter child-custody struggle that left her devastated and alone. I cherish the lovely jaclah turquoise beads that Rebecca left with me as a symbol of our friendship when she moved on to New York. I wear them as earrings with pride as a tribute to Rebecca's gallant but lost battle and in the hope that she will soon be reunited with Red Talon and Seven Gifts.

Rebecca's Northern Arapaho, Lakota, and Mexican-American heritage and her commitment to the traditional spiritual belief system of the Red Road provide a glimpse into remote worlds that are unfamiliar to those who come from a different culture than hers. This tale of an Indian woman whose life is marked by a violent yet beloved father and by her own alcoholism demonstrates how adultery can be incorporated into a man's battering agenda. It is also the story of a mother's despair at the loss of her children to her abuser.

At forty-one, Rebecca resides in Ithaca, New York, where she is enrolled as a fellow in a doctoral program in human services studies at Cornell University. It is her hope to establish a career developing community education programs for Indian youth. More important to her, however, is the day that she will be able to reenter the daily lives of her two young children.

Rebecca's father immigrated to "el norte America" during the 1940s from central Mexico. During that era the Immigration and Naturalization Department was more permissive, and he was allowed to pass freely through Brownsville, Texas. At this point Sergio Eustafio Morfin became Andres Caterino Maldonado. Only in the past ten years has Rebecca come to understand who her father was, where he came from, and how he has affected her life as an adult.

Sergio had been married to a woman from his hometown of Peawamo, Jalisco—a marriage that produced three children. He was an arrogant and promiscuous man who rode a motorcycle, worked primarily as a laborer, and in general lived by his wits. Eventually, Sergio was wanted for questioning in the murder of his first wife's lover, so he left Mexico, gradually working his way to Wyoming. There he met Rebecca's mother, Ruth Francis Spoonhunter, a resident of the Wind River Indian Reservation, which remains home to the Northern Arapaho and borders Riverton, a small ranching community.

Rebecca's mother's family is of Northern Arapaho and Lakota descent; both are Plains Indian tribes and practice what they call the "Red Road," the spiritual path of the People. Rebecca, her siblings, and her children are enrolled members of the Northern Arapaho tribe. Rebecca's mother was the oldest of twelve children raised on the reservation by her parents in a summer tipi and a two-room winter log cabin. With her father and siblings, Francis was expected to work around the clock managing a cattle ranch and farm while first attending missionary school on the reservation, then public school in Riverton.

This expansive federal reservation was dotted with Christian churches. It was at a Catholic mass that Francis first saw Andres. She had heard of his flirtatious nature and that a tribal member was pregnant with his child. A few Sundays later this twenty-nine-year-old man sat behind seventeen-year-old Francis at church service and began whispering in her ear. She eventually agreed to meet with him, and they began dating. Within a few months, she became pregnant with Rebecca's sister, Francesca. Rebecca's grandparents refused to allow their daughter to marry this Mexican national of tainted personal reputation. So the couple eloped the night of Francis's high school graduation.

Rebecca describes her father as an industrious and loving provider who managed to enjoy the early years of this marriage. She has photographs of the four-room frame house that he built in Wind River for his growing family. He worked as a carpenter, an oil-rig roughneck, and ranch hand when necessary. There are also photos that capture the strains in his life. Five children, one right after another, hard winters, and his own vices, involving fast motorcycles and women, probably contributed to his decision to leave Wind River.

Rebecca was four when her father traveled to Tucson to be near his distant cousins and search for work. Mines were booming in the 1960s and needed workers; within a few months he returned to Wyoming to relocate his family to Arizona. He had purchased a small house beforehand, and Rebecca recalls pulling up to the weedy unshaded yard and the deplorable heat. Recently she learned of her father's long-term involvement in drug trafficking and that the down payment for this house was probably acquired illegally.

Rebecca believes that her mother cooperated in these decisions that involved leaving her family only because there were no real alternatives. She had five small children, no employment skills, and very little patience. The family settled into a lower-middle-class, predominantly Hispanic suburb of Tucson bursting with children, dogs, and music. Rebecca remembers her mother's days being consumed with domestic tasks. Francesca was delegated responsibility beyond her years and bore the brunt of their mother's impatience and frustration. At the same time she was entrusted as their mother's confidante, which confused household roles. One minute their mother would be screaming at Francesca for having done something incorrectly; the next minute the two would be off shopping together. Rebecca recalls a distance between herself and both of them that lasted till well into her twenties.

While her mother toiled indoors all those years in Tucson, Rebecca's father worked outdoors to expand and beautify their homes and grounds. Within seven years the original house had grown to include three bedrooms, two baths, porches, landscaped yards, and a separate workshop/garage. The family would move up the housing ladder twice; their third house was in a pricey suburb of Tucson. Rebecca's father found his moments of peace watering and pruning fruit trees; planting shrubs, gardens, and shade trees; and coaxing grass to grow in the desert. Typically, he rose well before sunrise and was out past dark with his work and his mysterious projects and friends.

Rebecca was the middle child. As a result of having three brothers and their friends around the house, she was at ease with boys right from the beginning. Her relationship with her sister, Francesca, remained strained, and she had few female friends through elementary and high school. Rebecca explains:

As long as I kept up with my younger brothers, I was allowed to play with them in their escapades. This meant racing our bicycles through the streets, building forts in the desert, climbing walls, and jumping off of canyon ledges. I was a little girl trying hard to be a little boy because there were more freedoms in the role. My older brother was protective and demanding while my younger brothers were competitive with me.

Rebecca learned early on to stand up for herself.

By junior high Rebecca had become quite withdrawn, and she became even more so by the time she entered high school. Gender roles confused and offended her: she saw boys as aggressive companions and girls as passive subordinates. In an effort to avoid peer relationships, she focused on schoolwork—and ultimately excelled. In high school Francesca and Rebecca's older brother, Mario, had established their own identities that were typical for the time. Francesca was the great conformer: a pom-pom girl, rodeo queen, class president, dutiful daughter. Mario adopted a more exciting approach to adolescence. He convinced their father to let him purchase a motorcycle with money earned from his part-time job. Rebecca observed with dismay as a clear double standard was enforced on Francesca and Mario. Mario used contraband drugs, chased girls, and ran with the boys. Eventually, as a sophomore, Rebecca hooked up with that same "hippie" element but was still able to maintain her grades. She began working part-time in a tortilla factory and spending fewer hours at home and more time with her new friends.

As a child, Rebecca was drawn to her father and often sympathized with him in the face of her mother's anger toward him. She recalls:

My dad taught me how to dance [at neighborhood and community festivities—weddings, baptismals, *quincinettas*.] because my mom would not dance with him. Her excuse was that she didn't know how and did-n't want to learn. As a child, I adored my father and wanted to be around him. Dancing was our way of excluding everyone else from the moment. Even then, I caught the expression on my mom's face when we became lost in the joy of movement and he sang some Mexican bal-lad out loud. I also saw the expression of shock on my dad's face when my mom threw hot coffee on him for flirting with my godmother.

Rebecca remembers domestic life in Tucson as fraught with interpersonal strife. As a child, she learned to watch others to deter-mine the mood of the moment. She noted the ever-present tension between her parents, and at the same time, saw her father interact-ing with the children as though everything were okay. Her mother was verbally aggressive, and her father was emotionally abusive to his sons and wife and ultimately violent toward Rebecca's mother. Sometimes after one of his episodes of rage, he would pile the five children into the car and take them for a ride to visit his friends or to go walking in the mountains. That provided brief respite from the never-ending undercurrent of anger.

Rebecca continues to reconstruct the mosaic of her parents' twenty-eight-year relationship, realizing in retrospect that her mother knew of her father's philandering. She also knew she had virtually no control over who her husband was or what he did. The secrets of his past handicapped her; his guarded life prevented any understanding and intimacy between them, and her jealous rages only prompted him to stay away longer during the day. By the time Rebecca reached junior high, her father was rarely home, and her siblings were off pursuing their various interests. Her mother began working full-time at the county hospital. That greatly improved the household climate: she mellowed out with Rebecca's father and with her work demands on Francesca. Later, as Rebecca entered high school, her mother enrolled in the local community college full-time and dropped back to part-time at the hospital. With that, things got even better at home. The episodes of rage decreased in frequency and intensity.

Through it all, however, paramount in Rebecca's childhood recollections are images of those summers back at Wind River. Whenever the frustration and pain of her marriage overwhelmed Rebecca's mother, she would collect the children and head for Wyoming and the home of her People. This was routine in the sum-mer, and they stayed with Rebecca's grandparents for several months at a time. The children were instructed to not discuss the fighting that provoked these visits. But that was of no concern to Rebecca—just as long as they could be together with her grandparents. She loved the country, the powwows and ceremonies, the music, swimming in the creeks—the respite from the chaos of city life. Rebecca places Wind River in perspective:

I am grateful for the love of my grandmother and great-grandmother in surviving my childhood. Their love and tenderness were unconditional, unspoken, and felt eternal. I can still smell the sage burning on the cookstove, my grandmother's cigarette smoke, and food in its various stages. My mother's family had few material possessions, but the traditions bound me to them more than I can describe. These family members took the time to sit with me and instruct me in ways that I carry with me today. I am an artist because my grandmother and uncle saw the spark inside of me and taught me the techniques. I soon found that I could escape with this medium and blocked myself out from the rest of the world on more than one occasion.

My Native relatives provided a foundation of culture for me that wove strands of truth for my present circumstances. They reinforced the fact that I was different from most other children, that my gifts were to be developed, and that I would eventually have a responsibility for others through my traditional experiences. I spend thousands of hours in beadwork contemplation, dancing at the center of circles, listening to older women talk, and witnessing the beauty of the natural world. I believe now that "my world is not of this world" and that I am my grandmother's grandmother. Had it not been for my relatives, I would not be grounded in the Red Road.

FIRST MARRIAGE AND OTHER EARLY INTIMACIES

As a high school sophomore, during her "hippie" stage, Rebecca showed some interest in boys—an interest limited to those who used marijuana and alcohol and in other ways conformed to her liberal lifestyle. They exhibited gentle behavior while under the influence of smoking and aggression while drinking alcohol. That was a dangerous combination for someone naive to the ways of romance. Periodically, one brother or another would attempt to steer Rebecca clear of a boy known to be unpredictable or violent. But she would have nothing to do with their advice; she preferred to make her own mistakes. At sixteen she was permitted to date in a public place chaperoned by one of her brothers. She spent a few months with a Mormon young man but recalls the relationship as nothing special. Having a boyfriend was not important; the rituals of coupling were boring to her.

Rebecca began her college career at Brigham Young University in fall 1971. Even though she had dropped out of high school at the conclusion of her junior year, her family's conversion from Catholicism to the Mormon faith secured a place for her at Brigham Young. She associated with a group of young women who also were experimenting, as minors, with alcohol and barhopping. They had false identification cards and would travel to Salt Lake City from Provo, Utah, to experience the weekend nightlife. It was in this context, at age eighteen, that Rebecca met Arnold, her first husband, a full-blood Navajo four years her senior. She lost her virginity to this man and, after agonizing with that fact for a while, thought she should marry him. Her parents disapproved on the basis that she should complete more education before marriage. They married in September 1973.

After completing three semesters at Brigham Young University, Rebecca transferred to the University of Utah, where Arnold was supported by a tribal educational grant. During their three years together, all partying ceased, and they settled into the routine of married college life. Rebecca always suspected that Arnold was a dry drunk, as was his father. He was the oldest of ten children, assumed responsibility for his siblings, and expected Rebecca to join him in that endeavor. Rebecca was nineteen years old, and Arnold wanted them to adopt his cousin's two toddlers because she was an alcoholic.

The couple separated, then divorced after Arnold completed his studies and began full-time employment as a probation officer for the state department of substance abuse. Rebecca initiated the divorce, she says, because she was too immature to communicate issues and needs and unprepared to accept the kinship responsibilities associated with that marriage.

After the marriage ended, Rebecca entered into a series of brief relationships with young men that never survived a few months of physical attraction. She completed her senior year of college and, staying on at the University of Utah, entered a graduate program in social work—allowing her the opportunity to delay adult responsibilities and to legitimately continue "boozing and cruising." As had been true in high school, she gained the reputation of "party girl" while maintaining respectable academic standards. Her drugs of choice became marijuana, wine coolers, and scotch on the rocks. The only blackout of her lifetime occurred when she was with a man whom she had begun to date seriously during her first year of graduate school. It was then that she began to suspect her alcoholism and self-destructive tendencies.

While completing her master's degree in social work (MSW), Rebecca dated men of various cultures and races. However, she was resolved to never date a Mexican national. But that is exactly what she did. She became involved with a graduate student on campus who was just like her father: attractive, smart, and controlling. Initially, she liked his take-charge approach, but in the end she grew intolerant of his passive-aggressive control and terminated the relationship.

THE ABUSIVE RELATIONSHIP

At age twenty-two and upon completion of her MSW, Rebecca's social network was limited to graduate students who, like her, used alcohol and drugs to handle academic stress. She knew that in order to eschew chronic alcoholism, so prevalent among her people, she must leave the community. In search of a culturally diverse climate closer to her family, she moved to Albuquerque, New Mexico, and took a waitress job until a professional materialized.

By this time Francesca had married and moved to the Cattaraugus Reservation in New York, and Rebecca sensed that she had replaced Francesca as their mother's confidante. During Rebecca's graduate career her mother had become a part-time student at the University of Arizona and had enjoyed hearing of Rebecca's academic program, meeting her classmates, and discussing her future. She repeatedly referred to Rebecca's father as an obstacle to her own personal and professional development and worried even now that Rebecca would encounter the same impediment. Rebecca felt as though she had become an emotional and spiritual mother to her own mother. Conversations extended beyond the subject of career to domesticity: Rebecca's mother began confiding more of her father's abuse of her younger brothers and hinted at the escalation of physical abuse toward herself. Clearly Rebecca's parents' marriage was spiraling downward.

After three months of job searching and waitressing, Rebecca applied for a position as a health educator for the local Urban Indian Center. Among the three interview committee members was the health care program director, an arrogant man who claimed Cherokee ancestry and had worked for several Native programs around the country. A few days later, Rebecca was offered the job.

Kane was twenty-seven at the time—divorced, handsome, and

quite charming. His former wife was a Navaho woman from Nashville, Tennessee, who, Rebecca learned only recently, had left him because of his emotional and physical abuse. Even then, before her own personal involvement with Kane, Rebecca was aware of several women in Kane's life in various stages of conflict and con-

trol. There was a pending charge of sexual harassment against him about which she was unclear. Kane assured her that the charge was totally ungrounded. The case was dismissed, and Rebecca never probed him regarding the motivations of the young woman.

Six months into Rebecca's employment at the Indian Center, she and Kane became romantically involved. Then, six months later, having spent two years there, Kane was terminated for insubordination and persuaded Rebecca to leave her job and relocate with him to Denver, where he had found employment. But two months later that position came into serious jeopardy, so the couple returned to Albuquerque, set up an apartment, and again Rebecca took waitressing work, this time as a temporary means of support for both of them while they sought professional work. Shortly thereafter, in December 1980, Rebecca and Kane married in a private ceremony in the chambers of a justice of the peace in Albuquerque.

Just days later Rebecca found employment with a residential boarding school for Native youth in Santa Fe and commuted for several months until she and Kane located an apartment there. Nearly a year later Kane was offered a government appointment with the San Ildefonso Pueblo,* a local Native Rio Grande village, as a tribal planner. For the next seven years he would work within that system, ultimately progressing to the top position of tribal administrator. They lived on the pueblo, first in a rented, then a purchased mobile home. Kane had been enrolled part-time in a master's program at the University of New Mexico in Albuquerque and, under Rebecca's tutelage, completed that degree while working at the pueblo.

The relationship unraveled quickly once the couple settled into stable employment and lifestyle. Only months passed before Rebecca fully realized Kane's addictive personality. All along she had known of his drug use, primarily marijuana and prescription sedatives, but had understood the indulgences to be moderate. Kane had developed daily habits of cigarettes and marijuana in high school. He told her that he had not used alcohol back then for fear of its interfering with his performance as an athlete. He had

* This and other Rio Grande pueblos are considered "land grant" areas, not necessarily reservations.

attended universities in Tennessee and Kentucky on baseball scholarships, but his athletic career ended abruptly when his vehicle collided with a farm tractor, killing that driver. The circumstances remain unclear to Rebecca, but she suspects that Kane was under the influence of some drug.

One day Rebecca returned home to discover Kane crying over spilled milk—literally. Sobbing uncontrollably, he explained that he had spilled the liquid on and consequently ruined a five-hundred-dollar bag of cocaine. It was a pathetic sight, indeed. After several such episodes, Rebecca threatened to leave Kane. She had dramatically reduced her own drug intake since graduate school and had no intention of living with a heavy user. But Kane always swore that he would quit and insisted that he could not live without Rebecca. At one point she demanded that he leave because she could never again trust him. But he stayed, and before Red Talon was born, Kane told Rebecca that he had renounced all drugs. Rebecca does not know if he really did quit for a while.

Kane was intolerant of Rebecca's family. A few months into the marriage, Rebecca's parents severed the relationship with Rebecca and Kane as a couple. Rebecca saw her family only if she visited them alone. In hindsight, she realizes that they recognized Kane for what he was long before she did.

Several years ago my mother told me about the first time my great-grandmother, Yellow Plume Woman, met my father. Great Gramma spoke Arapaho as her primary language; however, she was fluent in English. Around "others" she spoke only her native tongue. When my eighteen-year-old mother took my father to meet this elder, Yellow Plume Woman would not permit my mother to bring him any further than the front door. As he stood silhouetted in the fading light, my grandmother said to my mother: "He is evil and will bring you only death and destruction. Let him go on without you."

As my mother was relating this event to me, she concluded with how she and my father perceived Kane when they first saw him. My mother was reserved, yet cordial. My father's reaction was more obvious, and I knew he didn't particularly care for Kane. Later my father commented to my mother that there was something ominous and arrogant about Kane that he didn't care for. Of course, my father saw Kane as he himself was.

Kane is the product of an abusive father and a passive-aggressive mother, who both demonstrated the classic dominance/control agenda. As Kane's wife, Rebecca fell victim to their "dance." They tolerated Rebecca, primarily her Native ancestry, because this was whom their son had chosen. Beneath the surface of their genteel southern hospitality, Rebecca could see their tension, racism, and judgmental attitudes. She was acutely aware of her father-in-law's emotional abuse of Kane's mother and witnessed numerous public humiliations involving name-calling and remarks about her mother-in-law's appearance. Meanwhile, he was flirting with every waitress whose attention was for sale. Early on, Rebecca feared that with age Kane would grow into the image of his father.

At twenty-eight Rebecca became pregnant with Red Talon. She hoped the pregnancy would breathe life into the marriage and dissolve the unspoken tensions. That did not happen, and neither did Seven Gifts bring spiritual relief or the anticipated family "balance" with her arrival two years later, in 1985. While the children introduced untold joy to Rebecca's life, there was a downside. Since late adolescence Rebecca had harbored a fear of unknown origin—a nagging premonition of bearing and loving her children and then having them taken from her, leaving her brokenhearted. All this ambivalence intensified as Rebecca welcomed Seven Gifts into the world.

Four months into her first pregnancy, Rebecca left her job and enrolled as a part-time student at the Institute of American Indian Arts, to refine her artistic skills. At Red Talon's birth, she was entrenched in her beadwork and well on her way to enjoying privileged status as an accomplished artist. Invitations to show and exhibit in Phoenix and eventually the Santa Fe region followed calls from Pueblo and Navajo people requesting special orders. Contacts placed her work in high demand, and within four years she was trading up and down the Rio Grande. Recognized Native artists prefer to trade rather than sell; they resist assigning monetary value to their work.

So Rebecca's home became filled with priceless original Native rugs, baskets, pottery, and jewelry. Her status and that of her family were elevated considerably by her talents and their fruits. Kane's reputation in the San Ildefonso community and his ascendance within its governing hierarchy were enhanced by Rebecca's accomplishments. As a non-Indian, he was awarded entrance to the Native community by having a Native wife, and a high-profile one at that.

When Red Talon was eighteen months old, tragedy struck. Rebecca received word that her mother was in critical condition with multiple stab wounds. Rebecca's father had attacked her and her companion in the middle of the night and had eluded the police. Rebecca's parents had divorced just months before, and though she had maintained minimal contact with them, Rebecca knew that her mother feared retaliation for having escaped the control of her abuser. Rebecca's father had carried out his threat. Rebecca's mother survived, but her companion died in the emergency room next to her. Rebecca's father was never located; she has reason to believe that he died recently under yet another assumed name in California. This case was featured on the television program *America's Most Wanted*, leaving his family with a painful legacy.

Rebecca likens life with Kane during the San Ildefonso Pueblo years to a "cat and mouse" game. Kane orchestrated a carefully calculated campaign of intimidation and control over her. She was expected to "read his mind" in an effort to satisfy his every whim. Rebecca elaborates:

I was very isolated. I never got off the pueblo, maybe once a week. He didn't want me to go back to work, we had no contact with my parents by then because I had no telephone. If we went to get groceries, he was there and he wrote all the checks and drove the car. It was a joint account, but he kept the checkbook and balanced it. The Saturday afternoon that we went to get groceries, it was a big deal. It was 28 miles one way to Santa Fe to do groceries, we might go out to eat. Once we got back to the pueblo it would start all over again. He would go into rages. There was always something wrong with the kids or the food or something. I couldn't do it all, it was too spread out. I felt like a blob trying to cover all the bases.

At this point the violence was not physical but, rather, a passive-aggressive undercurrent. Isolated at home with her beadwork, Rebecca gained seventy pounds and lost all self-esteem. She was an accomplished artist yet felt as though she were a fraud.

Both Rebecca and Kane made gestures toward leaving the marriage during this period, but out of different motivations. When Kane sensed vulnerability in Rebecca, he would walk out the door, threatening to abandon her with the responsibility of the family. Sometimes she feared him leaving. Other times she would announce her intention to leave because of the abuse; but Kane, aware of her fear of losing the children, would vow to win custody. Custody of Red Talon, that is. Within a week of Seven Gifts' birth, he made it clear that he already had his son and that Rebecca could have the girl. Rebecca always stayed.

When Seven Gifts turned eighteen months, life changed dramatically. In an effort to reclaim some control, Rebecca took a position at the pueblo youth shelter, helping to create a community youth program. She located reliable child care, lost her excess weight, and regained her optimism. About that time the San Ildefonso Pueblo administration came under investigation for misuse of federal housing money, and, as a result, several tribal administrators, including Kane, were fired for corruption.

GETTING OUT

Public sentiment demanded that Kane leave the area, so the summer of 1987 found the family relocating to Phoenix to assume temporary residence with Rebecca's brother Mario. Rebecca immediately secured a job at Sacaton, nearby village headquarters for the Gila River Indian Community, a reservation for Pima Indians. She was hired on a two-year U.S. federal grant by the Pima administration as a life management skills coordinator with the adult basic education/GED program. A year later, after a much-hated stint selling life insurance, Kane found an entry-level position with the Federal Housing Authority in nearby Mesa, and soon thereafter the family rented a house there. Rebecca continued to commute to Sacaton, now a one-hour drive. Kane considered himself overqualified for this job and quit within a year and a half.

During the year Kane was unemployed in Mesa, the abuse escalated to include physical violence. Once or twice a month he would push Rebecca to the ground and kick her, always careful to avoid her face. In the Arizona heat she would don long-sleeved, button-up shirts. For Rebecca, there was never a honeymoon period. Kane's version of making up was coerced sex.

Kane was relentless in his verbal attacks, which could last until morning:

I can still see him screaming at me, his eyes changing to a monster green and the veins on his neck pulsating with every breath. I learned to shut out the sound and observe the movements. This form of detachment saved me from the brutality of the words that spewed from his mouth when he had erupted into a screaming rage.

Sometimes Rebecca would escape by going to bed and trying to fall asleep. Infuriated with her having left the scene, Kane would burst into the room raging. On three such occasions he raped her. Rebecca always followed those rapes with a serious threat to leave Kane. She did leave him once. For six weeks she stayed away by night—in her locked car or in Phoenix with a woman friend or Mario's estranged wife—and cared for the children at the house (during off-work hours) by day. The children never knew; they were three and five. Rebecca reconciled with Kane out of fear of losing the children. Once, under Rebecca's threat to leave, Kane filed for divorce and tried to force her to relinquish custody. She recanted her threat.

When Rebecca's grant expired, she was offered the position of Native American counselor at Arizona State University. But it was then that Kane decided to quit his job and return to Santa Fe. Rebecca wanted to stay behind with the children, but Kane, of course, would not hear of that. So Kane secured a desirable position at the Institute of American Indian Arts and relocated the family to Santa Fe, where they purchased their first home.

But Kane lost that job as well as the prestigious position that followed at the Santa Fe County Housing Authority. A pattern was clearly established: the hubris of this man was rendering him unemployable. In the meantime Rebecca maintained three part-time professional-level positions until, after having spent three years in Santa Fe, Kane again uprooted the family, this time to be near his parents in western Kentucky. He was appointed director of a federally funded agency in a university town there, and the family bought a home in that community.

At this point the nature of Kane's abuse had shifted in some respects. He continued his emotional and physical abuse of Rebecca but desisted from raping her. Kane continued to blame Rebecca for his personal and professional limitations as well as for their marital problems. A predominant theme was her parental incompetence. At every turn he was compelled to show her how to deal with the children. And it was her fault that he could not hold a job. The most noteworthy change in Kane's behavior was toward the children. He was now venting his rage on them, especially Red Talon. His discipline was harsh and unrestrained; he hit Seven Gifts occasionally and took Red Talon into the bedroom for belt whippings. When Rebecca intervened, the rage shifted to her.

Within two weeks of having arrived in Kentucky, Rebecca was hired by the local university as a student health program coordinator. This job marked a transition in her career from Native- to non-Native-related work. Kane had nearly convinced her that she was not capable of surviving on her own in the general labor market, that the value of her work was limited to the Native community. As she excelled in this position and it evolved into full-time employment with respectable responsibility, her self-esteem soared. She was on her way up and out.

It was in Kentucky that Rebecca came face-to-face with Kane's philandering. Right from the beginning she had had good reason to suspect a continuous flow of other women in his life, but she had chosen the path of denial. That was no longer possible when, during a series of court hearings regarding temporary custody preliminary to the actual divorce proceedings, a young woman approached her at her office to confess a romantic involvement with Kane since his arrival in the community more than a year earlier. Emily shared her pain and remorse with Rebecca over the affair. She was aware that Kane was seeking primary custody of the children and offered to testify at the custody proceedings regarding his infidelity and fraudulent use of business travel funds. She had accompanied him on business trips at the expense of the local housing authority.

Rebecca left Kane in 1992, after a year in Kentucky and fourteen years in an abusive marriage. She had been victimized by every dimension of woman battery. She left when she did because the abuse had escalated to extreme brutality, the children were becoming directly involved, and Rebecca's newly found esteem had released her from Kane's clutch of intimidation, fear, and guilt. And there was another factor: parental mimicry. Rebecca had come to see her mother in herself and Kane's father in him. She wanted something better for herself and the children.

But her exit cost the ultimate price: she was denied primary custody of Red Talon and Seven Gifts. Her worst nightmare assumed a bitter reality after all. Kane operated through a merciless and aggressive attorney. That, in the context of a racist and sexist judicial system so reflective of the southern Bible Belt mentality, resulted in the ruling that Kane was the superior parent. Abuse, cultural issues, the wishes of the children, and Emily's testimony were dismissed from consideration. Rebecca was portrayed as a hyperemotional and crazed savage who claimed outrageous belief systems and practiced bizarre ritual.

REFLECTIONS

Through her Red Road lens, Rebecca reflects on her journey of progressive entrapment. Neglecting her own development, she allowed another human being to control her for his purposes. She became the food for another who was incapable of developing his own soul. She was his host; their interaction nourished him but depleted her. She was spiritually raped by this man's ravenous ego.

Rebecca has escaped that entrapment now: that journey is complete. But she remains entrenched in another: the pain of living apart from her children. No one speaks of that journey better than Singing Water herself:

Today I think about the ceremonies and the spiritual people who continue to pray with me during this journey, and I am reminded that I am never alone. For several years I have been suspended from the Red Road's "Tree of Life," anticipating release from the cords that have bound me. When I have prayed to this Tree, with the Sacred Pipe, I am blessed with the strength of the universe, knowing that I will be set free. Initially, the pain of the separation from my children was so great that I knew my heart and spirit were broken. Now the pain is subdued and the wind that blows through my heart is not as cold as before and the breath of Creator now heals my heart.

CHAPTER SIX

Emily

Emily and I first met in a waiting room as we anxiously anticipated our turns as witnesses in family court for Rebecca at her child-custody hearing. Emily was going to testify as a character witness against Kane, citing examples of his adulterous and otherwise inappropriate behavior as a father. I was prepared to testify as an expert witness on behalf of Rebecca and her children. The atmosphere was somber in that tiny room that held perhaps five or six people, reminiscent of a wake. I recall introducing myself to Emily in a whisper and sensing her embarrassment for being there in the capacity that she was. Her sense of guilt and remorse for her part in the pain that Kane had inflicted on Rebecca and the children was apparent. I respected her for coming forward and told her so. Later, when I learned from Rebecca that Kane had battered Emily too, we decided that I should invite Emily to join the *Getting Out* project to speak as "the other woman." Emily needed time to contemplate but contributed wholeheartedly.

Emily has survived a series of abusive relationships, including a failed marriage. The control she endured was rooted in a Southern Baptist tradition of conventional gender roles that dictates a woman's need for the romantic devotion at all times of a man. A woman without a man is viewed as not whole, and any man is considered better than no man at all. Emily learned that tradition primarily from her mother and is determined to not pass it on to her own child. Much of the abuse that she endured at the hands of Rebecca's husband was sexual in nature and quite different from the battering tactics that he used to control Rebecca.

Today Emily shares her Kentucky home with her son and enjoys a new career in business administration. At thirty-two, her priority is maintaining a rich and stable life for the two of them together.

Emily grew up in a tiny western Kentucky town in what she then considered to be the picture-perfect Baptist family. Her father was plant manager for the manufacturing firm of which he is now vice-president, and her mother taught school. Emily has no memory of her parents even arguing. Born four years apart, she and her older brother, Porter, were the closest of siblings. Never was their relationship marred by typical rivalries. Emily remembers Porter for his kindness and consideration—always offering to help her with tasks large and small. Porter and Emily were and remain sources of great pride to their parents. Emily's father viewed her as the "perfect angel."

Emily distinguished herself in adolescence both academically and civically. When not at school or cheerleading, she was at church. She served as manager of the football team and member of the Beta Club and was active in the church choir, musicals, and youth group. The mission team provided national travel opportunity during the summers. Throughout high school, she worked part-time as assistant secretary at her church. Unlike Emily, Porter had a rocky adolescence. He tangled with the law and dropped out of high school but with just the right parental discipline, support, and guidance has succeeded in charting a life rich in family and work satisfaction and in economic reward. Emily comments that Porter is ten times more successful than she—"and without a lick of college!" She beams with pride at her brother's accomplishments.

In spite of her seemingly idyllic youth—the involvements, the activities, and the friendships they produced—Emily always felt as though she were on the outside looking in. Her ulcer extends back to the first grade and signifies an unexplainable sense of loneliness that would persist into adulthood.

Beneath the exterior, Emily's parents' marriage was not what it seemed. Eventually Emily came to recognize the underlying tension and the associated long series of her father's adulterous affairs. Her mother, heavily entrenched in her own mother's conviction that the value of a woman lies in her ability to attract and keep a man, was a saint—always knowing, always loving, always forgiving, always taking him back. Emily recalls admiring her mother's selflessness—a woman to be commended for placing her marriage and family above her pride and vanity. Right to the end, as they waited together in the office of the divorce attorney, Emily's mother offered to try again. Emily expresses her Baptist sentiments:

She would always forgive him, and at times it looked like things were going good. I always thought that that was really neat that she was so forgiving and so loving, and that they worked it out, and you always forgive and make it work.

After more than twenty years of indulging shamelessly in his wife's degradation, Emily's father finally said no.

Once Emily began dating at age fourteen, she was never without at least one boyfriend. From the beginning, she followed the sexual-relationship pattern established by her father and his mother before him. When she became restless or unhappy, she would initiate another relationship on the side. Upon discovery, the original boyfriend would break up with her. Emily was never alone. A bad relationship was better than none at all. When speaking of these years, Emily repeatedly refers to the low self-esteem that influenced her decisions and lifestyle. Many of these men were arrogant and condescending; they might or might not call or show up as promised. Yet she was unable to stand up to them or leave. Typically her attempts to hold her ground failed; she would back down and end up apologizing.

There was one long-term relationship that extended from high school through Emily's two-year college career and represents her introduction to physical abuse. Emily and Frank had been friends for a while when they began dating; she was sixteen and he was a year younger. Emily claims to have loved Frank, but not "head over heels." She saw him exclusively at first, then, when away at college, secretly dated around while maintaining that relationship back home.

Frank was the third child of a "good" local family; his father owned and managed a motel, and his mother had recently died of cancer. Unlike his brothers, who became a computer programmer and a judge, Frank performed poorly in school. He preferred to fish and hunt. Later he would enroll in (Emily's) college for two semesters, party rather than study, and drop out. To this day, to Emily's knowledge, Frank continues to order his life to accommodate his fishing and hunting agenda. This is made possible by the fact that he works for his father at the local motel.

At first Frank was nice to Emily and they shared good times. But soon he fell in with bad company—including a married high school teacher who left his wife and infant for a high school girl. In short time Frank became arrogant and abusive; the relationship began to operate solely on his terms. He would arrive hours late or not at all. When arguments arose out of Frank's insistence on doing things his way, he would call Emily stupid and, sometimes, a whore. A few times he struck and pushed her. These were painful and tearful episodes for Emily, where she would struggle to repair the damage and smooth things over—whatever it took to hang on to Frank. The most severe and dramatic of these incidents yielded apologies and temporary deference from Frank. But soon he would regress to his caustic, self-absorbed persona. It was at this point in her life that Emily developed migraines, which she endured along with her ulcer.

The relationship with Frank persisted until summer 1984, six months beyond the completion of Emily's two-year secretarial administration program at a nearby public comprehensive university. It lasted for as long as Emily was willing to sustain the abuse and to expend the energy and subject herself to the humiliation necessary to reconcile with Frank once again. Over those four years she did that only when the alternative left her without a man. When she was otherwise involved, she could let Frank go—until that other relationship dissolved. Emily reflects: "I didn't want to be alone. Having somebody was better than nobody."

Eventually there did come the time when Emily just let go for good. It was simply no longer worth it. She had taken a job dispatching for the city police department in her university community. The breakup left her lonely and vulnerable—her college friends had dispersed, and she was beginning to establish home and family with her colleagues at the police department.

THE ABUSIVE MARRIAGE

After Emily had worked several months with the city police, a new supervisor was transferred to her shift. Peter was a self-assured and competent police sergeant, eighteen years her senior. Emily and Peter hit it off right away; soon he began calling and a courtship ensued. Those were wonderful times. Emily elaborates:

He would take me really nice places and he had a really nice house [that he had shared with his second wife]. He was settled and stable and paid for things when we went out. . . . He had been a sergeant for five years, so he told everyone what to do. He was very take-charge and in control—planned everything out. And I was so unsure of myself, and I didn't want to take responsibility for anything . . . so here was somebody who wanted to make all the decisions. So, have at it! It was the perfect match. . . . I thought he was perfect. He knew everything, and I just totally worshiped the ground he walked on. He was the most wonderful man that had come along, and, of course, he just adored me because I was adoring him.

After one year together, when Emily was twenty-two, the two were married.

From the beginning, Emily felt a deep sense of pity for Peter. His life had been riddled with abandonment, pain, and disappointment. Having been born and reared here in her community, he and his younger brother were placed in an orphanage when Peter was eleven. Their parents then relocated to another state with their two other children and never responded to Peter's letters. Eventually he was transferred to a foster home. From there he entered the navy, served in Vietnam, and returned home to become a police officer. He had endured two failed marriages and had no children of his own. Emily's heart ached for Peter; she wanted to turn all of that around for him—to rescue him from the unspoken pain.

During their courtship Emily developed an interest in becoming a police officer herself. Because the rule against nepotism prevented her from taking a position with the city, she applied to the campus security division of her alma mater in town. Her first two applications placed her among the top two or three candidates, but it was not until July 1986, two months after her marriage, that she was hired and began her training. Emily explains why she was finally hired with this third application: "They told me it was because I had changed so much. Peter had been such a good influence on me and had changed me so much." She owed it all to Peter!

The first three years of marriage produced little conflict because Emily deferred at every turn. At Peter's insistence she moved into his house rather than their getting a home of their own. The drawers and closets in the master bedroom were occupied, so she kept her things in a spare bedroom. Clearly it was Peter's house. And when she referred to it in those terms, people were amused and reminded her that it was her house too.

Within months Peter withdrew from Emily: he quit taking her out and lost interest in her sexually. He did as he wished, making few if any concessions for her. Early on Peter began accusing Emily of being incapable of doing anything right. She recalls their painting the living room together and Peter telling her to go get something to eat because she was not painting correctly. They kept separate checking accounts because Peter did not trust that Emily was capable of keeping a balanced account. He thought she would "screw it up," in spite of the fact that she effortlessly balanced her own to the penny each month. With time Emily came to believe Peter—that she was incompetent and needed him for her very survival.

In the meantime Emily excelled at work and loved her job. She had graduated second in her class at the academy and was awarded timely promotion to sergeant. Consensus had it that she performed exceptionally as a police officer, but deep down that was simply not believable to her. She lived with the distantly nagging fear that her incompetence, always taken for granted at home, would become apparent at work.

It was with Scott's birth in July 1989 that Emily first believed she could do something right. That single event altered her self-concept and, as a result, changed the dynamics of her marriage dramatically and irreversibly. She was a natural at motherhood right from the start. Everything fell into place as she joyfully and seemingly effortlessly took over the care of her son. Criticism and even advice were not acceptable; she knew exactly what to do. Emily relays an incident that reflects this time of transition:

I was sure of myself. I knew what I was doing; I am the world's most devoted mother. I remember one time, [Scott] must have been about six months old . . . I was fixing his breakfast one morning, and, you know, I had been doing it for however long he had been on solid foods . . . and he came in and said, "You're not doing it right. That's not the way he likes it." He had never fixed his cereal before and I was doing it every day and he was eating it. And I was like, "Excuse me, you know he is eating it every day, you know, and did he tell you this? He doesn't talk, you know."

It did not take long for the foundation of the marriage to crack beneath this revised power structure. Emily was no longer totally subordinated to Peter. In fact, she had taken charge of a critical life component: parenthood. It is not that he was seeking primary caretaking responsibility of Scott—Emily could have that. What he wanted was to maintain Emily's subjection. And now a piece of that had escaped him. He did not accept that loss gracefully.

Peter intensified his intimidation tactics; he was now more than ever "in Emily's face," cutting her down incessantly. She recalls preparing sandwiches and his returning the can of tuna to the cupboard, claiming it was the wrong kind. Another time he criticized her ability to use the stove properly: she had put the pot on the wrong burner. If Emily tried to reason with Peter, he would pat her on the head and quip, "It's just all in your head." He told her she was just too emotional. And all this time Peter was withdrawing further. She longed for him to hold her, but instead he spewed insults. Then, when Scott was about a year old, Emily became romantically involved with a longtime friend and fellow police officer. She explains:

[Peter's] work was always more important than me and his friends knew it. It was his work, then his fishing, then his hobbies—anything himself—then Scott, then me. He made it so hard. He never made love to me. He always put me down. Then, when I got depressed, I gained weight, and he'd say, "Why would anybody want you? Look at you." But, you know, he didn't want me when I was a knockout. I'd get all dressed up in a slinky gown and makeup and hair and stuff—and try, and he'd say, "Well, just wait till the news is over." And that hurts. So I ended up going out on him.

Emily fell in love with Mark. Initially, he appeared to be everything Peter was not. She confides that she might not be alive today were it not for Mark's caring intervention. They spoke of marriage and children. But soon Mark wanted Emily to quit her job. He thought the climate of police work was unsuitable for her and that she should find an office job and allow him to "come first" as a police officer. She should be willing to give up the profession for him. Besides, the nepotism rule would not allow both to remain on the force once they were married. So after four rewarding years of police work, Emily resigned her post in favor of an office position at the university. The next step on the agenda was for Emily to file for divorce.

But it was not that easy. Emily was deadlocked in guilt and fear. She adored Mark but remained drawn to her marriage out of a combination of moral compunction—considering Peter's background, how could she abandon him and take his son?—and that eternal fear that she was incapable of surviving without Peter.

In a desperate attempt to rescue her marriage, Emily sought therapy, which continues into the present. Under advisement, in order to draw Peter's attention to the critical nature of their marital problems and also to gain leverage with him, she moved out of the house and into an apartment with Scott. From that vantage point she was able to negotiate a reconciliation within two months, just prior to Christmas 1991. When Peter agreed to marriage counseling, a joint checking account, dresser and closet space for Emily's belongings, and time alone with him at least one evening per month, she returned home.

But Peter followed through on only one condition of the agreement: Emily did move her things into the bedroom. He still never made love to her or even held her, and he kissed her good-bye as he did Scott—with a peck on the cheek. He was totally entrenched in his job: happy to spend twenty hours a day there upon request but too tired to do things with Emily. Nothing improved. Taking after her mother, Emily was ever patient, ever loving, ever forgiving. She recalls that tortured existence:

Everything I did was wrong no matter what I did, and I kept trying to please him. I laid in bed every night and thought, "Oh my gosh, what are all the things I didn't do that day that maybe would make him happy?"

In April 1992 Emily assumed a position for increased pay with a drug prevention center. Soon after, the schizophrenic character of her personal life incited her to action. She was ready to move on the divorce, then settle in with Mark. She requested of Mark that they separate until the divorce was final. Leaving her husband while seeing another man was not an option; this was something she must do on her own. Besides, having the best of both worlds "medicated" her, neutralized the passion she needed in order to break free of the marriage. Mark would have no part of such a plan. Unable to continue with life as she knew it, Emily was forced to sever the three-year relationship with Mark. In retrospect, she realizes that Mark was much like Peter after all. He was controlling and treated her as a possession. The partnership with him had been totally on his terms.

KANE

August of that year brought a new colleague into Emily's professional community. Kane and Emily met in the context of their overlapping responsibilities related to drug prevention. Emily describes the first time she saw Kane:

I walked around the corner—I'll never forget, there he was. We walked in behind him, and he stood up and turned around, and he just took my breath. I went back down to my office, and someone said, "Have you met the new housing director?" and I said, "Oh my God, he's a Greek god!"

Within two weeks, Kane was making passes at Emily. His flirtatious manner was flattering and provided Emily with a much-needed ego lift. At this point she was overweight and deeply stressed. She was incredulous that someone of Kane's caliber would show an interest in her, especially considering that they were both married.

Soon Kane was stopping by Emily's office daily with some excuse or another. Then one day the conversation turned to his marital problems and pending divorce. Emily reciprocated by confiding about her troubled marriage. Kane told Emily of his attraction to her and that he hoped to know her better. Over that first month, they continued to talk at work and took a few country drives. Kane spoke of Rebecca's shortcomings: she was self-absorbed and irrational and didn't care about the children. Soon she would be returning to New Mexico. Kane was lonely, and Emily assured him that she understood all the ways he felt. She thought his marriage was like hers.

In September, when Rebecca was out of town, Kane invited Emily to come by the house after the children were asleep. That was their first sexual encounter. For more than a year, until January 1994, they continued to meet periodically in town and Emily accompanied Kane on business trips. They comforted each other and spoke of marriage and children of their own. That was particularly important to Emily because she wanted children—mothering was her strength and joy—and Peter had decided they would have no more. Emily envisioned herself and Kane helping one another through their divorces. Rebecca was always about to leave for New Mexico. Kane understood Emily perfectly; he always knew how she felt. And he was gorgeous and wanted only her. It was too good to be true!

Emily would do anything to please Kane and believed all he said. Anything to keep him. Once Rebecca summoned the state police to their home on a violence complaint against Kane. He denied the abuse to Emily, claiming that Rebecca had goaded him to hit her until he finally pushed her away. Emily bought into Kane's story and expressed sympathy for him. She jeopardized her reputation by phoning a state police friend to advise him that Rebecca was lying and "nuts."

In November, after years of depression and under the advice of her therapist, Emily committed herself to a local psychiatric center because she had developed suicidal tendencies. Her marriage was depleting her, and the affair with Kane compounded those troubles with guilt and the intense fear of losing him. Peter virtually ignored Emily during her two-week stay, visiting her only once and giving her an endless series of excuses. When she phoned him at the post to confront him about it, he left her on hold until she was compelled to hang up. Emily's time at the center fortified her temporarily, but on her release she had to face all her troubles again and to apply the insights that she had gained there.

The close of 1992 brought nagging doubts of Kane's honor and sincerity. He began to fail to call Emily as he had promised and to stand her up. He would freeze her out then reel her in, as she struggled to hang on to him. Rumor had it that he was seeing other women. Once he asked that she alter a hotel bill in order to allow him to be "reimbursed" fraudulently by his employer. And she discovered that he had been collecting reimbursement for meals that she had bought. In January Emily broke up with Kane. But a month later, when he phoned to say he missed her, she regressed right back into the turbulence. She was hooked and they both knew it.

Kane's abuse intensified. Until summer 1993, when Rebecca and Kane separated, he had been a gentle and considerate lover. Then he began inflicting pain by biting Emily and insisting on anal sex. When Emily protested, he quipped, "Oh, you know you like it," then went on to have his way with her. Soon thereafter, Kane's requirements escalated to a new level. He believed Rebecca was a lesbian and wanted Emily to seduce her on videotape. Emily suspects that he intended to use the tape in his effort to gain custody of his children. He also wanted to arrange for Emily to have videotaped sex with his buddy. Kane hoped to observe both trysts from a closet.

Both suggestions repulsed Emily, but she was not in the habit of saying no to Kane, so she stalled for a month or two. Finally, when pressed, she refused and suffered harsh consequences. Kane flew into a rage, accusing her of being inconsiderate, which sent her fleeing his office in tears. He pushed too hard that time; the incident elicited one of Kane's few apologies.

That summer banished all doubt relating to Kane's philandering. Emily overheard a conversation at work that clearly linked him to another woman in the building. Word had it that this woman was involved with a controlling, married man who shoved and hit her. Emily was becoming progressively hard-pressed to trust Kane. At the same time her fear of losing him intensified. The more she tugged, the more he withdrew. He stood her up more often now, and the fights were acidic. By year's end Emily was once again prepared to do whatever necessary to keep Kane.

It was in January 1994 that Kane "cashed in his chips," betraying and humiliating Emily to the breaking point. For two grueling weeks he pressed her, under direct threat of abandonment, to partake in an unspeakable scheme that, to his benefit, would violate every fiber of her morality. Her ultimate compliance signified the pinnacle of his control and her subjection to him that had characterized the relationship from its inception. He had ravished her and now had no choice but to discard her. She was far too angry with him to be of further use either sexually or in his unscrupulous campaign to quell Rebecca, gain custody of his children, and ascend professionally. From then on Emily's passion for Kane was funneled into vengeance, as she joined forces with Rebecca to help Rebecca keep her children and with the city commission to have Kane fired. It was too late for Rebecca and the children, but not for the city. Rebecca lost her children and Kane lost his job.

GETTING OUT OF THE MARRIAGE

Emily used the two months away from Kane to make a "wholehearted, 100 percent, nobody-else-involved last attempt" to make her marriage work. But Peter insisted that he had no intention of changing: "I am what I am!" His condescension and intimidation remained as brutal as ever. When queried about possible physical abuse from Peter, Emily is quick to point out that Peter never hit her because he didn't have to: he was trained in intimidation tactics and taught unarmed self-defense at the police academy. His posturing was as effective at intimidation as was another man's beating; it debilitated her.

Peter remained unaware of Emily's extramarital activities until she was forced to tell him about Kane because of her commitment to testify against him on Rebecca's behalf in March 1994. At first Peter was understanding, referring to the fact that everyone makes mistakes and assuring her that they would get through it. She was encouraged that he held her for the first time in years. A day or two later, however, he turned on her. He became rude, distant, and evasive regarding the affair and Emily's upcoming testimony. Once when she spoke of them, he retorted, "I'll deal with you when this is over," suggesting that he was blameless in the turn of events and that the situation would be addressed on his terms alone.

Emily was outraged; it was her first time to experience the luxury of anger toward Peter. On the spot, that anger neutralized the pity, fear, and guilt, releasing her from his captivity. Emily says:

I was furious for the first time. Before, I never thought I could get mad, and I didn't think I had the right to. I would ask someone, "He did this. Do you think I should be mad?" I'd question my hurt, but this time, I knew he had no right.

How dare he judge her: had he been there for her, she would have been spared all this extramarital abuse. How dare he—especially in light of the later discovered fact that he too had "stepped out" on the marriage. The anger propelled Emily to the divorce court. She filed the next day; the divorce concluded the nine-year marriage. Scott was five.

REFLECTIONS

Emily attributes the inner resources necessary for her eventual escape from male dominance to her long-term therapy, which helped her reverse lessons from her childhood. While growing up, she admired her mother's capacity to forgive her father. In retrospect, she realizes she was learning to be a "doormat for men." She was learning that women are inferior to men and that a woman must have a man, any man, in order to be whole. Emily embraced her mother's ideology and, with it, low self-esteem. Now she knows that she does not have to endure a climate of condescension, humiliation, and self-doubt. She has a right to require respect and is justified in becoming angry or leaving. And she can care for herself and her son, without a man, if necessary. Emily is proud of her hard-earned wisdom and offers these words of inspiration:

You can get out. When I left him, I had no job, no home, no money. All the things I thought I would have to have, I didn't have any of those. I wouldn't say just go and rush out. You need to plan it out in order for it to work, but start with yourself. Just start working on you, as we women allow a lot of this because we are low in self-esteem and socialized to believe it's okay. And [we] make the marriage work, keep it together, no matter what. . . . Start working on yourself and getting your inner strength. . . . See a counselor—somewhere, somebody. . . . There are programs that will help. . . . I don't have a lot of money . . . but I'm so much happier. I respect me. And I think even if you can't do it for yourself, if you've got children, you need to do it for them. Scott sees a strong mommy that does things and makes decisions and works and takes him places and that's responsible. I think I'm a much better influence on him and a better role model. . . . If I had never left for myself, I would still have to leave for his sake to show him a better way because you're going to just keep on repeating things until you can learn healthier ways. He's never going to learn healthy problem solving from his dad. . . . You can get out, and you need to for yourselves and your kids.

It is instructive to note that, while Emily's father supported her divorce, her mother offered resistance, which placed a wedge between them. Emily's mother thinks Peter was all a husband should be: he provided well for her, including a "lovely hundred-thousand home." How on earth could she walk away from something like that: nothing could be that bad. When Emily and Peter separated, her mother persisted with comments about how much Peter loved her and how hurt he was. She seemed to not mind or perhaps not understand that those were piercing words of blame. Emily resents that her mother would invite to join the family at Christmas dinner at *Emily's* home a man who had driven her to near suicide. Her newfound sense of independence and personal well-being has been achieved at the expense of the respect and admiration she once held for her mother regarding that unconditional "devotion" to her father.

Part IV

FAMILY AND FRIENDS
TO THE RESCUE

CHAPTER SEVEN

Lee

Lee responded to my nationwide mailing to abuse shelters. She was and remains shelter manager for Battered Women, Inc., in Crossville, Tennessee. After reviewing her autobiographical essay, I accepted an invitation to visit her for a day or so for an interview session. That brief stay in Fairfield Glade, Tennessee, a picturesque village nestled in a section of the foothills of Appalachia known as the Cumberland Plateau, where Lee spends weekends with her mother, brother, and three-year-old niece, turned out to be an idyllic winter getaway. Lee and her family extended to me the warmest welcome and most gracious hospitality. We toured the community and Lee's nearby shelter and dined elegantly. Then Lee and I spent most of the remainder of our time together poised at opposite ends of the living room couch with a tape recorder centered between us. There, settled comfortably into mounds of pillows and quilts and bundled warmly in big socks and flannel nightgowns, we embarked on a tumultuous journey into Lee's past. We persevered into the wee hours, breaking periodically for a kitchen run to refuel on the homemade cake and other delights prepared by Lee's mother for the occasion or sometimes just for a smidgen of quiet time. An aura overcame the house that this space and time were reserved for Lee and me alone. The room fell awkwardly silent when intruders passed through. It was clear that no one was welcome. We stopped when we reached exhaustion, then finished up in the late morning. This story of Lee's life is a product of that marathon of sorts.

Lee's story is one of close and loving family ties that somehow were not enough to keep her (or her brother) safe. It is a tale of clinical despair and substance abuse in the context of a young woman's perceived parental failure and its associated guilt. Lee's account of battering provides a disturbing glimpse into the Michigan outlaw militia associated with convicted Oklahoma City terrorist bomber Timothy McVeigh.

Today Lee is a young doting grandmother who has made peace with her son, who now resides in Florida. She continues living with her mother, brother, and niece in Fairfield Glade and thriving as shelter manager in nearby Crossville. Lee remains active in shelter issues statewide and is destined to enter university life soon.

Lee speaks in superlatives of her early years. They were the best times of her life, and she describes her parents as the best humans imaginable. Though both parents had sprung from dysfunctional families, they merged to produce a solid domestic climate that brought Lee much security and happiness. She remembers the great respect that her parents showed each other as well as each of their children.

Like her parents, Lee was born and reared in Detroit, Michigan. She was the oldest of three children and the only girl. In retrospect she realizes that home life was quite progressive, free of oppression and domination and conducive to critical thought and expression. Both parents earned respectable incomes: she as a secretary in a brokerage firm, he as chief custodian in the East Detroit public school system. The family thrived in a nice three-bedroom home in a suburb now called Eastpointe. Long before it was fashionable, Lee's mother was a "liberated woman." Lee's parents operated as a team; she watched both of them cook, clean, iron, bake cookies, and change diapers, all the while assuming that this was just the way families were. She learned early that it takes "two" to make marriage work.

Lee thinks of her parents as loving and gentle; they sheltered their children from what she refers to as "the horrors of life." She counts on one hand the times that a child in that household got a "swat." Her father was soft-spoken and easier when it came to discipline. Her mother was louder, with cool stares and pointed lectures destined to "make anyone break down and tell all." Lee's mother taught her the joys of femininity and that her gender need not block her accomplishments. Education was a critical tool to be used wisely. The greatest tragedy of Lee's life is the recent death of her father.

Lee recalls that both parents viewed her as hardheaded, stubborn, sometimes rebellious, but kindhearted. She seemed drawn to the helpless and dependent, to the underdog. At first she brought home stray cats and dogs, then eventually it was people. Her mother discouraged that, however. Some were a bit dangerous—a few, drug users—and Lee learned from them that she was not equipped to save everyone. Lee's mother often said of her that she marched to a different drummer. Both parents respected her unconventional views while maintaining subtle control.

Lee was always close to her youngest brother, Chris, six years her junior. One of those underdogs, he always had problems. She devoted much time aggressively but unsuccessfully attempting to mold him into the little boy, adolescent, and man her parents expected. With Nick, the middle child, the relationship was more typical of brothers and sisters. Nick is calm, kind, and a bit withdrawn. For years Lee and Nick fought and could not stay in the same room together. Lee claims that Nick still picks on her. Chris was likable, but selfish, judging people by what they could do for him. Lee was always protective of him, right up until Chris's suicide in 1993. Chris died an angry and troubled young man. Lee finds solace in his passing.

School left Lee uninspired. In high school her grades were average but her attendance was not. She preferred hanging out with friends during school hours. When she put her mind to it, Lee could skip three weeks of English, then ace the final. She never completed high school.

Lee's interest in boys began in junior high, but because she was small and underdeveloped, they took little interest in her. Her girlfriends had boyfriends before she did, and she longed to fit in but took consolation in her many platonic friends of both sexes. A serious romantic relationship blossomed in junior high and continued off and on into high school, but because of Lee's Catholic upbringing, there was no sexual intercourse, only a lot of "fooling around." Everyone thought they would eventually marry, but instead Lee's head was turned by the most handsome man in her universe.

LEAVING HOME, RETURNING TO THE FOLD: MARRIAGE, MOTHERHOOD, DIVORCE, DEVASTATION

Lucian was Italian American, one year older than Lee and quite reserved. He was a high-school student who worked at his father's construction company on weekends. Lee was not concerned that she and Lucian shared no interests or that he did not talk much—

his looks said it all. She was proud to show him off. Under her parents' protest, Lee and Lucian married in November 1970, when Lee was eighteen. Her parents begged her to complete high school and promised to subsidize the university education of her choice. But Lee was anxious to be free of school and of her parents' watchful eye. Both she and Lucian dropped out of their senior year of high school. They moved into a mobile home; he worked full-time for his father, while she stayed home and became miserable. Lucian indulged Lee, but she was bored. In February Lee faced an unplanned pregnancy, for which she and Lucian were totally unprepared. Christopher, named after Lee's brother, was born in September 1971. After being married less than two years, Lee and Lucian divorced amicably. Lee still thinks highly of Lucian; she recently enjoyed dancing with him at their son's wedding.

Lee returned to her parents and brothers with Chris in tow when she was twenty and he was eighteen months old. For twelve years she would be trapped in a downward spiral of lethargy, guilt, nonproductivity, and dependence—in a word, depression. She had left home seeking freedom and returned more shackled than before. For two or three years Lee mothered Chris and enrolled in night school toward the completion of her high school diploma. Then, at twenty-three, while still in school, Lee applied for a position as trader in a brokerage firm. She lied her way through the interview: in reality she had not graduated from high school, she did not know how to type, and she did not know the difference between a stock and bond. Nevertheless, she did well, commanded a good salary, and thrived on the intensity for the next six years, when health problems forced her to quit.

While Lee loved her job, she found off-time at home unbearable. Her mother had taken over the care of her child—and Lee had let her. There was all of the guilt associated with that, coupled with the sense of failure at having quit night school just four credit hours short of the diploma. And then there was the dependence: day by day, her son's life became progressively entrenched in the world of his grandparents and uncles. And associated with his entrenchment was her own. She was suffocating in it all. At one point Lee wanted to move out with Chris, but her parents resisted. While her parents were on vacation, she and Chris rented a house six blocks away. But that did not really change anything, and they were back at the homestead two years later. Lee was just not ready to leave; letting her parents take care of her and Chris was just too easy.

During these years, for recreation and diversion Lee hung out in bars with friends and dated married men. She was drawn to the danger of a married man's circumstances; then she tired of him and left in boredom. Soon she would find another. Married men consumed her; she welcomed the distraction from the agonizing realities of her life. These men could be with her on weekends only, but her week revolved around being ready for them when Friday night arrived. They became desperately dependent on her; she liked hearing how much they needed her. Bob was an older man, a mon-eyed stockbroker who introduced Lee to a life of privilege. When he asked her what she would do if he were to leave his wife, she told him that because she had watched him cheat on his wife, she would assume every time he walked out the door that he was doing the same to Lee. Basically that ended that relationship. Then there was Joe. Lee had never much liked her high school acquaintance, Josephine, but in their late twenties, the two became friends. Josephine had married Joe, an Italian immigrant. When Joe and Lee became lovers, Joe told Josephine that he was leaving her to be with Lee. Josephine then confronted Lee with knowledge of the affair, causing Lee to break off the relationship. Joe became violent, began stalking Lee, and broke into her home once and hit her while her parents were away. Lee took out an assault warrant. Joe stopped bothering her and ultimately reconciled with Josephine.

When Lee moved in with her parents after the divorce, she had trouble sleeping. Once, under the influence of a cold, she took Nyquil, which is 20 percent alcohol, and discovered that it allowed her to sleep. With time she was sending her son to the store for Nyquil and consuming three bottles per night. She reasoned that an over-the-counter product could not possibly be dangerous. Lee was addicted. Bottles were stashed strategically all around the house. Then she began mixing the Nyquil with beer. Alone in her room at night, she believed her secret was secure. But the family knew, even little Chris. She remembers passing many evenings and nights with the bedcover pulled up to her head—numbed by the Nyquil and beer—then dragging herself out of bed for work the next morning.

Six years of this lifestyle took its toll on Lee's health. At twenty-nine she was diagnosed with cervical cancer and submitted to a partial hysterectomy. Her temporary work leave turned permanent. The surgery had terrified her, and she was too depressed to return to work. A rash of tumors appeared in her breasts and uterus—all benign. She was not eating properly. Now she was home alone, depressed, intoxicated, and sleeping twelve to fourteen hours a day. She attempted a series of jobs with brokerage firms, finding no satisfaction there. Of those days, Lee says:

I knew my son was being well taken care of by my parents, but the feeling of complete failure was overwhelming. My son would become very upset with me. He always knew he could never really depend on me as a parent. But at least he had his grandparents. Thank God for that. I would go out with my friends to different clubs, meet men, and later say to myself, "Why bother!" I think what bothered me most was that all my friends were on their own (with or without partners), and here I was still with my parents. But I needed to be there and I knew it. I felt so much guilt because my son really needed me and I wasn't there for him. It was too easy to let my parents take over and solve all my problems—just like when I was a child. And they were good at it. I made promises to my son I knew I could never keep. But I knew my parents would. My parents had so much love in them; I knew they would do well for my son. I just gave up. I still don't really understand fully what was bothering me then. But here I was at home, with a child, still in my parents' home, nowhere else to go!

THE ABUSIVE RELATIONSHIP

At the end of October 1985, when Lee was thirty-three and Chris was fourteen, she met Tony at a neighborhood tavern. He was quite the gentleman that night: reserved, polite, chitchatting with Lee and her friend and buying them drinks. He was six years Lee's junior, very neat and quite handsome. Everyone seemed to like him. So she took his phone number and called two weeks later. They agreed to meet again at the tavern. That night she learned of Tony's close-knit Italian-American family. He was the third of four sons and currently living with his parents and waiting to close the mortgage on his own three-bedroom brick home. Lee would come to know Tony's parents as kind people who maintained an attractive, well-kept home. Tony earned a good salary working for his brother, who owned a van conversion shop. He spoke with pride of his seven years stationed in San Diego as a Navy SEAL (a special combat operations unit). It was the GI Bill that was allowing him to build the new house. That night Tony told Lee of his former marriage to a woman who had turned alcoholic, stolen money from him, and hocked jewelry and furniture to support her addiction. He had loved her and tried to no avail to help her. Of course, this story was later called into question and invalidated by Lee. In the conversation at the tavern that evening, Lee told Tony of her upcoming court date with Joe, the former lover who had stalked and assaulted her. Tony was appalled at Joe's behavior and offered to accompany Lee to court as a protective gesture.

Lee and Tony became heavily involved immediately. Tony was financially secure, kind, fun, and easygoing. He drank too much, but Lee reasoned that he was a happy drunk, a social drinker. Within five weeks Lee joined Tony in his new home. She was thrilled with this opportunity to be normal at last. About that time, Lee's parents retired and relocated to Tennessee. That left no choice for Lee's son, Chris: he had to leave his grandparents to live with Lee and Tony. In spite of Tony's efforts to befriend him, Chris intuitively disliked Tony. He was respectful but distant; the undertone was clear, and that relationship never improved. No doubt Chris was unhappy. In retrospect, Lee realizes that she was ignoring him as she devoted all her energies to Tony. Chris sulked around the house, got a part-time job, took driver's training, and essentially escaped the scene once he had free access to a car. He aggressively sought to create a solid bond with his father, who by now had remarried and established a financially secure and stable lifestyle.

In the meantime life was pleasant enough for Lee. Tony quit his brother's shop for a lucrative position as plant manager. The job demanded long hours, up to sixteen a day. He phoned often from work; she was flattered at how he missed her—and was so in love. Tony discouraged Lee from returning to the workforce; she took that as a gesture of generosity. Because he did not care for her friends and Chris remained aloof, her social network was limited to Tony, his family, and his friends.

When February rolled around, Tony showed interest in joining an outlaw motorcycle club called Hell's Our Home, part of the complex network of Michigan right-wing militia. He and Lee spent an evening of dinner and conversation with one of his biker friends and his "bitch." Lee was totally unable to relate to these people and their club-related accounts of misogyny and violence against women. She heard reference to "bitch slapping" and such and wondered what these women had done to deserve this talk and treatment. But Tony persuaded Lee that the club was harmless: just a bunch of guys who get together to ride motorcycles. Besides, they did MDA (Muscular Dystrophy Association) and Toys for Tots runs! Tony was initiated into the club shortly before Lee and Tony married in April 1986. The wedding was a simple civil ceremony, with just their families and a few of his friends in attendance. They came to the house afterward for sandwiches, lunch meat, and vegetable dip. Everyone had left by 5:00 P.M., including Chris, who was staying with his father for a couple of days. What happened next set the tone for marriage:

The next thing I hear, it sounds like motorcycles from hell; you can hear them pulling up. I think fifty-five of them showed up. I am thinking, "Well, I am going to meet these guys, his friends." You should have seen his friends. The whole neighborhood is looking out. So they all pull up and get off their bikes, and some of them have their "bitches" with them. So I am totally freaking out, and I am thinking they are monsters. Some of these guys are six feet tall, and their hair is down to the middle of their back, and it is all braided. They got the tattoos and the leather jackets with the bike club emblem on the back, what they call "colors." Their emblem was a motorcycle with a devil on it and the name Hell's Our Home. They also had their personal names on them: Froggie, Mouse, Hotdog, etc. So Tony rips off his wedding clothes and puts on these jeans that look like they haven't been washed in six years. His club name is Maniac. Now I am thinking: "Wow! This is our wedding and these people from hell are over here." This one biker walks in and he had to be 6'8" and probably weighed four hundred pounds, and the meanest-looking man. And I read his name: "Zeke." He walks over to me and just crushes a beer can in his hand and lets it drop. I am like, "Excuse me; that is my carpet." He says, "Are you Maniac's old lady?" And I say, "No, I am not his old lady; I am his wife." And he says, "You are his bitch." Now I am getting a little frustrated. I say, "I am not his bitch; I am his wife." He says, "Oh well, you better be nice to me or I will fuckin' rape you." My heart slipped to the bottom of my feet. . . .

It is now about 8 or 9 o'clock at night, and they are still leaving to buy beer, and there are just people everywhere. I tell Tony that his friends need to go home: "My God, this is our wedding night!" He turns and looks at me and says, "But these are my friends; we party all night." So I am thinking I have got myself into something. They are there for two days. Two days! I am totally out of my mind by this time. Nobody sleeps. They do too many drugs. I had never seen anybody shoot up. They were big cocaine traffickers and did "crank." I went to my bedroom upstairs and shut the door. I was furious; it was my wedding night. Nobody bothered me in my room. Now I realized, "My God, what the hell have I done!" This man has lied to me. These are not do-gooders. These are not the kind of guys you want over on a Sunday dinner. Tony knew all along.

From this wedding-day scenario, the abuse took hold and escalated: the yelling, the condescending manner, the cruel name-calling, the first face slap, the accusations of lying and wanting other men. Tony even asked the man across the street if anyone (meaning a man) were coming over while he was at work. His mind-set had changed drastically with his introduction to the club. Lee became frightened as she saw women associated with the bikers shoved around and beaten. These men were filled with rage toward the world in general, as well as toward women.

The longer Tony associated with the club, the more violent he became and the heavier he drank. He began using contraband drugs and missing workdays; the company became concerned. When it came to partying with the club, Tony knew no limits: a couple of hours would turn into a couple of days. Sometimes Lee did not know his whereabouts or if he were alive. Bills went unpaid; the utilities were periodically disconnected. Tony would blame Lee, telling people that he had given her the money. By eighteen months into the relationship, Lee was subjected to severe physical violence, including being punched in the face, shoved down two flights of stairs, threatened with a knife at her throat, and raped. The beatings intensified in frequency and severity to two or three a week. But the emotional agonies always overpowered the physical.

Home became intolerable to Chris, so at age sixteen he left to live with his father. He could not understand how Lee could let Tony do this to her. Lee recalls the sense of devastating betrayal the day Lucian came for Chris. Her absolute need to please Tony prevented her from grasping Chris's perspective, why he was abandoning her. For a short while Chris phoned Lee periodically, but he then became unwilling to hear the lies about how Tony was so much better now. Lee did not see Chris again till two years later, when he sought her out at work to say that he was leaving for college in Florida. Tony repeatedly told Lee that the reason Chris had left was out of disdain for her. He said Chris had confided that he would have happily stayed with Tony if Lee had gotten out of the house. Lee became convinced that it was she who made all of their lives miserable.

As a result of his absenteeism and drug use, Tony eventually lost his job. Financial problems intensified, and the bank finally repossessed the house. Again Tony blamed Lee, telling family and friends that she had squandered his money. Lee and Tony moved to a substandard rental home and subsisted on his unemployment benefits. Six months later he got another factory job but lost that a year later because of absence and bad temper. Then there were unemployment benefits again, then nothing. Tony remained unemployed. It was then that Lee took a series of menial jobs to pay the bills, but they were not worth the trouble. She ran out of explanations for all the injuries and bruises she suffered. Tony would call her at work with complaints and sometimes just appear there demanding whatever money was in her purse.

By now, Tony's appearance was startling. His lifestyle had hardened his features; he looked every bit as cruel as he was. The abuse now left Lee with broken bones and eardrums, a broken nose, and eyes so bruised that she was unable to open them for days. Half a head of hair was pulled from her scalp. On several occasions Tony nearly killed her; in her mind death was imminent. Just as destructive were Tony's words: she was stupid (without diploma), fat (increased from size three to five), skinny (back to size three) and totally unlovable (even her son had left her). Lee told no one; she lied to physicians.

In our five hours of taped interview, Lee's eyes watered only once: when the subject turned to her one friend through this ordeal, her beloved dog, Nasty, an Austrian shepherd. Nasty suffered through Lee's abuse and beatings of her own. She hated Tony and eventually would tear into him during Lee's "punishments." Tony would torment Nasty by placing meat in front of her, then forbidding her to eat it. He had her trained to sit alone in a room for hours with meat left untouched. Nasty would just look up at Lee while Tony was kicking her, and when Nasty bled she would come put her head in Lee's lap, and Lee would cry. Today a framed photograph of Nasty is displayed on Lee's bedroom dresser.

Lee existed in total captivity. Tony dead-bolted her in the house while he was away (sometimes without food because she was "fat") and taped the edges of the door to alert him to tampering. Lee was instructed to not touch doors and windows. Tony sometimes took the phone with him. He would warn Lee that she could never escape, that he would find her and put her six feet under where she belonged. He was omnipresent. Even when he was gone for days, she was afraid to leave; she knew he would find her. She had no money or car and had alienated her friends and son. Her parents were virtually out of the picture. Lee remained unaware that Chris had informed them of much of this abuse. Never had they believed the outrageous tales that Tony had fed them when they phoned, describing Lee as mentally incapacitated and Tony as the devoted caretaker. Nor did they believe Lee's feeble efforts to placate them—on those rare occasions when Tony allowed her to speak, always in his presence.

Tony's mother knew of the abuse and sometimes confronted him, but that only made it worse on Lee. She counseled Lee to leave, assuring her that Tony would never change. But Tony was saying something different. After each episode, he promised to attend AA and begged her not to leave. He offered gifts of cigarettes, junk food, and trinkets, and groveled for hours, convincing her how much he loved and needed her. He threatened suicide. Lee wanted so badly to believe him; she needed to believe him. He never changed.

In his effort to convince the world that it was Lee who had ruined them financially, Tony sent her to a psychiatrist. After two sessions with Tony and four or five with Lee, the psychiatrist phoned Lee to tell her to get out of there as soon as possible, that there was no money missing, and that she was not the cause of the marital and financial problems. He told her that she was in danger because she was a battered woman. Lee was incredulous. Tony would never really hurt her—she said with both legs in casts. Besides, she had nowhere to go. And most certainly she was not a battered woman. She had seen the television movie, *Battered*; Tony was not like that! But at another level and for a while now, Lee knew that somehow she must leave.

GETTING OUT

After they relocated to the rented house, Lee made between twelve and fifteen feeble attempts to leave Tony. None was well planned, and some took her out of the house for only a few hours, so went undetected by Tony. Sometimes she went to her friend Lynn across the street and sometimes to Tony's mother, but mostly she went to her longtime friend Joyce across town. Sometimes she packed a bag. The longest she was away was two weeks at Joyce's. Lee recalls missing Tony, being miserable. He phoned her and demanded that she come home lest he "blow up that goddamn house." She went back. Many times Tony sensed when Lee was thinking of leaving, and he reeled her back in with his charming side. While there were good times in the beginning, there were none anymore.

In October 1990 Lee's mother phoned her while Tony was out. Lee was so excited; she had not heard her mother's voice for three years. Her mother invited her to come to Tennessee to spend a few days at Christmas with her parents and brothers. She offered to send a round-trip ticket by restricted delivery registered mail (only Lee could sign) for departure December 21 and return December 27. Lee could not believe her own voice when she said yes. Her mother closed the conversation saying she was anxious to see Lee and loved her. Hanging up the phone, Lee realized this was her way out *if* she could pull it off. She needed Tony to go along with all of this and to drive her to the airport. If he even suspected this to be an escape, he would dash her plans. She was overwhelmed with it all. Could she convince Tony to let her go and was she really ready to leave him?

I knew I had that ticket coming. My mind, it was like, "Okay, you have this ticket coming. You can get away." But now I am thinking, "How can I get away, because how am I going to get to the airport? How am I going to do all this? I don't want to call my friends. I am scared to death, and I have to do this. This is my opportunity to get away, but how am I going to do it? The way out is there, but it is still unreachable. I still have to find a way to get out of the house to the airport and onto the plane." I was confused. I just kind of blocked it a while, thinking that this was October and it isn't going to happen until December. In the meantime maybe he will calm down; maybe he will go and get help; maybe he will stop this so I don't have to do this, because I really don't want to do this. Now I know that I have to do something, but I don't want to do it at the same time.

On a weeknight in November, Lee and Tony joined another couple at a local bar for drinks. Lee did not say much that night. She was always reserved when out with Tony; he criticized most of what she said. They were all tired and left early for home. The evening had been nothing out of the ordinary, and on the way home neither Tony nor Lee spoke. That was not unusual either. Lee was deep in thought about her plane ticket. They pulled up to the house. Suddenly, out of the dark silence rushed Tony's rage. With a single gesture he locked the car doors and windows and screamed, "You know, you really make me sick. You don't like my friends. You sit there. You don't talk!" He lunged toward her, punching her in the face and screaming, "You're going to die tonight, bitch!" Restrained by the locked doors, Lee just did her best to block his fists. He cracked the windshield with her head. Blood was spurting and blinding her, and the swelling was obstructing her breathing. She felt her eyes closing up and she tasted the blood. Then somehow she was out of the car and running for the back door. That beating terrified Lee more than any of the others, not because it was the most severe but because she had now changed. Now she had that plane ticket. She had a way out. For the first time something inside her said, "Run, get out!" It was a new emotion that would carry her through to the end.

Lee was unable to join Tony at his family's Thanksgiving dinner because her bruises were still noticeable. So she stayed home and planned her strategy. Tony was in a generous mood; they were in the "honeymoon stage" following that last beating. So when Tony returned home from Thanksgiving dinner, Lee told him that her parents had phoned that day to say that her father appeared to have cancer and her parents wanted to send her an airline ticket for what might be his last Christmas. She assured him that she hated to leave him during the holidays, but he had his family and she really should go. Tony said he would think about it; then ten minutes later he announced that he would let her go. Soon she had the ticket in her hand. Now she worried that the "honeymoon" would end and Tony would tear up the ticket.

But fate was on Lee's side. On December 13 Tony's father died unexpectedly of a heart attack. The entire family, including Tony, was devastated. Lee milked that situation: Tony was vulnerable now, and Lee was emphasizing how important it was for her to see her father this one last time. So far, so good. Now she was focusing on what to pack and on finding Nasty a new home. On December 20, at a gathering at her mother-in-law's home, Tony's mother took Lee aside to ask her about her father's health and to wish her well on the trip. She had always known of the abuse and advised Lee to get out, so Lee took this opportunity to level and say good-bye to a kindred soul. She blurted: "There is not a damn thing wrong with my dad!," to which the woman replied, "I know, and I love you, but don't come back because he will kill you." And there was more: she assured Lee that if necessary she would drive her to the airport herself the next morning.

Morning came and, acrophobia notwithstanding, Lee got onto that plane:

[Tony] knows I am afraid of flying, and I am a wreck. He says, "You don't have to be afraid. You are safer on a plane than in a car." I am a wreck. We get to the airport and I am saying to myself, "Oh my God, I am here!" And I am literally shaking. He says, "Don't worry; it is not going to crash." I am ready to vomit. I am thinking, "Hurry up; hurry up and call my damn flight before he changes his mind." I was a mental case. He sat right next to me. Finally they call my gate number. I am so anxious to go at this point. He is saying, "Well, wait, I will walk you there. Give me a kiss good-bye." I say, "Okay, you can go now." He said, "No, I want to watch the plane take off." Inside the plane, I go directly to the window seat so I can see this man. While I am sitting there, I start rocking, and I am thinking, "Hurry up, get off the ground, close the doors." People were looking at me on the plane. There are only maybe ten people on this plane. They are looking at me not only because I am rocking, but I am talking to myself. They are probably thinking we have got a psycho on the plane. I am saying, "Go, go!" The stewardess comes over and says, "Can I help you with anything," and I say, "Can we just leave?" She says, "Ma'am, the pilots will be taxiing to the runway." I am at the window, and I can vaguely see him, and I had visions of him running after the plane yelling "STOP!" I am giving him the finger through the window and saying good-bye. Now the stewardess is up to me going, "Are you having problems?" We are taxiing now and I say loudly, "Not anymore!" Then I become this sane person again, and they are looking at me and thinking I was psycho. It didn't even enter my mind that I was making a scene because the energy level was totally unbelievable. Now I start thinking that we are going to crash, and I am going to have to go back [to Tony]. I am not thinking that I am going to die. I am afraid that we will crash and that I will live and have to go back to him. I land in Nashville and my mom and dad and brother are there to pick me up.

Lee never saw Tony again. All along, her parents had intended the trip to be one-way. They were prepared to refuse to drive her the 110 miles back to the airport. But that was not necessary.

REFLECTIONS

When Lee reflects on her life choices, she sees a clear pattern of needing to rescue. In childhood, she tried to save stray animals, troubled adolescents, and her brother. Later, it was married men, then Tony. She realizes now that it was all an expression of her own dependence and need to be needed. Those people whom Lee rescued did not change in the conventional ways that Lee hoped; instead they exploited her energies in their domination and control of her. She realizes now that she needed them as much as they needed her and that they were pulling her down rather than her pulling them up.

Lee is certain that without the wisdom and thoughtful strategy of her parents, she would not be alive today. They understood her circumstances and waited patiently and silently until the time was right. Earlier Lee would have resented their intrusion; later she would have been dead. And a more forceful approach would have provoked her. They seized that window of opportunity, took the necessary risks, and gave it their best shot. And luck was on their side.

CHAPTER EIGHT

Annette

Annette was quite deliberately recruited for this collection. I wanted Hispanic women to be represented, and none had responded to my national search, so I set out to find one in my own Bowling Green, Kentucky, community. Annette preferred that all of my information collection be done by interview; she opted against writing an autobiographical sketch. That meant that I would spend more personal time with her than most of the others. Our regular meeting spot was her cozy upstairs apartment in a big old colonial-style house in a section of town that smacked of an elegant past. Sometimes our work was lightened by the presence and antics of Annette's beautiful dark-eyed and curly-topped toddler, who resembled his mother remarkably.

Annette tells a compelling story about the worst and best of families that begins in an impoverished Hispanic community in Los Angeles. She is a child of illegitimate birth, adoption, neglect, foster care, and, ultimately, battering in her late teens. It was a foster family that finally rescued Annette from oblivion. Annette's story provides glimpses into the unseemly worlds of baby smuggling and drug trafficking.

Today Annette is twenty and has achieved independence—freedom from poverty, drugs, and abuse. She supports herself and her young son by working as a beautician in Bowling Green. Annette's foster family, who took her in as an aimless adolescent, remains her mainstay.

Annette never knew her birth parents. Born in Los Angeles, she was the second of a Hispanic woman's three children who would be adopted and reared together by a Los Angeles Hispanic couple. Her birth mother was incarcerated when she delivered Annette at General Hospital. She kept the baby with her in the jail for three months, then gave up for adoption both Annette and her four-year-old brother, Tony, who was living with relatives. When released from jail, this woman became pregnant again, and a year-and-a-half after Annette's birth, there was a second brother, Angel, who joined Annette and Tony's adoptive family. Annette does not know if her birth parents were married; she does know, however, that she and both her brothers have the same father listed on their birth certificates.

Annette believes that she, Tony, and Angel would never have learned of their adoption had it not been for an act of indiscretion on the part of Tony when he was seventeen and Annette was thirteen. Tony broke into an always-locked drawer in their mother's room to discover birth certificates and adoption papers. A bit later Annette found a photo of her third birthday party, and when she inquired about the identity of a stranger in the photo, she was told simply that it was their birth mother. Perhaps because Tony is older than Annette and Angel and remembered their birth mother, he once took an interest in locating her. The search was unsuccessful: he found no trace of her or her parents, including death certificates.

Annette's adoptive family consisted of her mother, an outgoing woman active in church and community activities; her father, a quiet, withdrawn man who worked as a truck driver; her two brothers, Tony and Angel; and three other adopted children, a set of siblings who were the offspring of her birth mother's sister. So there were six children in all: two sets of three siblings who were biological cousins. Annette notes that this family of six children was not peculiar in terms of size when compared with other Catholic Hispanic families around them.

When Annette was six, the family moved south from Los Angeles to Escandido, just outside San Diego. Though they would establish a pattern of moving from place to place, they were to remain in that general area for seven years. Only in retrospect does domestic life during those Escandido times make sense to Annette. She surmises that while her father continued to work as a truck driver, both parents were heavily entrenched in drug use and trafficking. And periodically they smuggled Mexican babies into the U.S. to join their parents, who had entered illegally. Annette recalls her parents piling their six children into a van for a day trip to Mexico and returning with a couple of extra children. In the confusion of so many young faces, without fail the border patrol would hail the family through with the show of a few birth certificates.

What remains outstanding to Annette about those Escandido days is the excess of money and lack of child supervision. In some ways life was normal: the family lived on Elm Street and attended mass regularly, and the children walked to school. At the same time, however, the children virtually raised themselves. They got themselves up and out in the mornings without supervision. They were given plenty of money for food and movies and were expected to go to school, perhaps play in the neighborhood park, return by dark, take baths, and go to bed. While their parents issued typical parental admonishments such as "You're supposed to do this and you're supposed to do that," they rarely followed up. The children could come and go without their parents knowing or caring. This was when they were between the ages of six and thirteen. Annette recalls much neglect but no abuse.

These six children of the street became entrepreneurs of sorts and transgressed into minor delinquency. With money from their parents they would buy candy in bulk and sell it on the school grounds for profit. It was a game to stave off boredom. Also as a game, they engaged in petty theft on a regular basis. After school hours their mother sent them all to a therapist whose office was within walking distance. En route a pair of them would stop at the nearby Pic'n'Save to steal licorice, granola bars, and chewing gum. They would compete for who could get out with more. Annette recalls these and other desperate attempts by her and her siblings to conform to their parents' request that they stay occupied away from home. Even now, that typical send-off resonates back to Annette's consciousness: "Okay, you all go outside and play." In Escandido the children never skipped school, though they had no interest in academics. Annette remembers looking forward to recess.

When Annette was thirteen, the family relocated to Metcalfe County, Kentucky. It seems as though the move had been planned years in advance. Her parents had purchased the large old two-story, five-bedroom house on a hill years before and rented it out. They would travel across country periodically on trucking trips to visit its occupants, a family who appeared to be friends of her mother. Then, this particular summer, they stayed forever. The children were distressed upon realizing that they would not be returning to California. They hated the isolation and the big old house with its wood-burning stove, stained old-fashioned wallpaper, and general state of disrepair. Definitely a step or two down in their eyes. Annette recalls vividly her initial impressions of Kentucky the year she moved here:

We didn't just move to the country; we moved to the forest! All you could see were woods and a highway. . . . Here's Edmonton—we were like eighteen miles out of Edmonton. So, I mean, we pulled up; we were like, "Why were all of these animals out of their cages!" Cows, they were just wandering around. The closest store was like three miles away. You know, it was just awful, like a ghost town.

Annette surmises that this move to rural America represented an escape from the California legal system and the transfer of her parents' drug activities to a remote and safe environment. It is as though they were in hiding. To this day, her father rarely leaves that house on the hill. He stayed in trucking while Annette remained with the family, but he now works at a lumber yard two miles away. He works and then comes home, avoiding Edmonton, where his wife is socially entrenched. Many people continue to disbelieve that Annette's mother is married.

Moving to Kentucky signaled a powerful and destructive turnabout in family dynamics. People would soon begin splintering away; Annette was to stay with her family only nine months more, till age fourteen. The parents became demanding of the children in terms of work, and they evolved into harsh disciplinarians. Annette recalls being told to clean the large bedroom she shared with her sister. If it were not cleaned perfectly, her mother would pull everything out of the closets and drawers, and Annette would have to stay up all night cleaning it up again. This would happen two or three times a week. She remembers the children digging a huge pond and mowing the yard with a push mower—up and down the hill. All of this was a far cry from life in Escandido.

A particularly intriguing hierarchical structure within the family manifested itself with this new rural lifestyle and the work that it entailed. It became clear to Annette that the darker-skinned children, she, Tony, and Angel, were separated out for heavier work and harsher discipline. And they were referred to as "niggers" by their particularly pampered (and particularly light-skinned) sister.*

---

* At age twelve, diagnosed with vitiligo, Annette began losing skin pigmentation. By age fourteen, she had become light-complected, but that did not alter her position as "nigger."

Perhaps reinforcing that hierarchy was another family secret to be divulged much later—the fact that the adoptive mother was more closely connected to the birth mother of the lighter-skinned set of children than to Annette and her brothers' birth mother.

FOSTER CARE

A few months after having relocated to Kentucky, Annette was nosing around the thirty-two-acre homestead and entered the remote and forbidden trailer to which she had heard much reference—to discover that it was housing the production of "crystal meth," or "crank," which is a form of speed. She caught her mother in the act, along with some Latino and Mexican people from California who had formed a "farm" nearby. It was then and there that the mosaic of Annette's childhood fell into place. The dynamics of her Escandido lifestyle and the subsequent move to rural isolated Kentucky finally made sense. Immediately upon this discovery, Tony, who was now seventeen, left home to live in nearby Edmonton. Four months later Annette followed suit, after losing out on an ultimatum she had given her mother: it was either the drugs or Annette. Her mother chose the drugs and admonished Annette that if she left, she should never return.

Tony, Annette, and Angel had learned of their adoption soon after settling into their Kentucky home; that knowledge loomed heavily over them in an already difficult situation. Annette's mother had caught her studying the photo of her birth mother at Annette's third birthday party and quipped, "I hope you drop dead looking at that picture." It was time to go. So Annette walked out that night—two miles to the nearest phone, where she called Tony, who brought her to the house in town where he was staying with friends. She deeply regretted leaving Angel behind. She had asked him to come along, but he had declined. Though Annette sent cards and letters to Angel over the next few years (which he never received), she did not see him again until shortly after his eighteenth birthday, when he appeared on her doorstep.

Tony was unable to keep Annette with him. Besides, she needed to create distance between her and her parents. A phone call to Metcalfe County social services and a request to be removed from that county landed her in a Bowling Green foster home. She would remain in and out of that home over the next five or six years. To this day Annette sees that as her only real home and the people who lived there then as her real family. This was her only experience with what she considers to be a regular life—family outings, Easter egg hunts, family feelings. Her foster mother, Judy, worked for the health department as a resource person for pregnant teenage girls. Fred, her foster father, was a truck driver. They had two natural daughters. The older daughter, Tonya, and Annette were the same age, became fast friends, and soon entered their first year of high school together. During Annette's stay many other foster daughters passed through the family.

Entering high school, Annette was an outgoing child with a circle of girlfriends. From her Metcalfe County days she continued her moderate experimentation with alcohol, marijuana, and sex. And from her Escandido days she continued attending school for its social rather than academic benefits. Her petite frame notwithstanding, Annette had always been a fighter; she fought with boys and girls alike—and won. In Escandido her parents had taught her to fight in defense of her siblings as well as in self-defense. All in all, Annette avoided serious trouble and recalls those initial months with her foster family as the happiest time in her life.

THE ABUSIVE RELATIONSHIP

This first segment of life with Judy, Fred, and the girls lasted only thirteen months—until Annette spotted Billy off in the distance on his motorcycle at Judy's family reunion. Billy was a distant relative of Judy, the offspring of its only Hispanic member. While Annette had dated casually, Billy would become her first real boyfriend and ultimately her husband. Annette and Billy were instantly attracted to one another. She thought he was very handsome—and he was several years her senior. Immediately upon seeing Annette at the reunion, Billy phoned one of her older foster sisters to learn all about her. Annette and Billy spoke on the phone, and soon he began dropping by for visits on his motorcycle.

Billy's age, coupled with the fact that Annette was under sixteen, the age at which Judy and Fred allowed the girls to "car date," introduced tension between Annette and her new family. Fred and Judy vehemently opposed the relationship—to no avail. Billy convinced them to allow him to simply visit Annette at the house—that he was happy to wait until her sixteenth birthday to take her out. So the relationship progressed, though not in accordance with established rules, until Annette's relationship with Fred and Judy snapped under the strain. Judy forbade Annette to continue seeing Billy. Annette responded that she would rather leave home. So Judy requested social services to transfer Annette to another home, where she remained for three days. Then, partly out of fear of being placed in a group home, Annette married Billy in a quick civil ceremony. Getting married was Billy's idea, and Annette thought that option was as good as any. They had known one another six months; Annette was fifteen and Billy was twenty. After two weeks in a motel, the couple moved in with Billy's mother, stepfather, and stepbrother.

During their "courtship," Billy had always been charming and caring of Annette, or so she had thought. Only in retrospect are the nuances of progressive entrapment apparent to her. Ever so subtly his flattery, jealousies, and control isolated her and reeled her in. She recalls now that he would not allow her to go anywhere or do anything without him. He expected her to be home when she was not in school or with him. When she would tell him of plans to go somewhere, he would announce that he would be by that night to see her. And when she mentioned an intention to do something with a friend, he insisted that she do it with him instead. He offered her rides everywhere she wanted to go. A clear source of aggravation to Billy was Annette's enrollment as the only girl in an auto mechanics course.

Billy resented Annette speaking on the phone with friends. He would beep in on the call-waiting system, then tell her that he wanted her to hang up on the other person. Telephone contacts went from one extreme to the other: first he would indulge (even annoy) her with their frequency, then he would worry her with their absence. Annette also remembers Billy chipping away at her relationship with her foster family. They had made her feel a permanent part of their lives, but he introduced and perpetuated the idea that she was, in fact, expendable to them. Comments such as "What are you going to do when you turn eighteen?" or "What are you going to do if Judy and them decide to send you off?" or "What if they pick up and decide to close their home?" slowly but surely detached Annette from her new family. Billy helped compound that alienation by pushing his and Annette's relationship against Judy and Fred's wishes. Eventually, Annette was skipping school and sneaking out at night to be with Billy and, in general, becoming very rebellious at home. All the while, Billy was placing Annette on a pedestal, assuring her repeatedly of her extraordinary beauty and of his lifetime love and devotion. Little by little Annette found herself alone in the world—with Billy. She had even forsaken her beloved foster family, which left her unsettled right from the beginning.

Within a week of marriage, the darker side of Billy appeared. He decided that Annette need no longer attend school because she was married. He forbade her to wear makeup and nice clothes and to fix her hair. When they were in the car, he always drove and she was to hold her head down and keep her eyes to the floor. She was to remain confined to the house during the day while Billy and his stepfather were off at work (Billy was an outdoor seasonal worker) and Billy's stepbrother was in school. Billy's mother was home with Annette on days that his mother did not visit her own mother, but that was a burden rather than a consolation to Annette. Billy's mother's attitude regarding his abuse of Annette was simply, "Billy is just Billy." On the days that Annette was home alone, Billy took the phone with him to work, and he always left her with no car.

Perhaps ten days into the marriage, when the couple was still living in the motel, the physical abuse began. In retrospect the incident was predictable—it fit the pattern—but at the time Annette was left confused and longing for her foster family. Annette was no stranger to fighting; it was the betrayal of trust that hurt her so deeply. Going back home would have been too humiliating, and Billy had shaken her belief that she would be welcomed. There was nowhere else to go, and she had no car. And at that time it was impossible for her to know that her foster family would stand by her through the entire ordeal of that marriage. Those relationships have in fact endured uninterrupted into the present. But back then Annette was convinced that she needed Billy for her very survival.

Billy's violent tendencies toward Annette were unveiled while the two stopped at a nearby convenience store before a visit with his family. Annette went inside while Billy remained in the car. Annette's school friend worked in the store, a boy who all along had warned her against associating with Billy. He seemed happy to see Annette, asked her if she would be returning to school, inquired about the marriage, then assured her that he would be there working if she ever needed anything. Upon Annette's return to the car, Billy was livid: "Who's that—the guy at the cash register you were talking to?" He grilled her aggressively as they motored along and as she, in a fit of surprise, fear, and anger, explained that the boy was just a friend from school.

Continuing his tirade, Billy then moved on to the subject of another of Annette's friends, whom she had not dated but who had called her at the home of her foster family. Billy referred to that friend as "nothing but a male whore," to which Annette retorted, "No more than you!" With that, Billy halted the car and flew into a heightened rage. A beating episode followed, involving first an attack in the front seat. Billy grabbed Annette by the hair and slammed her head against the dashboard. Then he pulled over to the side of the road, got out of the car, and jerked Annette to the ground to continue the beating. All the while he was hollering that he had gotten her away from her foster family and that she was going to act as though she had some sense—she was not going to talk with other people so as to make him "look stupid."

When the couple arrived at the home of Billy's family, his mother walked back to the bedroom with Annette, who was visibly shaken, bruised, and weak. Her hair was in disarray and filled with dirt and leaves. In mild disgust, Billy's mother called out his name. That was the extent of the support Annette received from her in-laws. And it was symbolic of what she could expect. Billy's mother had been physically abused by his father until their divorce when Billy was six. This women was wise to the ways of battering.

Thirty minutes after their arrival at the house, Billy joined Annette in the bedroom to apologize and to clarify that she was to blame. She had made him "look stupid" by talking to people, like her old boyfriend. She needed to grow up. Annette offered her apologies in return. In the recesses of her mind she knew that this was not right—her father had never hit her mother. But she was immobilized. She believed Billy when he said that it was her fault and that he would not hurt her again.

Annette is quick to admit that, like Billy, she is violent. In fact, she hit him once. The first occurrence of physical violence between them was inflicted by her before they were married. She hid the car keys to prevent his driving while drunk, he called her a bitch, and she punched him. And while the two of them may have been capable of inflicting comparable harm on one another (though Annette is certain that she is a better fighter and could now and always have "taken him physically"), the associated motivations and meanings were quite distinct. Annette used violence as a means of expressing specific anger. Billy, on the other hand, employed it as a means of maintaining an undercurrent of control over Annette, based on fear.

Another incident early in the marriage relates to Annette's use of birth control. In response to Billy's sister-in-law's inquiry about her reproductive plans, Annette stated that she was currently using birth control. Billy was furious and, in that group setting, threw a shoe at Annette. He instructed her to not use birth control—he was sterile, so she did not need it. Because, in reality, Billy never did believe he was sterile, one can easily interpret his demand as one more gesture of dominance and control: he would control her reproductive system; perhaps he wanted her pregnant to reinforce her dependence on him.

After having spent three months with Billy's family, the couple got their own apartment in Bowling Green. With Annette's insistence that they needed the second income and that there could be no males competitive with Billy's interests there, she was allowed to work from 11:00 A.M. to 3:00 P.M. six days a week at a nursing home. About that time Billy attained a more lucrative job at U-Haul, from where he was able to monitor the apartment parking lot when Annette was there.

Life continued in the same vein: still no makeup, nice clothes, or fixing her hair. Annette recalls once curling her bangs for work, which elicited criticism from Billy: "Who are you trying to impress?" She never bothered again. Annette was expected to be with Billy when she was not at home or work. Billy transported her between the two locations, leaving his job briefly to get her in the afternoons. Each time he entered the nursing home to pick her up (he did not allow her to wait outside), he unobtrusively checked her time card. He continued his practice of removing the phone when Annette was home alone, and he leaned a newspaper against the outside of the apartment door to alert him to its having been opened in his absence. He also pulled the shades and positioned them in an identifiable way.

Annette was forbidden to shower when Billy dropped her off after work. She waited until later in the day when he was home. To Billy, Annette's showering while alone in the apartment suggested the possibility of illicit sex. Annette was not allowed to have visitors in the apartment, even in Billy's absence. Judy and Tonya visited, as did Billy's brother and sister. Judy and Tonya were barely tolerated because of their open disapproval of Billy, as was Billy's brother, because he was a young male. In spite of the restrictive lifestyle he imposed on her, Billy continually accused Annette of adultery.

Over the sixteen months that Annette and Billy lived together, the violent episodes decreased in frequency. They occurred nearly daily in the beginning. Annette surmises that he was trying to control his violent behavior. Rape was an integral and frequent part of their relationship. After four months of marriage, every sexual contact was rape. For Annette and Billy, the rapes were independent of the beatings.

Annette describes Billy as a bipolar personality, a man of extremes, a "Dr. Jekyll/Mr. Hyde." On the one hand he was charming and fun to be around; on the other he was brutal. She remembers especially the small gatherings in their apartment. Billy would greet guests at the door, offer them something to drink, and chat pleasantly. Then, after closing the door behind them, he would rant on and on: "What are they coming over here for? Are you planning something?" While the stated "reasons" for Billy's rages centered primarily on his fear of Annette's adultery or her leaving him, there were incidents over other issues: running out of money, cold food, the wrong food, her appearance—she was ugly. She relinquished her entire paycheck to him, cleaned, and cooked every night. If dinner were not to his liking, he would slam her against the wall.

In the beginning Annette told no one of the abuse and violence. She never informed the police, and on the two occasions that she admitted herself to the emergency room, she claimed to have slipped in the shower. But the battering became apparent with time. Well aware of Annette's elaborate grooming practices, Judy and Tonya took notice of her now unkempt appearance, and her weight loss became evident. Eventually, Billy would beat her in the presence of his family and friends. He would simply take her back to their bedroom when the urge struck. The battering quickly became common knowledge, and Annette's people continued pressing her to leave. In fact, Tonya did so in Billy's presence. Annette would suffer severe beatings after a visit from Tonya because of Tonya's outspoken hostility toward Billy.

Eight months into the marriage, Annette realized that her birth control had failed her and that she was four months pregnant. While Billy was pleased with the weight gain and its associated reduction in sexual attractiveness, the pregnancy incited a flurry of accusations of infidelity and physical assaults on the unborn child. He claimed that the baby was not his.

The most frightening beating incident occurred when Annette was about six months pregnant. It took place in their apartment, began in the presence of Billy's mother, stepfather, and stepbrother, and was sparked by Billy's belief that Annette had belittled him in the eyes of his family. Billy's mother commented, "Oh, Billy, you are losing so much weight. Is she not feeding you?" To that, Annette quipped, "Well, if that's the way you think about it, take him back home!" By the time Annette realized what she had done, it was way too late. In front of his family, Billy aggressively verbally challenged Annette's comment, at which point she retreated to the bedroom, then to the walk-in closet, and then on into the bathroom, locking all three doors behind her and barricading the bedroom door as best she could. Billy beat on that outer door, threatening Annette, for hours before removing the hinges. The other two doors were easier to penetrate. The expected beating commenced. Another particularly brutal incident occurred very soon after the marriage while the two were staying in the motel: Billy put a knife to Annette's throat, daring her to breathe.

After the assaults or beatings, Billy delivered weak apologies, but he never accepted blame. Instead he mounted tirades and litanies of Annette's shortcomings that had caused his transgressions. He told her that he had not meant to hurt her but that she had made him do it. And he told her, "It's not that I don't trust you; I just don't trust the world." About a third of the time Billy claimed that he remembered no such incident at all. "Case closed!" The beatings typically took place in the bedroom. When he was through, Billy left the room, often to watch television, leaving Annette behind to rock in her rocking chair.

GETTING OUT

When Annette was six months pregnant, Billy lost his job at U-Haul, so now Annette was employed but he was not. Two months later he tested positive for drug use, which violated his probation, and was taken to jail. Annette worked up till the time of her delivery, and during that final month she was without car and phone. Billy had taken the car keys and arranged for his mother to have the phone disconnected. Annette walked to work. Billy phoned every night from jail, and his family checked up on her constantly.

Fabian was born November 10, 1992. He was and remains healthy and beautiful. Both parents were present. His father was brought shackled from the jail to the delivery room for the occasion. Because of the arrival of the baby, Billy's legal charges were dropped, and he was allowed to go home with Annette and Fabian. Life improved for a while. Billy was reinstated at U-Haul, and Annette remained home to care for and enjoy Fabian.

When Fabian was three months old, it all started in again. Billy arrived home from work one afternoon to the typical scene of cooking and bottle feeding. The tirade began: it was always the baby; she spent all of her time with the baby; and the baby wasn't his anyway! Annette was just rising from the couch, holding Fabian as he was dozing off, when Billy shoved her. Etched in Annette's memory is Fabian's startled expression as the bottle was jerked from him and Annette lost her balance. That was the turning point for Annette: she would not subject her child to this life. It was at that exact moment that she decided to leave Billy. She had left a couple times before but had returned within hours. Billy had always warned her that if she ever left and stayed out overnight (implying sleeping with another man), she should not come back. She had been afraid to stay away. But this time was different. This was the only time that Annette stood up to Billy—and she did so both verbally and physically. The bout of mutual combat produced no serious injuries.

The following weekend would bring Valentine's Day. Annette was determined to make her exit then, when Tonya would not be in school and could help Annette and Fabian escape. She phoned Tonya the evening of that last confrontation with Billy, and the two conspired over the getaway. Tonya arrived late Saturday, as planned, to "spend the night." Throughout the evening, as Billy drank and otherwise occupied himself, Tonya was ducking into the bedroom periodically to pack Annette's belongings. Annette had prepared Fabian and his things. The two women planned to leave after Billy had gone to bed. But it did not work out that way. Billy caught on. In front of Tonya he dragged Annette down the hall into the bedroom, where behind closed doors he punched her and for the first time choked her to near death.

Eventually Billy passed out as he stood in a blocking gesture in front of the double-locked door. The two women collected their courage, pulled his limp body from their exit, unlocked the door, and ran with the baby and one bag of his essentials. Tonya's car had been disabled by Billy, so they ran on to the local convenience store, where Tonya called the police. The police brought them back to the apartment and arrested Billy on "probable cause." Clearly, Annette had been beaten brutally, and Billy was sitting in the living room, stone sober, exclaiming, "Honey, what happened to you? Where have you been?" Annette and Billy had recently purchased a second car; Annette grabbed the keys, and she, Tonya, and Fabian drove to Tonya's house. Annette was home again—back with her foster family. She turned eighteen that month and would remain with her family for a year and a half while she got her life in order.

Annette had engaged in heavy use of alcohol and marijuana when she was with Billy and began using cocaine after they separated. When Fabian was seven months old and she was preparing for her GED exam, she committed herself to a drug rehabilitation center. Having completed the rehabilitation program and earned her GED, she took a job at another nursing home and enrolled in and graduated from beauty school. Billy is currently in the process of relinquishing paternal rights to Fabian. Annette's foster family has supported her and cared for Fabian through all her efforts to change her life. Though she and Fabian have had their own apartment for eleven months, they remain strongly integrated into that family.

REFLECTIONS

Annette's feelings about her time spent with Billy are effectively expressed through her story of a very recent incident. She stopped by U-Haul, where Billy still works, to tie up some lose ends on legal matters relating to Fabian. Billy and his new wife and their infant daughter live in a trailer on the premises. As Annette and Billy chatted in the parking lot, the wife drove up to the family trailer and proceeded to struggle with baby, baby belongings, and new purchases as she began unloading the car. Billy made no gesture to walk across the lot to help her. Annette approached the woman and offered to hold the baby while the woman settled in. At that moment, with infant in arms, Annette dissociated—part of her consciousness pulled away and she saw her earlier self in this women: the unkempt appearance, the pallid complexion, the numb silence. As she was leaving, Annette handed the little girl to her father. She noticed how Billy awkwardly held her away from his body. Annette was overwhelmed with relief that that part of her life was behind her.

Part V

FACES OF
SHELTER LIFE

CHAPTER NINE

Sharon

I first met Sharon as the capable mind, friendly face, and soft-spoken voice behind the office management desk of the women's studies program here at my university. Her enthusiasm and sense of direction set her apart from the crowd.

I feel a strong sense of gratitude to Sharon for her willingness to break a traditional edict of silence among Black families to keep their private matters to themselves. And I am honored as a White woman that this Black woman chose to place her trust in me as a vehicle in her effort to free battered Black women from the shackles of secrecy and isolation. Sharon's story is a gesture of activism. She hopes that other Black women will follow her lead in breaking the silence so that they can get help for themselves and their children.

Today Sharon is in her early thirties and operates as team leader with her two adolescent children as they struggle to achieve educational standards that will ensure them the life of productivity and dignity to which they aspire. Together as a family they live in a lovely country-style home that clearly reflects Sharon's loving and artistic touch. Sharon continues to work for the women's studies program and is a part-time college student destined for a career in law or organizational and corporate communications.

Sharon is the youngest of five children. Although her father was a decorated army veteran of the Korean War and the first Black to graduate from the local business college, he remained a foundry worker until she was nine and after that worked for the railroad. Her mother attended a semester of college in Tennessee, then joined the Women's Army Corps. Sharon's parents met in army training, married, and moved to Flint, Michigan, to be near her father's family and childhood home and to raise a family of their own. They did just that and remained there until her father's death, which occurred when this essay was in progress. Her mother worked in retail for seventeen years and later at a local bank. Sharon's father was an alcoholic and her mother a strong Christian, a highly volatile combination at times, but one the family learned to cope with and to never discuss. There is a traditional edict among Black families that states simply, "What goes on in this house, stays in this house."

Sharon's family was more than kin to her; they were her life. She was a shy child. Neither she nor her siblings had many outside friends, so they became friends to one another. It was rare for one child to do anything without at least one other tagging along. Their isolation stemmed from the protective and rather restrictive nature of their mother, especially toward her four daughters, coupled with the family's neighborhood reputation as elitist. Sharon's family set themselves apart from their mostly Black neighbors by the parents' advanced education, their employment in the labor force rather than dependence on government assistance, and the sense that their children were college-bound. Sharon enjoyed school and maintained a B average throughout. Serious dating in high school was out of the question—her mother would not allow it. Boys knew that in order to get to her they had to go through her mother; they opted to just stay away.

The intimacy with her siblings that brought so much comfort and pleasure to childhood made adolescence difficult because they had all left home for college or career, and Sharon missed them. The hardest time was the summer of 1977, just after the completion of her freshman year, when her sister Wanda went off to college, leaving Sharon alone with her parents. She recalls the loneliness:

During that difficult summer of 1977, I began to withdraw. Music became my best friend, and most of my paycheck went to support that love. Many nights I would climb out on the roof outside of my bedroom window with my headphones on and just sit while letting the music take me wherever I wanted to go. At a time when I felt no one else was there for me, "my" music was. I could imitate the best of them: Donna

Summer, Tina Marie, Patti LaBelle and the Bluebells, Minnie Ripperton! My private dream was to be a singer. I was good!

To assuage the loneliness, Sharon worked part-time at Kmart beginning her freshman year, then managed the girls' track team during her sophomore year. She hoped to play volleyball her sophomore year, but a broken ankle prevented that.

Sharon's mother insisted that all of her children finish high school without having any children of their own. And they did. All except Sharon went on to college, and three of those four siblings eventually graduated. Their parents were unable to offer financial support for advanced education, so the children helped one another out down the line—until Sharon came of age. No help was forthcoming, and Sharon's school climate, in the midst of Reagan cutbacks, was not conducive to the aggressive pursuit of a college education. Fewer than 7 percent of her graduating class of 350 were college-bound—that included only three Blacks. For Sharon's siblings, college was a way of getting out of the house. One by one they helped plan each other's escape. As the only child remaining at home, Sharon had no coconspirator.

Sharon's three best friends in high school were Stine, who was Black, and Cindy and Diana, who were White. They had great times together doing "the cruising thing" at lunch break and while skipping government class now and then. Other school acquaintances were "fair-weather friends." It was under the influence of one of those acquaintances, a girl bent on convincing Sharon of her mother's overprotective nature, that Sharon decided to "get out a little." As a result, she began "talking to" and eventually attending a few movies and parties with a male cousin of this passing acquaintance. That illicit relationship was short-lived and inconsequential.

When Sharon was fifteen and had completed her freshman year, her parents separated for a few months. At that time she and her mother relocated sixty miles away to Pontiac to live with Sharon's oldest sister, Linda, and her husband and children. It was in Pontiac that Sharon discovered "boys." Linda's friend had a daughter, DeeDee, from whom Sharon became inseparable. One day at DeeDee's house, Sharon met Broderick, DeeDee's uncle. Broddy and Sharon hit it off instantly, and soon he was calling regularly. When Sharon went to DeeDee's house, she made certain that Broddy knew it. Broddy ran with a clique who quickly accepted Sharon. She remembers Broddy mostly for a single statement that she believes contributed to her later involvement with her abuser. When Sharon told Broddy of her isolation and loneliness in Flint, he said, "You learn more by watching your surroundings than by being part of the action." She was touched by the irony: a gregarious and socially entrenched person longing for solitude. At that moment, Sharon redefined in a more positive light her own isolation and isolation in general. Perhaps there was truth in Broddy's observation. Perhaps loners were to be admired for their wisdom.

Sharon spent the first semester of her sophomore year at Pontiac Central and loved it. Even though she and DeeDee spent lunch hours checking out guys, they studied hard and maintained good grades. Soon after Thanksgiving Sharon's parents reconciled and she returned reluctantly with her mother to Flint. With sixty miles between them, she and Broddy lost touch. Back in Flint, Sharon realized that she no longer fit in at school and was no longer compatible with her Black friend, Stine. But Diana, Cindy, and Sharon picked up where they had left off. They enjoyed good times together—ballgames and track meets—but after graduation went their separate ways.

THE ABUSIVE RELATIONSHIP

Although Jesse had played pickup basketball with Sharon's brother when the two were in school together and had visited their house once or twice, Sharon did not become aware of him until she began her daily neighborhood jog. He would usually be in his yard tinkering with his car, and they would exchange waves and hellos. Sharon was eighteen and Jesse was twenty-two when they began dating. He was always the perfect gentleman: opening car doors, walking on the outside at the curb. She liked him, but that was the extent of it.

Sharon was seeking a life plan, something beyond Kmart. One weekend she took the train to Kalamazoo to visit her brother at college. On the train she met a young man who was to become one of her truest and long-lasting friends. Today she consults with him on raising her son and on her dating relationships. Larry was the on-board electrician; he was twenty-eight, single, and very fine. They talked nonstop that trip and exchanged phone numbers. He lived in Chicago and worked a run to Flint every other day. Sharon became accustomed to those alternate-day phone calls. If he had a chance to spend a day or two with her, they would go bowling, sight-seeing in Canada, out to dinner. They enjoyed being together. After about six months, Larry was transferred. Brokenhearted, Sharon tried desperately to hold on to an older man and a long-distance relationship, but at nineteen her attempts at love were feeble.

It was during that time of confusion that Sharon began to look at Jesse differently. She elaborates:

I was impressed that he was a "loner," and much like me. He had a solid job with a major utility company, lived on his own, and loved to have fun. Our dates would frequently involve watching basketball or boxing on television. It was nothing for us to drive thirty miles to Mount Clemens for White Castle burgers or to Detroit for shopping or to a concert. It was on one of those shopping trips that we picked out my engagement/bridal set. We talked about living together; he wanted to buy a house with just a few acres of land and just live quietly.

Jesse had moved to Michigan from Alabama in 1977. His parents divorced when he was six, and he was deposited with his mother's aunt when his mother moved to New York and remarried. Although he visited his mother occasionally, he did not wish to live with her and his half brother and sister. Only rarely did Jesse speak of his father, and when he did it was with little or no emotion. Sharon recalls Jesse telling the story of his dad always carrying two wallets. When Jesse spotted his father around town and asked for money to buy something for school or a toy, his dad would pull out the wallet with a dollar in it and say, "Junior, I don't have any money," but would then proceed to the local "juke joint" and drop five or ten dollars on the spot. Jesse's father had a third-grade education and worked as a mechanic; his mother had quit school at sixteen to marry Jesse's dad and raise a family. During the six years his parents were together, Jesse spent most of his time with his cousins and aunt. His parents were heavy drinkers and argued and fought constantly.

Jesse asked Sharon to marry him when she became pregnant. On April 5, 1981, the two married and spent the next week in Toronto on their honeymoon. A week later Sharon quit her job at Kmart and during the next few months settled into the routine of married life and housewifery. Going out as a couple came to a screeching halt: Jesse now saw that as a waste of time. While Sharon loves a clean house, she came to feel married to the apartment rather than to a man. Life became a meaningless and endless cycle of cleaning up the bathroom after this man, vacuuming, fixing dinner, and ironing work uniforms.

After one particular weekend of strenuous housecleaning, Sharon went into labor six weeks early, and the next morning Jordan was born. Jesse and Sharon argued in the hospital over a middle name. She preferred Michael; Jesse refused because that was the name of one of Sharon's early crushes. That established the marital climate and the emotional abuse that lay ahead. Returning home with that tiny, five-pound, jaundiced baby, Sharon was challenged with keeping him alive and fattening him up. With three months of nursing she had a nine-pound healthy baby boy. It was with the passing of Jordan's health crisis that Jesse changed almost overnight and the subtle abuse became apparent. Because Jordan and Sharon were now able to get out and about—walks downtown, half-day visits with her parents—Jesse began accusing her of sleeping around. Often, while Sharon was breast-feeding, Jesse would walk by and yank her breast from Jordan. She wanted to continue nursing but began bottle-feeding when Jordan turned five months.

The emotional abuse began penetrating Sharon's days to the point of depression, then action. She elaborates:

Like many Black women, rather than seeking out counseling (which most of us can't afford or health insurance does not provide), I turned to food for comfort and emotional soothing. The verbal abuse continued, but at the same time, I could not separate what was common marital stress and what wasn't. If Jesse came home from work and dinner wasn't on the table, he would go into a rage and start screaming he wanted a divorce. He began drinking a "half man" of dark Bacardi rum every other day. But if the baby needed milk or diapers, he had to borrow the money. I started looking at my life and I wasn't happy with what I saw. After a year of constant accusations and arguments, I had heard "I want a divorce" for the last time. I visited an attorney one day while Jesse was at work. The information he gave me would one day save my life. While walking home with Jordan in his stroller, I made up my mind that one day Jesse would have his divorce.

Things were relatively uneventful for the next six months, but the drinking escalated to a pint of Bacardi or Hennessey cognac every other day. The family moved from the apartment to an old farmhouse where the only source of heat was a Warm Morning coal-burning heater. The house had four bedrooms and a big backyard, so the trade-off was acceptable. Sharon bought every *Country Living* magazine printed and began collecting baskets and using the country look to make the coal dust bearable.

In December 1983, a second child was born: Jessica, a healthy, nine-pound baby girl. Sharon loved being a stay-at-home mom, chasing a toddler who never slept and caring for an infant, but she was exhausted. Jesse rarely fixed a bottle, changed a diaper, or soothed a crying baby. He fathered from a distance and differentiated between the children, and ultimately a contempt for Sharon and Jordan began to fester. Jordan was a left-handed child, but because Jesse was not and neither was anyone in his immediate family, he began to disclaim Jordan as his son. On more than one occasion he would publicly refer to Jessica as his baby and Jordan as his "maybe." Jesse would force Jordan to eat and draw with his right hand, and when Jordan would forget, Jesse would quickly remind him by yelling or by plucking him on the fingers.

Sharon always stepped in to protect Jordan, which shifted the abuse to her. She was too fat; she used to look good; she used to dress better; she cared about the kids more than him; she babied Jordan too much and was going to make a sissy of him. Sharon became an emotional wreck. The more upset she became, the more she ate, and the cycle intensified. Whenever she declared that she was going on a diet, Jesse arrived the next day with cookies and ice cream in hand. Eventually she tipped the scales at 248 pounds. Everyday at 4:00 P.M. Sharon would become sick to her stomach in anticipation of Jesse's arrival home.

Sharon and Jesse's social activities were limited to associating with one married couple, Charles and Michelle. Jesse and Charles had worked and drunk together for the past three years. While Sharon enjoyed getting out with other adults, those occasions brought a painful and predictable outcome, a barrage of condescending comparisons: why couldn't she dance like Shell or wear a swimsuit like Shell or cook like Shell? On the few occasions when Sharon would challenge Jesse by warning that if he didn't like her as she was, someone else would, he would halfheartedly apologize and bring her a card as a peace offering. Sharon knew she had to get out and remembers formulating escape plans back then.

Life was agony and was sustained on four hours of broken sleep per night. Now added to Jesse's drinking was a nickel bag of reefer every three or four days. Payday was Thursday, and by Monday he was borrowing money to put gas in the car for work. If Sharon bought a basket or other trinket for the house or a new game for the kids, she was "blowing his money." Jesse believed he was doing Sharon and the children a favor by providing for them. Sharon knew that she could not live like this forever:

Many were the nights I went to bed thinking that there was no way I was going to spend the rest of my life with this man. I realized I had married a man just like my father, and I was not going to wake up thirty years down the road and wonder what the hell did I do with my life. I wasn't going to become my mother.

Michigan winters are bitterly cold and can be deadly. Some mornings Sharon would awaken to find Jesse had left for work with no coal in the house, no kindling in the wood box, and no fire in the stove. Sometimes the back door or bathroom window would be left wide open to air out the house because he had smoked a joint. If Sharon called him at work to inform him of his carelessness, Jesse would apologize sarcastically and quip, "I'm not cold; after all it is 110 degrees in the plant." During those dark winter days Sharon became her strongest; the survival of her and her children depended on it. She bundled up and went out to the coal shed, where she would "empty ashes and sling tears at the same time." She would burn blankets and old clothes to ignite the coal and some hard wood logs. And through it all, her attorney's words kept playing in her ears: "When you've done all that you can and you are sick and tired of being sick and tired."

One night in February 1984 Jessica woke up in the middle of the night crying. Sharon dragged herself out of bed to fix a bottle (she was afraid to nurse the baby while Jesse was in the house). That night, out of frustration, she began slamming doors—the bedroom door, the bathroom door, the cupboard door, the refrigerator door—until Jesse was awakened from his drunken stupor. He ran from the bedroom shouting, "What the hell is wrong with you? I thought someone was trying to break into the house!" Enraged, Sharon enumerated all that was wrong with her—each item relating to Jesse.

That night was a turning point. As she rocked and bottle-fed Jessica, Sharon took stock of her surroundings and her life. From the outside, the family appeared to be thriving. They had all the major appliances, solid oak furniture, two cars—all symbols of comfort, safety, and well-being. It was a lie and she knew she had to let it go. Returning the baby to her crib, Sharon went into Jordan's room and kissed his forehead as usual. Then downstairs she ran her hands over the pictures, the baskets, the homemade country curtains and pillows. Recalling the incidents that had ensued with the purchase of each basket and piece of fabric, suddenly it all looked so ugly. Sharon sensed that she must begin detaching herself from all the stuff.

That night she climbed into bed with the realization that it would be easier to care for two children alone than three or more. The next morning she arranged to have her tubes tied. She had the surgery in early March and by April had developed a severe yeast infection. Whenever she took her medicine and prepared the Monistat, Jesse began his berating ritual—if she hadn't been screwing around, she wouldn't have all these diseases. The verbal warfare was relentless. Sharon is unsure of when or how she became aware of Jesse's sleeping around, but she knew as only a wife can. She quotes a saying among older Black women (her grandma's age) that a man will always accuse you of what he is doing. Certainly that was true of Jesse.

That July employees of the power company where Jesse worked went on strike. Sharon got a job at a convenience store in order to pay for diapers and groceries. Jesse claimed that he was unable to work because of his erratic picket schedule. It was when Sharon refused to supply him with liquor and reefer money that the abuse turned physical. Jesse squeezed Sharon's wrists until circulation stopped. He would twist her arm behind her back, holding it there until she was in tears. Many times Jordan would just stand there and yell at his dad, "Jesse, don't start tuh mess." It hurt Sharon to watch her innocent baby horrified and crying. Many times, if she complained to Jesse about her wrists hurting, he would explain it away by saying that she carried the kids around too much or by saying that she was whining.

One night the family went out for pizza. During the meal all was quiet, but when they were leaving the building they met up with a group of Sharon's high school acquaintances, and Jesse went ballistic. The first thing out of his mouth was, "That's why you wanted to come here so you could fuck around with your buddies." He was so crazed that in leaving the parking lot he nearly hit a man on a bike, and a few blocks from home he ran a red light at about fifty miles an hour.

Sharon was beginning to fear for her safety. The more she was able to emotionally detach herself, the more intense Jesse's abuse became. He began to demand that Jordan call him "Mr. Daddy." Sharon recalls: "I went to bed one night and cried myself to sleep— the best sleep I'd had in a long time. I knew it was time to go."

GETTING OUT

Sharon's sister Wanda was in town. She and her little boy had moved back home with her parents while her husband was in

Guam. The sisters began spending a lot of time together. On a whim one night, Sharon collected the children, picked up her sister and nephew, and took in the late show—*Indiana Jones*. They had a great time; it felt good to laugh. It was then that Sharon broke the code of silence. Edict or not, she betrayed Black tradition and divulged Jesse's abuse. She told her sister of her fear for her safety and that of her children and that she was making plans to leave. Wanda warned her to be careful.

When Sharon returned home, she was prepared for the worst. She slipped her car keys into her pocket and hung the rest on the key rack. Then she placed both sleeping children on the couch with their jackets still on. As she had expected, Jesse was in a state of outrage. Sharon recounts the life-threatening struggle that ensued:

He pushed me and demanded to know where I had been. He pushed me again, and I told him I was calling the cops. I went to the living room with him fast behind me. He pulled the phone, wires and all, out of the wall. Trying not to be intimidated, I went back to the kitchen and poured myself a glass of milk. He grabbed my left wrist and started to squeeze it; on pure instinct I threw the milk in his face. He let go long enough for me to run to the bathroom and lock the door. In what seemed like seconds, he was coming through the bathroom door with his hands aimed for my neck. As he pushed me into the metal towel rack, I could feel my head hitting the window and my feet giving way. I was not aware of time, only the thought that if the glass broke, it would go straight through the back of my neck; this man was trying to kill me. . . . I grabbed [a wire brush] and put all 248 pounds of me behind the blow, right into the back of Jesse's neck and head. When he felt the blood start spewing, he let go. . . . I ran from the bathroom with keys in hand. I snatched up the kids with adrenaline pumping and ran outside. Through fear, the shaky knees, and tears, I was somehow able to "throw" the kids in the car, and managed to get the keys in the ignition. I hit the power locks and ripped out of the driveway.

From her parents' home, Sharon filed a police report on the incident and visited her attorney, only to learn that she needed a three-hundred-dollar retainer fee to file for divorce. For three days she took refuge with her parents. It was during that visit that she told her mother of Jesse's abuse and that her mother reciprocated with similar tales from her own marriage. Sharon is convinced that knowing these things sooner would have informed her judgment better when she was dealing with Jesse.

Sharon returned home filled with fear but with a definite plan. For months she would leave in place the phone wires hanging out of the wall, the milk spots on the ceiling, and the broken towel rack—grim reminders of the task at hand. Jesse offered the usual apologies, and Sharon put on her facade. Her mom always had said that a woman is plotting while a man is sleeping. Surely that was the case here. For three months, while Jesse was at work, Sharon planned her escape. She packed a suitcase and left it in the basement of her parents' home. She sifted through belongings, throwing away old papers, pictures, cards, and her address book, and carried on as if she were just tired of so much clutter in the house and wanting things spruced up for the holidays. She stashed grocery money away, and when her brother came home for Christmas, he provided the remainder of the three-hundred-dollar retainer. Sharon filed for divorce, acquired a copy of the police report, and sued for custody—all the while taking great care that her actions would remain undiscovered by Jesse. She phoned the local women's shelter, explaining the abusive situation and that she and the children needed somewhere safe to go while her husband was being served the divorce papers. He would find them at her parents' home, and that would jeopardize everyone's safety. She learned the correct procedure to get to the shelter when the time was right.

The day the divorce papers were to be served, Sharon got the children up and dressed right after Jesse left for work. She showered, dressed, fixed breakfast, and washed the dishes. In spite of the foot of snow on the ground, she put the children in their wagon and walked those two blocks to "Grammy's" house. Her mother kept them while Sharon traveled back and forth with the wagon collecting all that she wanted to store in her parents' basement. Having unloaded her treasures, she put the wagon in the basement, retrieved the packed suitcase, bid her parents farewell, and called a cab.

Jordan was so excited; "Where are we going?" he asked over and over, as only a three and a half year old can. Jessica was now a little more than one year old, and Sharon was twenty-three. From the police station they were escorted into a patrol car and delivered to the shelter. The officer made small talk about the children and, after seeing Sharon to the door, set down her suitcase and wished her well. She wondered what he thought and how many times he had taken women to this shelter. She also wondered whether he, too, battered his wife.

The location of the shelter was a complete surprise. It was a place Sharon had passed many times, oblivious to its function. She registered, submitted to a brief orientation and screening, and then called her mother. Later that night, her mother phoned to say that Jesse had gotten the divorce papers and that he was beyond furious and frantically looking for her and the children. Sharon, Jordan, and Jessica were given a private room at the shelter, complete with crib and bunk beds. Sharon did a lot of resting and reflecting, and she joined the other women in the community responsibilities of cooking, cleaning, and childcare. When she came down with a severe case of the flu and was taken to the emergency room by one of the counselors, the other women cared for her children. Sharon learned that Jesse was calling her parents daily, insisting on his innocence and that Sharon was cheating on him. She did not care anymore. He could not hurt her again. She was changing.

After two weeks Sharon and the children left the shelter to live with her parents. Jesse had calmed down a bit, so they would be safe there. At her request, Jesse brought Jessica's crib to Sharon's parents' house. A few weeks later Sharon enrolled in a word-processing course at the local business college. For the next seven months she attended school while her mother cared for the children. She studied, played with the children, and began building a life for the three of them. She was stunned to receive the first child support check because of what it symbolized—her marriage was over, she was a single parent, she was a national statistic. With time, the children relaxed, and because her emotions were healing and under control, Sharon cut back on her eating and lost fifty pounds. Her parents gave her Wanda's old car, a 1976 Chevy Monza, a five-speed that she taught herself to drive.

Jesse saw the children on a regular basis, and occasionally they would all go out. He swore that he had stopped drinking and that he wasn't smoking reefer anymore, and Sharon believed him. In July 1986, after having been away about six months, Sharon returned to Jesse.

It was a combination of the political and personal that took her back that one last time. At a time when society and the media were playing up the dysfunctional Black family and the number of households headed by Black women, she was uncomfortable wearing that stigma. Typically, a Black single mother is assumed to be a welfare recipient and treated accordingly. Sharon was intimidated by the scrutiny she would be subjected to by Jesse and his relatives if her standard of living were to drop. She was fearful of her inability to pay the bills and of rearing an African-American male child without the benefit of a father. In addition, Sharon remembered the good times with Jesse: picnics at the lake, backyard barbecues, trips to the beach, nature trail hikes. He had taught her simple car maintenance and other useful skills, including how to negotiate repair bills, fish, and mow the lawn. Sometimes when he worked the afternoon shift, Jesse would bring home Chinese food, and the two would sit on the floor and play checkers into the wee hours. Those images stirred once again that perpetual hope for change.

Ironically, on the very day Sharon and the children moved back into the house, Jesse asked her to go to the store and buy him some liquor! She told him to go to hell and to take his liquor with him. The family took a "vacation" to Jesse's family reunion in Alabama after Sharon graduated from business school later that summer. She spent most of that week observing the posturing of those people who viewed Jesse as the good old homeboy who had gone up North and done well for himself. The whole scene was one to behold—Broddy's words churned over and over in Sharon's mind. She was watching and learning. Soon after that she found a vial in the front yard with a silver spoon attached. Then there was the aluminum-foil-packed hashish found shoved between the car seats. Her perpetual hope died for good at that moment.

Sharon was building up to the final exit. She worked for a temporary employment agency so had her own money. It was painfully clear that Jesse would never change, and she told him so. Her fear had dissipated; no longer was she afraid of losing Jesse or her material possessions. During the brief period of inactivity after the standard six-month waiting period (dictated by Michigan law), the divorce suit had been dismissed, but Sharon did not let that deter her decision. One Friday in September, when returning home late from work, Jesse quizzed her about her whereabouts. Gladly she told him that she had been to see her attorney and had paid to have the divorce suit reinstated; he could expect the court hearing in six to eight weeks.

Sharon reflects on Jesse's final and unsuccessful attempt to reel her back in:

For the next few weeks Jesse begged, pleaded, cried, and begged again for me not to leave him. He volunteered to go to counseling. The ploys did not work that time. I *really* wasn't afraid anymore—cautious but not afraid. He would often ask me if I loved him—all I felt was indifferent. He began sleeping on the couch, and I slept upstairs with the children. . . . On November 3, 1986, my divorce was final. Because he thought I would really change my mind and not go through with the divorce, he did not get an attorney to contest it. A default judgment, and I was awarded sole custody of the children . . . the car that was paid for . . . and all the household furnishings. Because we rented the house and I could afford the rent on my own, Jesse had to move out. I went home that day and cried over my marriage for the last time. Two days later, he removed his [belongings from the house].

REFLECTIONS

Sharon remembers her marriage as a combination of good and bad, but clearly the bad outweighed the good. She understands that Jesse was able to love only in the manner he had witnessed love and nurturing between his parents.

Sharon's reflections focus on that traditional edict of silence among Black families that was ingrained in her and her sisters by their mother: "What goes on in this house stays in this house." Black women are taught to not divulge personal information, especially to other Black women—not even their own kin. Sharon emphasizes that no one can help a battered woman if she does not break the silence. She urges women, and Black women in particular, to speak out, unite, and educate one another, profit from one another's experiences, and break the isolation. This is her message:

In the Black community [it is difficult to speak out], especially when you have been taught to not divulge information to other women because those are the main ones that will come after your man. (In some cases that might be good—let her take him off of your hands.) As Black women, we sometimes have limited knowledge as to what organizations are available to help, so we must educate ourselves. The phone book is a wealth of information. If you can't trust or don't feel comfortable with your church body, go to a White church. Call the police and ask for shelters; call the hospital and get names of organizations that deal with battering; call the local victims' rights advocate. Educate yourself and then share the information. I find it uncanny that usually a woman who has been battered can spot others in the same situation.

Sharon broke that code of silence and so did her mother eventually. But that was too little too late for Sharon's mother and surely too late to prevent much of Sharon's agony with Jesse. It is her hope that her story will lighten the load of other women.

CHAPTER TEN

Gretchen

Gretchen and her four small children were "under-ground," running for their lives from their abuser, when she responded to my national mailing to shelters. The five of them were stowed away at the mercy of generous strangers in a tiny and remote Kentucky community; this was their fourth sanctuary in the shelter underground since having been forced from their New York home only thirteen weeks earlier. Gretchen was reaching out for a meaningful connection from her isolated spot in these frightening circumstances in this unfamiliar place. Thinking that she would feel safe and supported here, I invited her to visit Bowling Green for a day to attend the upcoming annual university-sponsored women's studies conference (where I also met Netiva, whose story is told in chapter 2). Able to arrange childcare and the use of a vehicle, Gretchen took me up on the offer. There we met colleagues, attended paper sessions, had lunch, and developed a strategy for our work together on her biography. Later, on two occasions, Gretchen spoke to my classes about her abuse and her life on the run. Her presentations were inspirational.

Gretchen's story introduces us to a criminal justice system that fails battered women and their children, and in so doing reduces them to fugitives fleeing not only from a life-threatening man but also from the law. Isolation, fear, unemployment, homelessness, and instability prevent any semblance of normal life for these families. Also, Gretchen contributes to this collection a glimpse into the subtle evolution of one woman's recognition and acceptance of her own homosexuality, the antecedents of which extend back, perhaps, to her grandmother.

I do not know Gretchen's whereabouts or even that she is safe. She moved away abruptly one day without a word. But then, I was prepared for that possibility. She told me that I should expect that she and her children might again have to flee in the night but that she would contact me when she felt safe. It has been more than two years, and I have still heard nothing.

Star Lake is a town of six hundred people in the Adirondack Mountain Forest Preserve, a northern New York State park preserved as forever wild. Situated on a spring-fed lake scooped out by glacial activity and surrounded by the foothills of the small, young Adirondack mountain range, it touts three stop signs, a grocery, an eight-hole golf course, a sixteen-bed hospital, and a school, and serves as the "metropolitan" center of the northwestern part of the Adirondacks and the park proper. Small settlements, including Cranberry, Oswegatchie, and Fine, lie to the northeast and west of Star Lake. To the south there is nothing but predominantly virgin forest and mountains extending more than a hundred miles. There are more summer homes than permanent dwellings in Star Lake. People are attracted by the natural beauty of its setting and the isolation from world events.

All of this is home to Gretchen. Star Lake was settled in the 1700s by her father's family. She grew up there in the 1960s, when summertime flushed from the woods and mountain streams hermits, draft dodgers, and hippies to trade at Padgett's IGA. Timothy Leary lived in Star Lake for a few years during that time, before relocating to the West Coast.

Though neither completed elementary school, Gretchen's father's parents were the smartest people she had ever known. Her grandmother was an avid reader and freethinker and would become a feminist role model to her. In his youth Gretchen's father hunted, trapped, and guided tours into the south woods. As a well-known humanist and practical joker, he would bring poor children home for lunch, and after school would dump flour from the second-story window of the post office onto little old ladies.

Gretchen's father was a woodsman, intellectual, and idealist. Though six foot four inches tall and weighing 280 pounds, he could walk through the forest on a dry fall day without making a sound.

Under his influence, Gretchen grew up reading *The Federalist Papers* and other such works. Emerson, Thoreau, Carnegie, and Whitman were topics of discussion at the dinner table when Gretchen's grandparents were there. Always present in her childhood living room was the Bible, along with copies of the Bhagavad Gita, the Koran, and other sacred writings. Gretchen's father believed all religions held truth and was a passionate advocate of social justice. Gretchen adored her father and takes joy in the lessons she learned from him. He impressed on her the value of our natural surroundings. To him, education, stewardship, and service to others marked the fundamentals of a good life. Upon graduating from high school, Gretchen's father joined the air force, ultimately to be stationed in Simbach, Germany, where he met her mother.

Gretchen's mother grew up number eleven in a family of thirteen children in World War II Germany, where her father ("Oppa") was the primary contact in the south for the underground mechanism employed to free prisoners of Nazi camps. He was among Hitler's most wanted. She tells stories of terror and desperation in the context of outlaw involvement in a war that devastated her homeland. Gretchen's mother was a survivor.

Gretchen's parents met in 1958, when her father was stationed near her mother's hometown. He had been courting Gretchen's Aunt Gretchen, the youngest child; an engagement announcement was on the horizon. One evening at the family dinner table, Gretchen's mother announced that she was pregnant by Gretchen's father. That was impossible, but Oppa was now mayor, and Gretchen's father's commanding officer instructed him to marry the woman to keep peace.

They married, and within a month Gretchen's mother "miscarried." Because the relationship was strained, Gretchen's father sent his bride to Star Lake one year before he was to be discharged. Knowing the circumstances of the marriage, Gretchen's grandparents did not welcome her warmly; but they did house her, tolerate her, and teach her English. Gretchen is convinced that her mother used this pregnancy ploy to gain U.S. citizenship.

Upon his discharge in 1959 Gretchen's father returned to Star Lake, bought a small house, and attempted to forge a good relationship with his wife. It was through his compassionate prodding that she was eventually able to speak of her childhood. With time, Gretchen's parents came to love and care for one another. Gretchen was born in 1962, the first of four children. Her father named her after her Aunt Gretchen, which placed a permanent wedge between her and her mother. Christine was born eighteen months later, and John followed ten months after that. Cathy came as a surprise six years later.

Gretchen recalls her father as easygoing and content to work at the paper mill. But her mother wanted more, so in addition to shift work at the paper mill, he sold insurance and traveled on evenings and weekends to attend college seventy miles away in pursuit of a paper engineering degree. During those same years, the middle 1960s, he built her mother's dream home—a true American ranch-style house—flawless, but with one exception:

It was on the edge of town and our backyard was the woods. My mother would pile the furniture up against the doors at night, but still at least twice a year a black bear would tear down the doors and come into the house looking for food after it woke up in the spring. Mom would freak out, but all Dad ever did was lead it out of the house with a loaf or two of bread and slap it on the rump as it went out the door. Dad would laugh and Mom would scream. She hated Star Lake.

Upon completion of his engineering degree, Gretchen's father assumed a supervisory position at the paper mill and continued selling insurance. In 1970 he was offered two jobs. He had become a top salesman for Nationwide Insurance and was invited to transfer to the Albany office for a six-figure salary. At the same time he was offered a position managing the nineteen-acre, twelve-building Star Lake summer estate of the Scott-Brace family, whose fortune derived from Unguentine salve and Bayer aspirin. He chose the caretaker job and continued selling insurance. Gretchen's mother was furious, and her parents fought for months over this decision. Her father wanted a life grounded in his family and the woods. Gretchen says this is the only time her father got his way.

Gretchen never got along with Christine and John; there was much sibling rivalry there. But she and Cathy remain best friends. Gretchen recalls her mother claiming Christine to be the pretty one and removing Gretchen from her father's lap to replace her with Christine. Christine would continually mock Gretchen. She would say to their mother, "Look how you messed up with Gretchen; you're going to let me do what I want."

Whenever John misbehaved, he blamed it on Gretchen, who in turn would be chastised by their mother. After Gretchen's father died, when she was fifteen, their mother put John at the head of the dinner table. Once, while Gretchen was home from college and their mother's companion, Ernie, was a dinner guest, their mother served Ernie first. At that, John raged, "I'm the head of the house; you serve me first," then stormed around the table and slapped their mother across the face. All was silent. Their mother apologized to John, and dinner progressed uninterrupted. Gretchen has not spoken to Christine or John for years.

Gretchen loved school and was the first to arrive and the last to leave every day. When she was in the third grade, the administration attempted to place her ahead of her class, but her father insisted she remain with her age-peers. By the tenth grade she had aced every academic course and was accepted at St. Lawrence University, where she was bused forty miles three times a week for accelerated work in sociology and psychology. In the eleventh grade she attended Clarkson University for advanced chemistry and physics under a similar arrangement. Her senior year was a "washout"; school time was occupied with typing and study hall and off-hours with friends smoking cigarettes and sneaking sloe gin into sodas at the local teen hangout. In 1980 she graduated high school with her kindergarten class and was actively pursued by universities including McGill, Yale, and Cornell.

When Gretchen was nine, her family moved to the Scott-Brace estate, which calls up sweet memories of youth and of her father. For eight summers and those fall and winter weekends when the Scotts or Braces were there, she worked, cooking, cleaning, and waiting tables, saving every penny for college. Her mother was also employed by the estate—as head cook. Sometimes Gretchen worked into the night cleaning up after dinners for twenty to forty people, and sometimes her father would sneak down to the kitchen to help with the dishes.

This is one of Gretchen's favorite stories:

In November 1976 Hal Scott, a member of the Scott-Brace family, came to the estate on a business trip. At that time he was president of the US-USSR Trade. He arrived with fourteen Russians in tow. This was during détente and the grain embargo, and Hal was trying to smooth relations and keep trade going between the two countries.

All of the Russians were lodged "up on the hill" in the bunkhouses, and it fell on me and my mother to cook and serve them. They were there for a twelve-day stay of talks. Two days into the talks, Hal's wife went into labor with her first son in New York City. Hal had to leave, and for the next ten days, my father was responsible for the health and welfare of fourteen Soviet Russian citizens.

My father took them hunting, sledding, and hiking in the woods. He assured them that no KGB or CIA would be watching them, and he would sit and eat dinner with them.

I waited table and was brought into the discussion more than once. We gave them a good education on America. One gentleman was bald with a funny-looking mark on his forehead. He was the most outspoken of the group. He asked a lot of questions about politics and religion. One night my father invited a local priest, Father Rudy, and the Presbyterian minister, Mr. Goyette, to dinner with the Russians. The discussion got pretty heated, and I spent an extra long time serving dinner. . . . Mr. Gorbachev kept repeating he couldn't believe what he was hearing [that Americans were not afraid to speak their minds].

The day the Russians left, they gave us all gifts. I got two albums of Russian folk songs and everyone signed the cover. Every year after that, my father got a large box of Cuban cigars from Russia for Christmas. When my father passed away, the largest flower arrangement was from Moscow.

Gretchen's father was diagnosed with Hodgkin's disease in 1972 and died six years later at forty-two. Her mother, Christine, and John were with him the day he died. Gretchen wanted to be there, but she and the rest of his family were kept away by her mother. A hospital nurse later told Gretchen that her father had requested to see her. He had instructed this young woman, who was also his cousin, that it was now up to his family to care for Gretchen because her mother would not. And he was right.

Gretchen's mother took over as caretaker of the estate until she was fired in 1980. Her campaign of abuse toward Gretchen intensified to the point where she would lock her out of the house and deprive her of food. She would cook a delicious family meal but allow Gretchen no more than half a potato, saying that the reason Gretchen had always been so much trouble was that she had been given too much.

In October of the year her father died, as Gretchen turned sixteen, she moved in with her father's parents and remained there until time for college. She received Social Security survivor benefits, worked at the Scott-Brace estate whenever needed, and received financial support from relatives. She had many friends, and the car provided by her uncle enhanced her popularity.

After her father died, Gretchen sought counseling; a critical concern was her sexuality—or its apparent absence. She did not identify with "normal" femininity. Her grandmother told her not to worry about it, that she too had never harbored an interest in feminine things. She advised Gretchen to never marry. Repeatedly, she voiced her regrets over her own marriage and the wish that she had been born later, when opportunities and alternatives were available to women.

At seventeen, Gretchen enrolled as a sophomore in Potsdam State College. She elected to go there because it was only forty miles from home. She had opted for pre-med in her accelerated high school curriculum and wished now to pursue a career in psychiatry. College life suited her perfectly. She enjoyed classes, dorm life, and her new network of friendships. She smoked a lot of marijuana, but that was not of concern. Her grandparents had always raised hemp in the back woods, and the smell of "pot" had permeated the family gatherings of her youth.

She continued with the counseling and now began facing the issue of her possible lesbianism. By now she had experienced sex with a few men and found it cumbersome and unsatisfying. She had initiated a relationship with a woman, but that never took hold. She was not seeking romantic involvement. Her vision was to finish school and become established professionally before settling down. The image of her future was one of living alone in a nice apartment in a large city.

By the time she entered her junior year, Gretchen had evolved into a social and political activist. She penned the editorial column for the school paper and volunteered for its emergency hotline. Also, she helped out at the local women's abuse shelter. Her passions activated the ideals of her father and grandmother.

THE ABUSIVE RELATIONSHIP

John entered Gretchen's life in January 1982, as she began the second semester of her junior year; she was nineteen and he was twenty-eight. He appeared at the door of an apartment where Gretchen and some friends were smoking and hanging out. At the time he was in pursuit of the woman who lived there. They had met the previous semester before he had dropped out of school, and she warned Gretchen to keep her distance.

Gretchen disliked John on the spot but initiated a conversation to be polite. He was an odd sort, and she felt a bit sorry for him. He suggested they get out of the smoky apartment and go for a walk. She complied. Once outdoors, John immediately informed Gretchen that the moment he saw her he knew she was the one for him. That statement left her uncomfortable, but they walked around the block, then returned to the apartment.

Though Gretchen showed no interest in John, he continued to call and stop by her apartment. She recalls one incident. It was a cold February day; she had known John a month. He came to her door shivering with cold and bearing a six-pack. He was visibly shaken and asked if they could talk. It was time for class, but Gretchen stayed home to listen to him. John described his recent nightmare in which he was massacring women and children in Central American guerilla warfare and enjoying the process. He was upset by this and just knew no one could ever love him because he was so screwed up. At four he had been adopted by his mother's husband and had endured a horrible childhood at their hands. Gretchen describes how John reeled her in:

I was starting to be afraid of John. I tried to avoid contact with him after that, but he still kept persisting. By March John was calling me constantly. He always seemed to call just as I was leaving for class. I was starting to miss class, something I had never done before, and schoolwork was going down the drain. Whenever I mentioned to him I couldn't talk, I had to get to class, he would get upset and say, "See what I mean, no one really cares about me." John was monopolizing all my time. I was feeling sorry for him, and I thought that maybe if I gave this man a little bit of my time, I could show him that he was worthy of a relationship with someone.

Toward the end of April Gretchen had spent a particularly gratifying afternoon smoking and discussing politics with her socialist friends. They had composed and sent letters to President Reagan criticizing his budget cuts in education and his support of the religious right. Just as she was settling in with her anatomy and physiology, John stopped by. He was in a rare "up" mood and brought beer as usual. The beautiful spring day and stimulating conversation had put Gretchen in a good mood too. She even drank some beer; her inhibitions were down. The dialogue opened with Gretchen calling John a jerk and telling him she did not want to continue seeing him. He wept. She leaned over to comfort him with a hug, but he sobbed uncontrollably. Gretchen felt awful; she had crushed this poor fragile man. She hugged him again and apologized. John began to respond—sexually—resulting in their having sex for the first time.

The pursuit intensified dramatically after that. John told Gretchen she was the best he had ever had and that they were meant for each other. She bought it. In May she quit school and relocated with John to Watertown to be near his family. He rented an apartment and got a job delivering specialty items to grocery stores. This was his first job and his first time living away from his grandmother since high school. Gretchen found work as a hotel housekeeper. After a few weeks she quit her job because John wanted her to accompany him on his delivery route.

That was a fun summer—until July. Once a week Gretchen and John drove to Syracuse in the company truck to pick up the grocery supply. Then during the week they traveled over northern New York delivering the goods and picking up the next order. They were home only at night. Late one night John came home drunk, insisting that they make the run to Syracuse right away rather than waiting until daybreak. They left for Syracuse but never arrived. An accident with a motorcyclist left John charged with driving while intoxicated (DWI), his fourth offense.

John sank into a depression, repeating that he always screwed things up and that he fully expected Gretchen to leave him. She reassured him she would stay. Two days after the accident John came home drunk and tore into Gretchen. He threw her across the room and beat her until the swelling blinded her. The next day she called her grandmother to take her back to Star Lake. Learning of her pregnancy two weeks later, she went back to John and married him because of the responsibility she felt for him as well as for the unborn child. Her family and friends counseled her to abort, but she refused. She believed in a woman's right to choose, but abortion was not for her.

They were married in a small Catholic ceremony in September 1982, attended by family and friends. John was drunk at the altar. He had been convicted of felony DWI, fined and placed on probation, and fired as a result of the highway accident. So they lived on welfare and fought constantly. John would lash out at and hit Gretchen when he was drunk, and he raped her regularly. Later he would apologize—but always with the disclaimer that if she had not done or said whatever, he would not have been drinking. She felt guilty and ashamed, and she was trapped; he would not let her out of his sight, except when he went out drinking.

The pregnancy was particularly brutal. John resented any special attention paid Gretchen. She recalls, "If someone offered me a seat on a crowded bus, he would get upset because no one offered him a seat. He felt as though no one cared how he felt being an expectant father." Gretchen quit smoking and drinking during the pregnancy. John accused her of being selfish in her refusal to drink with him. Gretchen was plagued with morning sickness the entire nine months, and John would not let her forget that. For the six months surrounding Max's birth, John accused her of being unable to perform properly even the most basic act of reproduction. He accused her of having lesbian tendencies that prohibited her from functioning as a woman.

As part of his probation stipulation, John submitted to an alcohol rehabilitation program. He completed it and remained sober for nearly a year. Gretchen attended family counseling with him and also went to Al Anon. But Al Anon did not work for her because she was under John's control; if she did not enable him, he would hurt her. Once the children arrived, he used them as well as the beatings as leverage. Many times when Max was a baby, John threatened to hurt him if Gretchen did not comply with his demands. He would comment how easy it would be to break Max in half. It was while John was in rehabilitation that he first called Child Protective Services, claiming Gretchen to be an unfit parent. During their eleven-year marriage, he made six such calls. All reports were deemed unfounded.

John's alcohol rehabilitation credential qualified him for vocational rehabilitation; he enrolled in the electronics program at the local vocational school when Max was ten months old. They were living in subsidized housing, and three months later John's parents moved in next door. Gretchen describes life with her in-laws:

While John was gone to school, Dorothy and Raymond, John's parents, would come over to the apartment and threaten me. They told me that I was worthless and had caused their family a lot of pain. They would grab Max out of my arms and tell me that he was theirs, not mine. If I cooked a meal for John that Dorothy did not approve of, she would get upset. The few times we argued, she hit me with her fists. Raymond threatened to rape me a number of times. He said that what I really needed was to have my "ass reamed out" and he was just the one to do it. One night after midnight, they came to the door. It was locked and I refused to open the door. Dorothy called the police. She told them she was worried about her son, that I had been trying to poison him and she was trying to check on him. I opened the door and let them in. My house was not my own; it was an extension of theirs. Dorothy and Raymond had a collection of handguns and rifles. These guns, they said, were used to protect their own, not for hunting. They told me that if I ever tried to leave their son, I would be dead.

In spite of John's resistance, Gretchen returned to school in fall 1985. She enrolled at Empire State College, there in Watertown. John was finishing up his second and final year at the vocational school and struggling to stay sober. At that point he was able to make it six months at a time. Soon after classes began, Gretchen learned of her second pregnancy. Dorothy and Raymond accused her of infidelity.

One day Gretchen called John to say that she would be home later than usual because she needed to use the library. John flew into a rage and demanded that she come home immediately. She walked in the door to find the apartment trashed. Everything was destroyed, including her prized Russian folk albums. John was sober, but she was still beaten. Gretchen completed that semester. Over the next six years she would repeatedly enroll, then well into the semester be forced to drop out at the hands of John. She has yet to complete her degree.

Another difficult pregnancy produced Jonathan two months prematurely in March 1986. John finished school in June. He was released from probation but had resumed drinking. In September he was hired as an electronics technician at a medical facility. Then in December the family moved to a farmhouse outside Watertown. John's job was secure, and they finally had a car. Now Gretchen was more isolated than ever. John took the car to work, and she was home with the children. There was virtually no contact with her family. She was forbidden to visit her grandparents at the nursing home. John found fault with and would not allow her to speak to any new friends. The only people in Gretchen's life were her children, John, and his family.

John made fifty thousand dollars a year, but Gretchen had nothing. Employment was out of the question; he wanted her home "barefoot and pregnant." She was allowed one black skirt, three blouses, and a pair of sneakers—no underwear because that kept her embarrassed and more accessible sexually. She was given twenty-five dollars a week to feed and clothe the family—with no increases as the family continued to grow. Gretchen bought staples in bulk, baked bread, canned vegetables, and bought meat from a wholesaler. She could stretch a quarter of a pound of hamburger to two meals.

In the summer of 1988 Gretchen learned of her third pregnancy. Hearing the news, Dorothy handed her a coat hanger and tried to drag her into the bathroom. John forbade her to use birth control, then blamed her for the consequences. In the middle of January, with six weeks to term, John arrived home in a drunken rage complaining that it was Gretchen's fault that the baby had not come before the new year in time for a tax break. He kicked her down a flight of stairs, which left her in a coma for a week. Still, Gretchen felt too ashamed and guilty to speak of the abuse. Hannah arrived as expected in January 1989. Shortly thereafter, John faced another DWI conviction—complete with fines and probation.

GETTING OUT

In the summer of 1989, John joined a study group to discuss the writings of New Age guru Edgar Cayce. Gretchen accompanied him to the first meeting at the public library, where she met Diana, who would become a critical force in Gretchen's escape from John. Diana had exited an abusive marriage and saw all the signs in Gretchen and John. She taught Gretchen to see John as an abuser and to "store away acorns," kernels of truth that would eventually bring her freedom. Gretchen was now on her way out.

In June 1991, when Hannah was more than two, Gretchen received an unexpected visit from the parish priest. She remembers:

Father Hunt told me that John had been to confession, and even though he could not tell me what was said, he told me to leave immediately. Father Hunt helped me pack a bag and get the kids together. He drove us to the women's shelter for the first time.

John pleaded and promised, and three days later Gretchen was back home. Within two months John raped her, and she left again, this time by bus to visit her mother in Florida. Gretchen returned to the Watertown shelter two weeks later when she learned that John had sued for child custody and that New York law required children to remain in the county where custody is filed until the final ruling.

During that month at the shelter Gretchen learned she was pregnant, but she remained determined to not go back. She agreed to a marriage counseling session with John and told him then that she would not return. At that, John threw himself on to the floor, crying and banging his head against the door. Gretchen offered him a lift home, and en route he threw himself out of the van. She took him to the emergency room to be treated for a broken leg and knee. Because he was unable to kill himself, he vowed to kill Gretchen and the children.

Gretchen was awarded custody of all three children, and the judge recommended that she leave town permanently. She was transferred to the Buffalo shelter. Pregnancy complications set in, and at four months, Gretchen lost one of her twins. Her doctors recommended total bedrest, and the shelter determined that the children should be placed in foster care for the duration of the pregnancy. Gretchen refused and returned to John.

Things were different this time; John's abuse intensified and now included the children. He removed the phone and had his parents stop by during the day. He would beat Max when Max got up to use the bathroom at night. Jonathan was beaten for no reason at all, and Hannah would be pulled up the stairs by her hair when she cried. The children were hungry, and John would bring home snacks to eat in front of them. In the meantime Gretchen's weight had escalated with each pregnancy and left her miserable at 397 pounds. This was the situation into which Andrew was born in May 1992. For nearly eight months John drank heavily and abused everyone in the house. Gretchen complained to John's probation officer, who then placed him in another rehabilitation program, this time for alcohol and mental illness. But ultimately the abuse continued.

Then in June 1993, a year and a half after returning to John, Gretchen left again, this time for good. Raymond had phoned to say that he and Dorothy would be a couple of hours late coming by but that they would be calling every few minutes. Gretchen seized this opportunity to phone the police and have them deliver her and the children once again to the Watertown shelter. John and his parents phoned there repeatedly, threatening to kill Gretchen and anyone who got in their way. It was at that point that the shelter manager suggested that she and the children go underground.

Going underground meant moving to a shelter-related private residence elsewhere in the country. Many shelters have local volunteers for the underground. For Gretchen at this time it would also mean breaking the law: she did not have custody of Andrew. She had filed a petition for custody the day after she left, and wanted to remain in the state until after the scheduled hearing in two months that she assumed would rule in her favor. She knew she would be running from John; she did not want to be a fugitive from the state as well. Watertown was not safe, so they transferred to another New York county shelter. John found them in two weeks, so they relocated once more and were later placed in a nice apartment in Potsdam. Gretchen received full custody of Andrew, with no restrictions regarding leaving the state. The hitch was that John was awarded visitation rights, so Gretchen was bound by law to provide him with her address.

Within a week John quit his lucrative job at the medical facility in Watertown and appeared on Gretchen's doorstep with a U-Haul and threats to kill the children if she did not comply. They were legally married, and she had no alternative to allowing him to move in and then patiently await the transgression that would warrant an order of protection (OP). It took five weeks for John to come home drunk and hit Gretchen. She got her OP. He violated it repeatedly, which culminated in his arrest, a three-month jail sentence, and another several months in a halfway house awaiting trial. At the trial in June 1994, John was issued an OP that was to last nine months but that contained a provision stating that this order could not infringe on his visitation rights.

Gretchen and the children had now been away from John for a year. Time and counseling had strengthened them. Gretchen began to shed her excess weight. Sixteen months later she would celebrate the loss of two hundred pounds. Around this time, however, Gretchen was faced with yet another horror:

During counseling, it came out that the three oldest [children] had been sexually molested by their grandparents. Hannah started passing out whenever anyone mentioned how big she was getting and that she was growing up. While the grandparents were molesting her, they told her she was growing up and getting big.

Gretchen brought a case against her in-laws, but they denied the allegations, and ultimately the case was dropped.

In May 1994 the family was placed in a spacious town-house apartment in Potsdam. Gretchen was seeking a satisfying lesbian relationship and in that context developed a close friendship with a woman whom she had met at the shelter. Within six months Pam relocated to Pennsylvania to be with her family after exiting an abusive marriage, but that friendship revitalized Gretchen. Today, she misses Pam; they talk regularly.

A month after meeting Pam and about the time of John's trial, Gretchen took a part-time position as office manager for a chiropractor. She loved the job, though it did not free her of welfare dependency. The three older children were in school; only Andrew required day care. In an effort to economize, Gretchen accepted a boarder in exchange for child care services. Donna was another formerly battered wife; she was now recovering from the breakup of a lesbian relationship.

By January 1995 life was progressing smoothly. John had harassed Gretchen a bit on the phone, and Dorothy had done the same. Gretchen had Dorothy arrested; she felt empowered by the legal system. She could not afford to file for divorce but felt released from her commitment to John. There was a respite from fear; life was good; an intimate relationship with Donna was evolving; the children were happy.

Then John was released from probation and anticipating the expiration of the OP just a few months off. He was unemployed, on welfare, and drinking heavily. Word got back to Gretchen that when the OP expired, the lives of her and her children would be in danger. Just two weeks before the expiration date she was informed that the Potsdam Police Department could not protect her and the children and that they should leave the state. Gretchen contacted the shelter for directions to go underground.

Gretchen's first underground site was Jackson, Michigan. Her friend Beth lived there, with a husband and five children who welcomed her. Arrangements for the safety of Gretchen and the children were solidified between the Potsdam and Jackson shelters. With a tearful (and, it was hoped, temporary) farewell to Donna, Gretchen crammed nine boxes and four children into the car and headed for Michigan. Three Potsdam police cars escorted them to the county line. Nine hours later they arrived at Beth's, and Gretchen checked in with the shelter immediately.

After a month conditions became stressful in that three-bedroom house, so Gretchen explored options with the Jackson shelter personnel. She was connected with Billie, a longtime volunteer, who opened her home to the family for three weeks and helped them find a small house outside town in June 1995. Six weeks later word came from the Potsdam shelter that John had discovered Gretchen's whereabouts by using her Social Security number to trace her most recent credit check (for the house rental), and that he was on his way. It was time to move on.

The Jackson shelter connected Gretchen with Tom, a sixty-year-old divorcé who lived in Hopkinsville, Kentucky, and had helped a couple of other abused families. Tom drove to Jackson to pick up Gretchen and the children in August 1995. In the spirit of reciprocity, Gretchen cooked, cleaned, and bought the household groceries with her AFDC checks and her food stamps; Tom purchased a van for Gretchen's use. She enrolled the children in school, unsuccessfully sought employment, and became involved in local shelter activities. Within twelve weeks relationships with Tom became strained, and Gretchen and the children were again uprooted.

They moved to the home of a Clarksville, Tennessee, family, found conditions there inhospitable, and three days later relocated to the Clarksville shelter, where they spent a couple of days. Gretchen secured a subsidized apartment in that community and enrolled the children in school. When I last heard from her in November 1995, she was seeking employment in Clarksville.

Gretchen told me once that the Potsdam shelter would always know her whereabouts. My recent contacts with that shelter lead me to believe that Gretchen is still on the run and that life is still the same for her. I conclude this from the simple fact that I am not told she is dead when I write or call.

REFLECTIONS

After eleven years of abuse Gretchen left John, but I wonder if she will ever find the freedom she seeks. When I last saw her, she spoke of discrimination at every turn. It was virtually impossible for her to find permanent housing and stable work. No one wanted to rent to a single mother with four children; jobs were scarce for the same reason. She had been heavily in debt since John's 1993 incarceration, when all their debts were transferred to her. She could not afford the cost of bankruptcy or divorce. Clearly, Gretchen faced the real possibility of a lifetime of poverty, at least until the children were grown.

Gretchen spoke of being sometimes depressed and at other times angry, but there was one constant—fear. She realized that she was at high risk of being discovered by John again through the credit checks that are required for job and housing applications. She wondered sometimes which is worse for the children: the stability of an abusive marriage and father or the fear of him finding them. But really she knew and so continued on.

Part VI

WHEN THE
SYSTEM WORKS

CHAPTER ELEVEN

Raquelle

This book was in progress during the O. J. Simpson murder trial, when some attention became focused on domestic violence among professional athletes. I wanted to include a woman who had safely escaped an athlete and, to that end, located Raquelle through a popular magazine article on the subject. The magazine directed me to her agent. At that time Raquelle's story was being circulated in the television and print media, perhaps, at least in part, because she was a White woman whose batterer had been a Black man. Raquelle was enthusiastic about the prospect of being included in this collection. She wanted her experience to inform battered women and to compel them to get out. She was determined to use her pain in some constructive way, to ensure that it would not be wasted.

In addition to its setting in professional athletics and its element of interracial sex, Raquelle's story provides valuable insights into how a criminal justice system can liberate a battered woman (through enforcing mandatory reporting and arrest laws) but how, at the same time, public sentiment (in the form of jury verdict) can fail her. This is a story of what often happens when a woman cries rape and is willing to endure a criminal trial in her search for justice.

Raquelle is a warm and articulate woman who, at thirty, thrives in Denver, Colorado, among friends and in her career as a regional service agent for a reputable nationwide communications firm. Her ambition is to climb the corporate ranks. Raquelle looks forward to eventually marrying and having a family.

Raquelle grew up in a small Wyoming community, steeped in her own family traditions of ranching, farming, and Mormon worship. Born the second of five children and surrounded by four generations of kin, she enjoyed a rich family and spiritual life rooted in Mormon ideologies and values. Hers was an influential upper-middle-class family. Her father held important positions in the church and was highly respected in the community. In fact, Raquelle lived on a street bearing her father's surname.

Raquelle's parents were hardworking people devoted to the traditional Mormon ethic. Their priorities lay in family, work, and worship, all embraced in the context of modesty, immaterialism, and conservative attitudes toward race and gender. The family knelt nightly in prayer, observed the custom of "Family Home Evening," and tithed. Raquelle's mother was a homemaker and her father the undisputed patriarch and primary disciplinarian. Though her father was harsh, there was never any doubt regarding his love for and commitment to her and the other children, and he never laid a hand on them. But he remained an intimidating presence and, though he has mellowed with time and they have grown close in recent years, Raquelle harbors a nagging sense of her inability to measure up to his expectations.

Raquelle's youth was stable, patterned, and tightly structured. Clearly, her parents operated as a team in the management of family affairs. Her mother's simplicity in terms of needs, desires, and lifestyle is remarkable to Raquelle. Having married at eighteen and without benefit of a college education and the ability to support herself, Raquelle's mother emerged from adolescence a devoted wife and mother and an avid horsewoman.

Raquelle's father was devoted to the family business that he had tended with his father and brothers in his own youth, the full ownership of which was later passed on to him by his father. Raquelle characterizes her father as a workaholic; that grocery store and cattle ranch have always prospered and supported the family comfortably. Raquelle describes her parents' marriage as one where her father always had to be right.

Early in life Raquelle and her siblings learned the importance of responsibility, work, and family enterprise as, one by one, they joined forces with their father in the management of the store. When Raquelle entered the scene, she had to contend with the high-handedness of not only her father but Steve, the brother four years her senior. Under their scrutiny, she learned to do everything from processing ground beef to bookkeeping. She resented Steve's bossing her around and hated working with him. He carried into the workplace the controlling and sometimes torturous relationship from home that involved forbidding her to touch his belongings, chasing her, punching her in the arms ("big brother stuff"), and painful and terrifying episodes of tickling and suffocation with the big pillows that were kept in the family room. When Raquelle recalls working at the store, what comes to mind first is her father's periodic summons and the fear she felt of him. With reference to those, she states:

He was always working and my father was very serious, and my friend calls him Major Dad. If I had a snapshot of my dad back then, it wasn't a happy one. It is being at his store and him saying, "Raquelle, can you please come back to my office?" Anytime I got called to his office, I knew I was in trouble or was going to get a lecture. He was controlling and intimidating. My dad had that look that I knew I was in trouble.

When Raquelle was seven, her brother Paul was welcomed into the family. She took an active interest in his care and became his second mother. Then, when she was thirteen, along came a set of identical twin sisters. Raquelle was thrilled and redoubled her maternal involvement. At that point Paul began acting out his resentment at the transferral of Raquelle's attention from him to the twins and became a generally obnoxious child. As an adult, Raquelle has mended fences with Steve but remains a bit distant with Paul, who was ten when she left home for college. She regrets missing out on the later upbringing of Natalie and Nicole and is uneasy with the notion that they idolize her. She hopes they avoid growing up in her image—she has made too many mistakes.

Adolescence was a mixed bag for Raquelle. On the positive side, she socialized well with a wide variety of schoolmates: the intellectual types, the "straitlaced" students, and those a bit on the wild side. And, though barely average academically, she got along well with her teachers. One in particular, the school favorite and a church leader, took a distinct liking to her, and only much later did she realize that he had sexually abused her.

More on the downside, Raquelle entered high school feeling somewhat rebellious toward her parents and a bit of a misfit among her peers. While things were "okay" with her mother and she adored her baby sisters, her relationships with her father and brothers were difficult. Being larger and taller than her girlfriends, she often felt self-conscious and awkward—the odd one out. They teased her about the size of her hands and feet. Raquelle's outward response to such ridicule was simply to laugh it off. Similarly, when as a freshman she was taunted by a group of senior girls out of resentment for the attention she drew from their boyfriends, Raquelle never stood up for herself. Nor was she encouraged to. Regarding her aggressors, her always sympathetic mother advised her to "kill them with kindness." More and more, Raquelle came to feel like a doormat.

By sophomore year Raquelle was well on her way to exploring lifestyles antagonistic to that upheld by her family and church. She became fascinated with older boys—it was the danger that appealed to her—though she was not allowed to date before age sixteen and had no real boyfriends at all in high school. She fantasized at length about the worldly adventures awaiting her beyond the confines of childhood—worlds discovered in contraband issues of *Cosmopolitan* magazine. The seeds of liberation were sown.

Clearly, Raquelle was expected to graduate high school, move on to Brigham Young University, and from there to settle down and create a family with a nice young Mormon man. She would do none of that. Upon high school graduation, she moved to Laramie to enroll at the University of Wyoming.

College life did not suit Raquelle, so she left after only a year and a half—but not before partaking in an unconventional romance that would riddle her with pain and initiate a series of exploitive and abusive relationships destining her to a court of law and its associated media attention.

Early in the first year's football season, while observing the game from behind the home team bench, Raquelle made serious eye contact with jersey number 83. Following that flirtation came a visit from the water boy bearing the message that number 83 wanted to know her name and hoped she would meet him later that night at a particular nightclub. Raquelle was flattered and curious: he was a Black man and an athlete; he had noticed her in a crowd; and he had a beautiful smile. So off she went to meet him. It was an evening to remember. They exchanged phone numbers and the relationship took off. Allyn was Raquelle's first love; she had her first intimate experience with him at age nineteen.

From where Raquelle sat at the time, Allyn was a real catch: he was charming, popular, and funny and he treated her well—they never argued. Most importantly—he passionately adored her. The hitch was that he was committed elsewhere, to the mother of his infant daughter, which relegated to secrecy—and to secondary status—the relationship with Raquelle.

STRIKING OUT ALONE

Though having never met him, Raquelle's parents disapproved of her relationship with Allyn. At the close of her freshman year, they issued her an ultimatum: to stop dating Black men or assume full responsibility for her financial support. Raquelle returned to the university that fall fully expecting to pay her own way with money earned over the summer at the grocery store and through anticipated restaurant work in Laramie. But soon thereafter, having endured a year of intense struggle with a romance destined for tragedy, she dropped out of school and relocated to nearby Denver, Colorado, to begin anew. All along she had sensed she was a city girl at heart; it was time to test her wings.

Raquelle loved Denver on the spot and continues to thrive there. With a long series of filler-jobs and false starts behind her, she has settled in professionally as a regional service agent for a reputable nationwide communications firm. The relationship with Allyn persisted another three years, as a long-distance affair. Raquelle saw him through his draft into the NFL with the Detroit Lions and the subsequent back injury that released him from the team. In the wake of their parting, Allyn went on to marry and have another child. Raquelle continues to view Allyn as the love of her life.

In spring 1989, about six months after the break with Allyn and while waitressing in a sports bar owned by a Denver Bronco football player, Raquelle was invited out by the owner of the bar. Her subsequent involvement with him and another lover consumed the next four years of her life in a frenzy of exploitation and abuse that culminated in clinical depression and bankruptcy. Like Allyn, both men were Black, athletically built, and charming.

The first leg of her relationship with Mike, the Denver Bronco, lasted a year and was kept secret because of his primary involvement with another woman—shades of Allyn. Mike's pathological philandering and deception wore Raquelle down to the breaking point, at which time she severed ties with Mike and within weeks took up with Thomas, a part-time fashion model.

Thomas was separated from his wife and two children. He was a heavy drinker, a con artist, and an abuser. But just as significantly, he was gorgeous, soft-spoken, and charming—admired and pursued by an endless series of desirable women. Raquelle struggled to be the bright spot in Thomas's troubled life, to rescue him from his alcoholism and its underlying unhappiness. She wanted to turn his life around and to be adored by him in return. When he hurt her, she applied her mother's principle from years past and ever so patiently "killed him with kindness." Her perseverance would win him over. Raquelle was ever accessible to Thomas to the destruction of her social life; friends and social activities were sacrificed for his convenience.

Thomas lapsed into drunken rages, burning Raquelle with his cigarette, hitting her in the head, threatening to toss her off her apartment balcony, and, most frightening of all, suffocating her with sofa pillows (he knew of her childhood phobia). He cunningly persuaded her to charge things for him on her credit cards. When he was arrested at her apartment for assaulting his wife in violation of a restraining order against him, he and his family further persuaded Raquelle to take out a loan to post bail.

One night Thomas, livid with the realization that Raquelle had taken her phone off the hook, burst into her apartment, threw her out of bed, and suspended her by the throat and neck. When he then absconded with her car, she called the police. They could not arrest him for car theft because she had given him the keys, but upon seeing bruises on her neck, they were required by a Colorado mandatory arrest law pertaining to all levels of domestic violence to arrest him for assault. Ultimately, Thomas pleaded guilty to the misdemeanor assault and served six months' jail time, which ran concurrently with the two-year sentence handed him for assaulting his wife. Raquelle declared personal bankruptcy in an effort to recover financially from the two-year ordeal with Thomas.

Within months Raquelle was back with Mike, but nothing had changed—signs of women at every turn and no commitment in sight. In the space of a year, in August 1993, she had left him again.

WOMAN ABUSE IN THE CONTEXT OF PROFESSIONAL ATHLETICS

In July 1993 Raquelle was twenty-seven and working as a concierge for the VIP lounge of the Hyatt Regency Hotel, where she met Marcus, four years her junior. He was a recently promoted relief pitcher for the Colorado Rockies, the Denver-based major-league baseball team, and the downtown Hyatt served as official hotel for his ball-club. Marcus was in town reporting to the team, and Raquelle was charged with his care as a special guest.

Marcus was tall (six feet five inches) and, like the men Raquelle had dated before him, an athletically built and exceptionally charming Black man. He approached Raquelle for a recommendation to a jazz club, then invited her to join him. Raquelle describes what happened next and the beginning of her relationship with Marcus:

I declined. I told him that I worked days across the street as a waitress and evenings at the hotel. Marcus showed up for lunch every day that week so I could wait on him. He was persistent and kept asking me out. I finally accepted, and he took me to a club where there was a table reserved for us. I was very impressed. Marcus seemed very attentive and a total gentleman. We hit it off right away. I remember him showing up at my apartment to take me to breakfast one Sunday morning and surprising me with roses. All my girlfriends were very impressed with him and his charm; they really encouraged me to go out with him. Marcus never made me feel insecure with regard to other women. I remember a time when we were out at a nightclub and a woman passed him a note on a napkin. He didn't even open it; he just turned and handed it to me. That really made me feel secure. When he was in town, we were inseparable. When we were out on the town, he would always tell the service staff that I was his lady and to make sure I was well taken care of. He was always generous with my friends, buying them drinks and dinner or giving them baseball paraphernalia. When we were in New York City, he sent me shopping with his credit card. Another time, we were out and he was approached by a lady selling roses, and instead of buying me one rose, he bought me all of them (fifty to sixty). He had a real way of making me feel special.

In September, two months into the relationship, Marcus was planning a two-and-a-half-month stint in Phoenix, Arizona, beginning mid-October, to play in the off-season baseball league. He invited Raquelle to join him. She happily accepted and arranged a thirty-day leave from her job to accompany Marcus on the trip. Raquelle was happier than ever and, needless to say, hooked.

About three weeks prior to departure, Marcus's evil side surfaced. Raquelle describes her first glimpse into "Mr. Hyde":

I had gone to pick him up after a game, and I was waiting in the players' parking lot when the team owner's wife struck up a brief conversation with me. She asked me how long I'd been with Marcus, and I told her a couple of months. Marcus came out and saw us talking. When we returned to his apartment, he proceeded to ask me what we had been talking about. I told him it was small talk and she had asked how long we'd been together, and I told her a couple of months. Marcus SNAPPED!! (I think he had led people to believe that we'd been together a lot longer.) He started going on and on about me running my mouth, that I shouldn't be talking to these people, that they're always watching and trying to get into the players' personal business. I assured him that I was not saying anything personal about us. He threw my bag and dumped everything out on the floor and was stomping on it and breaking things. I started trying to gather up my things. As I did, he started throwing baby powder and lotion on me. I was upset and crying; I said I wanted to leave. He held a beer bottle in his hand and said, "If you try to leave, I'll bust you in the fucking head!!!" I couldn't believe this was happening. I sat down on the edge of the bed, crying. Then he knelt down in front of me and looked me in the eyes, and in a real nice and calm voice, he said, "Raquelle, you have to understand that you just can't be talking to people; you need to be careful. I'd really like you to be with me in Arizona. Now, come on, let me help you with your hair." He led me into the bathroom, where I accidentally knocked a plastic cup off of the counter. It made a really loud bouncing noise. Before I knew what was happening, he pushed me into the wall by my face and said, "We're not going that route!" (I'm still not sure what that meant.) Then he snapped back into the nice mode: "Now let me help you wash your hair." I didn't have a car to leave, so I stayed and went to bed. The next morning it was as if nothing had happened.

For weeks that transgression remained an isolated incident in the scheme of things. Raquelle could not yet know that it had set the tone and pattern for the remainder of a doomed relationship. Her anticipation of Phoenix was exciting, as were the first ten days there. She loved devoting her day to taking care of Marcus, cooking wonderful meals and doing whatever necessary to please him and make him appreciate her. When she reported to her mother her whereabouts and their surrounding circumstances, she was crushed by her mother's dire disapproval. But Marcus was quick to the rescue with seemingly heartfelt comfort and support, which escalated the intensity of her feelings for him. It was then that she became determined to make the relationship work.

Then it happened again. There was a simple disagreement followed by the silent treatment—freezing Raquelle out—and from there a tantrum, complete with Marcus throwing her belongings into a suitcase and demanding her return to Denver. Then an immediate reversal: wouldn't she come with him to the game in Tucson and on to Mexico for a romantic two-day holiday?—she had exactly five minutes to collect her things. At the game, he was ever so solicitous, sending her his jacket when noticing from the dugout that she appeared chilled. But later at the hotel he erupted with an angry interrogation into Raquelle's former lovelife, followed by a raging episode of grabbing, shoving, and abusive language. Name-calling would become an integral part of Marcus's campaign of degradation and terror: "stupid," "crazy," "whore." Raquelle's dramatic flight from their room to the lobby culminated in confrontation and public spectacle.

This type of exchange became a way of life for Raquelle and Marcus. She refers to his dark side as his "gangsta mode." He had been abandoned in infancy by his sixteen-year-old mother, to be raised in Oakland, California, by his maternal grandparents. Throughout his childhood, Marcus's mother had struggled to support herself and send home money periodically. Marcus never knew his father, an attorney and former college track star, and spent his youth resenting both parents as he negotiated the rough streets of Oakland. Marcus claimed that though he had never been a gang member himself, he had friends who were; and toward the conclusion of his relationship with Raquelle, he incorporated them into his terror tactics: "I'll get my boys to take care of you!"

Another episode in Phoenix sent Raquelle packing for home, but three days later Marcus convinced her to return for the remainder of the thirty days. After a month back in Denver, she revisited Phoenix for the Thanksgiving holiday, with plans to prepare a turkey dinner for Marcus and some of his teammates. It was the same old thing; the trip was cut short by disaster that left Raquelle stranded in the airport for hours awaiting a standby flight home.

Though the relationship remained active, Raquelle and Marcus were together only two days in the four months that followed— between Thanksgiving 1993 and April 1, 1994, when Marcus returned to Denver for the Rockies' season opening. During their months apart Marcus played winter baseball in Mexico, participated in a championship in Venezuela, visited Oakland, and spring trained in Tucson, Arizona, with the Rockies. The Christmas and

New Year season was particularly difficult: intense drama resulted in aborted plans for Raquelle to join Marcus in Mexico.

At the conclusion of the winter holidays Raquelle sensed that she needed to get out of the relationship. She attempted unsuccessfully to break things off with Marcus by telephone: he would hear nothing of it. He tried to persuade her that their problems had been rooted in job-related stress and now that he had a contract with the Rockies and was undergoing a great winter ball season, things would be fine between them. Marcus was doing his best to reel in Raquelle, so when he realized that she was resisting his appeal, he snapped. "It's not over till I say it's over," he raged. He insisted that she meet with him for a couple days in Washington, D.C. at the end of January, inferring that they would renew and perhaps escalate the relationship. Raquelle wanted to believe him; she wanted the old Marcus back.

Raquelle arranged to meet Marcus at the Denver airport, where he would arrive from Mexico. They had not seen one another for two months and would fly together to D.C. But when Marcus spotted Raquelle in the airport, he said hi, then kept right on walking. When she caught up with him, he was frigid. Then, during the several hours of the flight delay, he badgered her unmercifully about a date that she had accepted with Mike over the holidays. Upon boarding, she was in tears, and they hardly spoke on the plane. That night Marcus raped Raquelle anally as she cried in pain for him to stop and bled on the sheets. True to form, the next morning he behaved as if the rape had not occurred and laughed when Raquelle pointed out the bruises on her body. Marcus never apologized to Raquelle. He simply switched personas, which kept her confused and vulnerable. The trip ended on a sour note, with Marcus complaining about having to pay Raquelle half the cost of her plane ticket as he had promised.

At spring training in March, Marcus performed well, demonstrating his ability to make the major league roster. He was in a good mood, and he and Raquelle happily anticipated being together again soon. Marcus spoke of them having a baby together; when he returned to Denver they would plan the pregnancy so that she would deliver during the off-season. Raquelle was flattered but clarified that she could not plan a pregnancy outside marriage. She wanted to be married before starting a family. At this point she was hopeful that their bad times were behind them and life would resume with the charming and generous man with whom she had fallen in love.

But that did not happen. Marcus returned to Denver moody and irritable. Raquelle suspects that he was on drugs. He moved into a furnished luxury suite after, at his request, Raquelle had located an apartment for him in her complex and arranged for it to be furnished and decorated. Over the next three months the abuse intensified, and Raquelle was beginning to fear for her life. In addition to spitting and name-calling, Marcus shoved her up against the wall and, with her face in his hand, ranted about one thing or another. He again threatened to get "his boys" to "take care" of her. She recalls pushing her loveseat up against the door for protection. Once, in a threatening, backhanded gesture, he quipped, "Now I know why O.J. did what he did!" Marcus flipped like a switch, pushing Raquelle to the edge with his cunning brutality, then reeling her in: "Okay, I'll stop fucking with you; don't you know how beautiful you are?"

Raquelle was confused, depressed, and afraid. Any gesture to withdraw from Marcus, such as expressing the desire to spend a night away from him, incited his wrath. She knew better than to try to leave. And through it all, Marcus's mother was an influential force—always quick to remind Raquelle that Marcus was just that way, always ready with advice on management strategy.

GETTING OUT

Marcus was having a mediocre season when in July he was dispatched to the Rockies' AAA affiliate, the Colorado Springs Sky Sox—a demotion from the major to the minor league. He took it well: Colorado Springs was nearby, so he could keep his apartment and commute, and the adjustment was temporary, or so he was told.

Later that month while away on a road trip, Marcus pitched the worst game of his career, giving up ten earned runs and walking five batters. It was a humiliating turn of events, and Marcus was not one to accept humiliation gracefully. On the return bus trip to Colorado Springs (demeaning in itself, considering the major leagues always fly), he phoned Raquelle eight or ten times to harass her about one thing or another. He demanded to know where she had been when he had called earlier and insisted on a description of the clerk where she claimed to have been shopping. Another time he demanded that she take two or three days off work to be with him (she said she couldn't). His demeanor was intense as he vacillated between accusations of cheating and expressions of romantic sentiment. Finally, he demanded that she await his arrival in Colorado Springs that night to drive him back to Denver.

It was 11:30 P.M. when Raquelle arrived at the stadium. She was a bit late because Marcus's directions had been incomplete. It was a brutal ride back to Denver. She had been late, he insisted, because she was stupid and didn't listen. And her men friends no longer would be allowed to phone her—she would get an unlisted number. Then Marcus announced repeatedly that Raquelle would be disciplined. She tried to make light of the threat, but clearly he was serious.

Upon their arrival at Marcus's apartment, Raquelle nervously scurried about, helping with the unpacking and offering to do laundry. But Marcus remained fixed on the idea of discipline. Raquelle describes her final violent episode with Marcus:

He told me to take a shower, so I did. He put on some romantic music. As I came out in my nightshirt he said, "You're going to be disciplined, now get on the bed." All this time I was doing what he asked me to, but I was pleading with him not to hurt me. Out of nowhere he had a leather belt; he told me to get on all fours. I was afraid but I got up on the bed. Then he ripped off my panties and struck me on the bottom with the belt. He didn't strike me that hard, so I thought he was just trying to scare me, and it was working. Then he just started striking me *harder* and *harder* (*Keep in mind that this is a man that has the strength to throw a ball 100 mph, so even holding back, he was striking me very hard*). I begged him to stop, but he said if I screamed he'd hit me harder, so I just took a couple of strikes, holding back the screams. He stopped for a moment and said I was a smart mouth, that I never listen, etc. Then he flipped me over and continued to strike me on my bare buttocks. The final blow struck me between the legs. I remember bolting up in pain. The next thing I knew, he raped me and sodomized me (*all of the time, he was saying it was what I wanted, obviously trying to convince himself*). I was in shock. When he finished . . . he reached over and held my hand like nothing had happened. I got sick with dry heaves. I just pretended to be asleep. Meanwhile, I was trying to decide how I was going to get out of there.

At sunrise, Raquelle hit the snooze button in an effort to appear unaffected by the night before. Since Marcus had threatened to continue beating her into the next day and night, she wanted to be certain to get out. She was stiff and sore and incredulous at her reflection in the mirror—bruises and welts everywhere. Raquelle slipped out into the morning quietly, leaving Marcus in a sleepy daze.

Under the guidance of a sympathetic and wise cab driver, Raquelle went directly to her physician who, under the Colorado mandatory report law for physicians, was required to report the abuse to the criminal justice system. The police came to take her statement and photograph her. She was then escorted to Denver General Hospital for a rape kit, then taken home. She was instructed to file for a restraining order but arrived downtown too late to accomplish that, so she had to return the following day. Several voice messages from Marcus awaited her at home: "C'mon, girl, let's just go on about our business." Raquelle never responded, and she never again spoke with Marcus. It was a long difficult Monday, but well worth the humiliation and aggravation. To this day, Raquelle remains convinced that without that mandatory report law, she might never have escaped Marcus. Out of fear for her life, she would never have reported him.

The next day Raquelle met with the detective assigned to her case. Again, she gave her statement, and he informed her that the office of the commissioner of Major League Baseball had been in contact with the police to offer its cooperation. The next morning its representatives escorted Marcus to the police department to be booked for first-degree sexual assault and third-degree physical assault. A few hours later he was free on a twenty-five-thousand-dollar bond. His arrest made headlines. Marcus was booed when he walked on the field that night.

In June 1995, nearly a year after the beating and rape, Marcus was tried in court. That three-day trial resulted in a hung jury—eleven to one for acquittal on the sexual assault charge and ten to two for acquittal on the physical assault charge. Raquelle and her family were devastated. She had testified for five grueling hours and never wavered, and was certain the jury had believed her. Marcus had not performed well; even notoriously objective reporters predicted a conviction. He had remained smug and cocky throughout the proceedings. But closing statements for the defense "played the race card": the jury must be fair to Marcus, "a Black man accused of raping a White woman." And sports celebrity may have played a part. The lone "guilty" voter on the rape charge had this to say to the press:

Everybody said he was guilty. They didn't want to convict him. It was baseball that did it. They didn't want to push it with a baseball player, a celebrity. They thought being traded down to the minors was punishment enough.

This juror was referring to the fact that in April 1995 Marcus had been traded from Colorado to Cincinnati and was spending that season in Chattanooga, Tennessee, with the Reds' AA farm club. It was a long fall from his major league days in Denver. A spokesperson for the Rockies denied that the trade had been precipitated by the charges of rape and assault. Marcus had been traded down before his arrest, after all.

REFLECTIONS

Raquelle believes that she has been strengthened by her tragic experience with Marcus and that it has forced her to recognize and examine her patterns with men and to correct them while she is still young, before a marriage and children are involved. She realizes now that though her father has been an intimidating presence in her life, she has always respected his ability to take control. She recognizes that she always felt safe with him and has sought out men who, like her father, seemed self-assured and much in control. She knows that she seeks that safety again in a partner. What she understands now is that control can be exploitive and abusive, that all self-assured men who have grabbed control of their lives do not have the values, morals, and ethics of her father. They do not all have Raquelle's well-being at heart. Some feed on women by constructing a controlled, gendered hierarchy. Raquelle will continue to respect and seek the companionship of strong men, but now she will look deeper into the dynamics of their motivation. Raquelle comments on the aftermath of her abuse and escape:

I've come a long way since July 18, 1994 [the rape]. I still have moments of panic when someone approaches me from behind, and I still have occasional nightmares. I'm still dealing with the effects the publicity has had on my family. I'm not real anxious to meet any new men, and sex is the farthest thing from my mind. I gained forty pounds, which has actually been a sort of armor for me. I'm learning to trust myself and my instincts. I know that I'm a good person and that I didn't do anything to deserve what happened to me. I've also learned a great deal about forgiveness. . . . In time, I know I'll be able to take the forty pounds off. I felt it was more important for me to work on my emotional and mental well-being first.

CHAPTER TWELVE

Lucretia

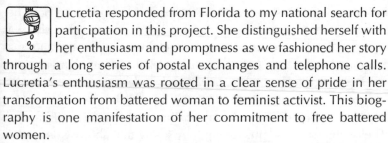 Lucretia responded from Florida to my national search for participation in this project. She distinguished herself with her enthusiasm and promptness as we fashioned her story through a long series of postal exchanges and telephone calls. Lucretia's enthusiasm was rooted in a clear sense of pride in her transformation from battered woman to feminist activist. This biography is one manifestation of her commitment to free battered women.

Lucretia's story is one of a close family network of women entrenched in a world impaired by racism, unemployment, poverty, alcohol and illicit drug addiction, and neglect. In addition to overcoming all of that, Lucretia has faced and comfortably settled into her homosexuality.

Today Lucretia is an active single mother, a full-time executive secretary, and a heroic figure in the surroundings of Clearwater, Florida, where she facilitates her healing process by speaking publicly to abused and sometimes hopeless women about her own recovery and of hope for theirs. At thirty-seven, the obstacles that once fettered her now mobilize her to realize her fair place in a compromising world.

Lucretia is the second of four daughters of a Florida family. One day, at age eighteen, she was kidding around with her younger sisters, Charlezetta and Janet, in the family room of their Miami home, while their mother Jeanette relaxed on the couch engrossed in a favorite novel. Charlezetta called Lucretia ugly, to which she responded playfully, "Your daddy!" (inferring that any ugliness was sourced in Charlezetta's as well as Lucretia's father because they were one and the same and, therefore, that Charlezetta must be equally ugly.) With that, Jeanette peered over her book, announcing to Lucretia, "He's the only father you ever had, and you better be grateful." She proceeded to explain that the girls' father, Dike, was not Lucretia's natural father, and that he had adopted her when she was four.

Jeanette went on to tell the sisters that at age twenty she had conceived Lucretia with a young man named James Weaver, whose family had viewed Jeanette as poor trash and, therefore, dismissed her when she informed them of the pregnancy. The young man and his family immediately left Georgia for New York, and Jeanette had heard nothing of them since. It was now up to Lucretia to locate her natural father if she wished. Lucretia now learned for the first time that she had inherited her height and left-handedness from this man and that her dark skin was beyond explanation because both her natural parents were light-complected. She learned that she was without the heritage that she had claimed all along and was reminded once again of the regrettable status of her pigmentation.

It was a critical moment, now two decades ago, in Lucretia's life trajectory. She was redefined on the spot by her two sisters: "No wonder you're different!"—taller, thinner, smarter, left-handed. They expressed disdain, saying they knew that she was Jeanette's favorite daughter and that she "made them sick." Those sister relationships never totally recovered. Nor did Lucretia's relationship with her mother, whose betrayal cuts deep and involves lies of commission as well as omission. Lucretia recalls being eight when her cousins informed her that her older sister, Angie, and she were adopted. But Jeanette had continued over the years to deny the allegation. Lucretia also remembers a wedding when she was four years old, and when she learned that Dike had in fact adopted her, she realized that she had been in his and Jeanette's wedding. When questioned again on that day of reckoning, Jeanette admitted to it all and apologized for her deception. Prompted by this incident, Lucretia left home that year.

That same day Angie learned that she had been fathered by yet a third man. Jeanette said little of him besides the fact that he had been short and crazy. Angie inquired no further. Charlezetta and

Janet vented no anger toward Angie for having a different father, as they had toward Lucretia. There was no jealousy involved; clearly Angie was not a serious competitor for their mother's affection; she had always been and was to remain psychologically distant from the family and a loner.

Until age ten Lucretia lived with her family in a predominantly Black Jacksonville neighborhood, in a modest three-bedroom, two-bath rental home. Dike and Jeanette were alcoholics and drug addicts and sometimes seriously neglected their daughters. Their parental availability was inconsistent and sporadic—especially during these early years. Family life lacked structure, boundaries, and love. The children were provided no instruction to bathe, brush their teeth, attend school, or adhere to a set bedtime. Discipline was harsh and lacked continuity: punishment would be withdrawn before completion. Beatings with belt buckles were the rule, and hunger was common. In those days the parents were unconcerned when a child missed school or became injured. Lucretia and her sisters learned early on that they had to take care of themselves. They found no joy in childhood; they were too focused on merely surviving.

Lucretia's earliest images of her mother include long hours of her toiling through nursing school, then as a hospital nurse. Jeanette was an intelligent and attractive woman, though always sullen and depressed. Her children clearly were a burden to her, and she suffered emotional and physical abuse at the hands of Dike. At age forty her professional career all but collapsed when she was caught stealing drugs for her own consumption and to sell under Dike's coercion. Her license was revoked, and she was fired by the hospital. When five years later her license was reinstated, she assumed private-duty work.

Lucretia and her sisters witnessed immeasurable abuse in their early years and endured much of their own. Dike had been dishonorably discharged from the army when he and Jeanette married in Georgia and relocated to her original hometown of Jacksonville in search of work. He was of stocky build and mean disposition, and jealous and possessive in his relationship with Jeanette. Lucretia recalls the violence of her childhood:

If Jeanette were a few minutes late coming home from work, [Dike] would beat her; if she talked back, he would also beat her until she became unconscious. He oftentimes hit her after he had been on a drinking binge, for no apparent reason. This was a typical day at our home. As young as age six, I began hiding in the closet and praying that Dike wouldn't kill her. I cried many times because when Jeanette was beaten to an unconscious state, I thought she was dead. I couldn't understand why he hit her so hard and made her bleed from her head and/or mouth in the presence of me and my sisters. By age ten, I began to resent Jeanette because I didn't understand why she wouldn't leave him. Whenever we screamed and asked him to stop hitting her, he would beat us with belts or curse at us to leave the room. I internalized that I should not voice my opinion or I would be severely punished.

Lucretia was a responsible child and an A student because it was expected of her and she feared the repercussions of behaving otherwise. Though her parents generally neglected their children, especially when the children were very young, they insisted on good grades because, Lucretia believes, those grades reflected their parental competence to the community. Because Angie was immature and incapable of doing so, Lucretia assumed the role of oldest daughter. In that capacity, she was cleaning house and preparing meals for her sisters and herself by age six. A peer friendship evolved with her mother, who burdened her as early as age eight with talk of financial and marital problems. By the time she was ten, Lucretia was bicycling around town paying utility bills and on occasion hiding money from Dike on Jeanette's behalf.

Because of her family responsibilities, Lucretia had little time for elementary school friends, and besides, friendships were risky because they could lead to embarrassing disclosure or discovery. What if it became known that wearing those long-sleeved shirts and long pants in the summer was intended to cover welts and bruises? What if someone asked about the dirty clothes and matted hair? Much of the time Dike and Jeanette were passed out at home from abuse of one drug or another. No one should know the family lived this way. Then there was the most devastating secret of all: the sexual abuse that both Jeanette and Dike imposed (sometimes both parents together) on the four daughters, unbeknownst to one another. That all surfaced at an angry and tearful 1991 gravesite anniversary reunion of their mother's death. How could Jeanette have violated them that way, and why had not she protected them from Dike? All these family realities denied Lucretia the opportunity to develop stable peer networks in her childhood.

When Lucretia was ten, Dike accepted a job as conductor for a railroad company, and the family relocated to Miami. Lucretia remembers that job as Dike's first steady employment. Jeanette was the family's economic mainstay. The family occupied an apartment for six months until they were able to purchase their own home. Dike was fired for truancy shortly after the move, then spent most of his time between jobs and in local bars. Jeanette was working and going to school. That was a difficult time for Lucretia: relocation compounded the familiar parental absence and general family turmoil.

Then in 1969, while in sixth grade, Lucretia was faced with another major adjustment: the Miami school district desegregated. Black children were apprehensive, and parents expressed opposition to their being bused to White neighborhoods and schools. Lucretia recalls that critical juncture in her life:

I can remember Jeanette sitting me down, explaining this transition. She told me White people were no better than me, but that I would have to work extra hard to prove myself. When this transition took place, I was readily accepted and admired by White girls partly, I feel, because I was very smart and seemed to impress them.

In the seventh and eighth grades, Lucretia's teachers entered her in the local spelling bee, and under Jeanette's tutelage, she won both times. Jeanette was proud and Lucretia's Black schoolmates, envious. White classmates took notice and wanted to befriend her, so Lucretia doubled her efforts to impress them with her grades and other intellectual accomplishments.

By this time race had become a critical issue for Lucretia. She had come to understand what it meant to be Black rather than White. Her words stand as powerful reminders of what racial prejudice can do to a child:

Jeanette bought us White Barbie dolls when I was a little girl, and I admired their long, blond hair and white skin and hated my coarse black hair and dark skin and wished I were White.

While being Black had become a great source of pain to Lucretia, her efforts to escape that status brought additional discomfort. Lucretia explains:

Most of my Black friends soon began calling me names, "Oreo" and "Whitey," and immediately separated themselves from me. I cried on many occasions because I didn't understand the aversion and why I had to [endure] such ridicule. I felt isolated from my Black friends.

Jeanette always reiterated my Black friends were jealous of me. She told me not to succumb to the pressure and to continue to befriend Whites if I wanted to. To date, many of my close friends are White.

Those early Miami days found three resourceful sisters hard at work to keep food on the table. Charlezetta, Janet, and Lucretia bagged groceries and stole food from stores. They charged neighbors ten cents admission to the tree house that Dike had built for them and a quarter admission for the Saturday fashion shows hosted in their backyard for three consecutive summers. Donning Dike and Jeanette's party clothes and accessories, including high heels, makeup, and jewelry, they sang and danced for their young audiences to recorded music and their own choreography. The clothes and adornments were always returned neatly to their places without suspicion. For refreshments the girls sold juice, Kool-Aid drinks, and homemade coconut candy.

In the meantime Dike and Jeanette hosted parties of their own, always with twenty to thirty friends. They cooked crabs and conch, served plenty of alcohol and marijuana, played cards, and filled the house with great music. Dike would become inebriated and fly into a jealous rage if he saw a man talking to or even looking at Jeanette; often he hit her in the presence of friends. Lucretia recalls the embarrassment of it all. Those parties often featured orgies with bedroom doors ajar. As young children, the girls were exposed to provocative sexual behavior, as, for example, when Jeanette's best friend, Eunice, periodically joined Jeanette and Dike to form a "threesome."

One of the happiest days of Lucretia's life was when, at fifteen, Jeanette left Dike. But even after the divorce Jeanette never seemed happy. Dike had introduced her to drugs during their marriage, which led to her untimely death at age forty-six in 1983. After the divorce Dike remained in Miami and continued to attempt a reconciliation with Jeanette. But she had had enough, even though she still loved him.

EARLY SEXUALITY IN THE CONTEXT OF RELIGIOUS CAPTIVITY

When Lucretia was fifteen, she and her sisters joined First Faith Cathedral, a Pentecostal church a thousand members strong, ministered by Pastor Milton Baker and located in downtown Miami. In the beginning the church provided them with a welcome diversion from their troubled family life. They became involved in the youth program, which sponsored field trips to Disney World and other popular entertainment sites, as well as local activities. As a group, these young people washed cars and sold candy to fund these events. Lucretia joined the choir and played tenor saxophone in the orchestra. She expresses appreciation to the church experience for its enforcement of structure and discipline—a welcome change from her chaotic childhood. The sense of extended family provided many wonderful friendships, and church conventions offered her the opportunity for out-of-state airline travel.

Three years after Lucretia joined the church, Pastor Baker informed the congregation that the Holy Spirit had directed him to relocate the church to the Tampa Bay area. Within a year the Miami church building was sold, and about three hundred families had sold or rented out their homes and moved to Tampa. Lucretia and Charlezetta elected to go, while Angie and Janet remained in Miami. In Tampa, Pastor Baker had purchased four homes in which single women of the church shared living expenses and for which they paid rent directly to him. Lucretia and Charlezetta shared one of these homes with three other women. A strict lifestyle was imposed on these women: no television, gentleman visitors, makeup, pants, or jewelry—and a 10:00 P.M. curfew. Jeanette strongly disapproved of her daughters' move to Tampa; she resented Pastor Baker's control over them.

It was during these years under Pastor Baker's rule that Lucretia first faced important sexuality issues. Her first sexual experience had occurred at age twelve and involved a ten-year-old neighborhood girlfriend. They had maintained a close friendship for three years, until Pat's family moved away, leaving Lucretia devastated. It was then, at age fifteen, that she had faced her homosexual tendencies but had been afraid to disclose them. She had assumed that something was wrong with her, and the inner struggle persisted through a long series of unspoken attractions to women.

Then at eighteen, while attending a junior college in Miami, Lucretia became involved with her first boyfriend. Larry was in her humanities class—tall, handsome, and one year her senior. She was particularly impressed with his command of Scripture. They had lunch together, and he invited her to his church to hear him preach. Larry was Lucretia's first heterosexual partner, and Lucretia found sex with him to be unsatisfying and painful. He was emotionally abusive, resorting to name-calling and embarrassing her in the presence of his mother by inviting her to visit, then ignoring her. When he asked her to spend the night, he left her alone and slept in bed with his mother. At the urging of Charlezetta and Janet, Lucretia severed the relationship after four months.

Within months, at age nineteen, Lucretia fell victim to attempted stranger rape, which seriously affected her sexuality, at least temporarily. She recalls:

I was in McDonald's eating lunch, and he asked me if he could join me at my table. We talked about school . . . and his job. He said he only lived a few minutes away and wanted to take me home. When I got in his car, he began talking about the weather, and a minute or two later, he locked the doors, and I became extremely nervous. I told him I wanted to get out. He told me he was going to take me home and fuck me. I was so afraid; I began to pray in the car. [When] we got to his house, he grabbed my arms and made me go inside. He began pulling at my clothes and I started crying and screaming, and one of the neighbor's dogs began barking. When he looked away, I ran towards the door and got out. I ran for miles and miles until I got home. I never told my mom. I was too embarrassed. Because of this experience, I was afraid of men, and consequently became celibate until I met Johnny, my ex-husband, when I was twenty-four.

Shortly thereafter, in Tampa, disaster struck again. Lucretia developed a serious attraction to one of her roommates and sensed that her sentiments were reciprocated. Then when Gail began dating a man and withdrew from her, Lucretia became despondent and attempted suicide by ingesting rubbing alcohol.

In the meantime Lucretia's sentiments toward Pastor Baker were souring. She came to view him as a shrewd White man who had garnered control over much of his predominantly Black congregation. Women were placed in subservient roles in the church hierarchy and discouraged from furthering their education and pursuing careers. They were admonished to obey their husbands and assume traditional domestic roles. Pastor Baker employed terrorization tactics in order to maintain dominance: if one did not believe in Christ and had not been saved, that person was doomed to hell. Salvation required relinquishment of all worldly possessions to the church and total devotion to the work of the Lord. Pastor Baker also instructed members to toil long hours for the ministry and to tithe. Many double-tithed or contributed extra earnings to the church. Clearly, Pastor Baker was orchestrating a hostage-type enterprise for his personal benefit. Particularly debilitating to Lucretia was

Pastor Baker's perspective on sexual orientation: homosexuality was immoral and blasphemous.

As she turned twenty-one, Lucretia was depressed. She was unhappy with her life, agonizing over sexuality issues, and resenting Pastor Baker's control over her and his congregation. Another suicide attempt, this time using Tylenol, landed her in the hospital, where her stomach was pumped before release later that day.

GETTING OUT

Three years later Lucretia was ready to break away from Pastor Baker's cultlike operation. She was suffocating. She confronted Pastor Baker with his misrepresentation of Scripture to support his personal belief system and was excommunicated on the spot. Lucretia remembers:

Pastor Baker said, "No one talks back to me. If you don't agree with my doctrine, you need to leave. You will not upset the balance and the order of my church." He ordered me out of his rental house by twenty-four hours. I didn't have anywhere to go. By then, my sister Angie had moved to Georgia and was raising her family; Janet was living with an abusive boyfriend while raising her young son; Jeanette was living with an abusive boyfriend; and Charlezetta was married to an abusive man and still very much a part of the church—therefore [she couldn't associate with me].

On Gail's advice, Lucretia moved in with Gail's cousin Carolyn, who lived in Tampa. Carolyn aided Lucretia in her adjustment to the world outside Pastor Baker's church—helping her to deprogram from a decade of life devoted to sacrifice and preparation for heaven. Lucretia realized that she had been stunted socially and needed to learn how to think for herself and to participate in conventional culture—movies, dancing, restaurants. This was a particularly lonely period of transition. The sense of Pastor Baker's betrayal cut deep—that after so many years of devotion, he would toss her aside for simply standing up to him. And, for Lucretia, critical life issues remained unresolved.

ANOTHER ABUSIVE RELATIONSHIP: THE MARRIAGE

Still twenty-four and while working as a medical transcriptionist at a Veterans Administration (VA) hospital in Tampa, Lucretia met Johnny, a licensed practical nurse five years her senior. The attraction was immediate for Lucretia. She says:

Johnny was a tall, handsome Black man with the most beautiful eyes. Physical beauty was far more important to me at that time than inner qualities. We became romantically involved rather quickly.

Johnny was kind and quiet in the beginning; Lucretia felt fortunate to have found him.

The oldest of five children, Johnny had been born and raised in Kosciusko, Mississippi. When he was nine, his natural father divorced his mother, then died in an alcohol-related car accident when Johnny was seventeen. Johnny numbed the pain with alcohol and other addictive substances. He resented the man his mother married when he was eleven because that husband beat her and also abused alcohol. When he was eighteen, Johnny fought his stepfather for hurting his mother, and the man never touched her again in Johnny's presence. Johnny left home at nineteen. Before having met Johnny, and only weeks into her employment at the VA hospital, Lucretia accepted a secretarial position at the University of Nebraska. Even though she was smitten with Johnny, she followed through with her plans to relocate to Lincoln. After only two months away, however, she returned to Tampa under Johnny's relentless campaign to get her back. He overwhelmed her with all the right words. Having arrived in Tampa with nowhere else to stay, and again at Johnny's persistence, she moved in with him "temporarily" at the home he shared with his brother, the brother's girlfriend, and their child. Lucretia found work as a word processor at Amica Insurance in Tampa. Even though there were clear danger signs from the beginning, including drunkenness, name-calling ("Black nigger bitch"), and possessiveness (Johnny hated Lucretia's family and friends and insisted that she limit her associations to him), the temporary living arrangement became permanent.

Though totally unprepared for motherhood, Lucretia was pregnant within a year. Johnny had made sure she missed gynecological appointments to get birth control pills. He knew she did not want children initially, but he insisted the pills were unhealthy. Lucretia took them anyway—sporadically. Johnny disallowed an abortion. The physical abuse began with that pregnancy. Lucretia describes the context of the first assault:

The first time he slapped me I was a few minutes late from work, and he accused me of sleeping with another man. I was dumbfounded, yet I lacked the courage to leave him. By this point in the relationship the emotional abuse had already taken its toll on me, and my self-esteem was very low. I felt ugly; I was losing weight because he would have me on an emotional roller coaster.

Johnny hit and slapped Lucretia and remained missing without explanation for days at a time. Apologies and broken promises always followed the violence. Over the next decade Johnny remained physically and emotionally abusive in the context of alcohol and drug addiction; it was a replay of Dike and Jeanette's relationship—except that Lucretia was not a drug user.

When Lucretia was six months pregnant with David, her mother suffered an untimely death at forty-six of a drug overdose. Johnny discouraged Lucretia from attending the funeral and in general was unsupportive. As a result she was unable to grieve the loss until many years later during therapy. Then, seven months into the pregnancy, Johnny injected cocaine into Lucretia's arm, claiming that he was God and supposed to make her feel good. Afterward, she walked for miles in an effort to neutralize any effects the drug might have on her or her unborn child.

Johnny proposed marriage to Lucretia when she was thirty, David was four, and their second child was expected. They had left his brother's home to buy their own in a predominantly White neighborhood three years earlier, in 1985. The wedding occurred there in October 1988, and their daughter Rasheka arrived the following May. Johnny continued to work at the VA hospital and was promoted to cardiac catheterization technician in 1989, and Lucretia was promoted to lead word processor at Amica in 1990.

Lucretia married Johnny even though he was abusing her and she did not love him. She describes her mind-set at the time:

I married Johnny even though I didn't love him. I felt a moral obligation to do so since I already had one child out of wedlock. I was too afraid to deny his request to marry because I was afraid of him. Also, I was emotionally dependent on him and didn't feel I could adequately function without him. Johnny cooked, bought groceries, and paid the bills. . . . Shortly after the wedding, Johnny became very possessive and the abuse escalated.

Johnny had taken over Lucretia's life, including child care and total control of their finances; he insisted that even her paycheck was his money. His possessiveness had intensified over time; often he made the direct claim that he owned her. He was raping her vaginally, orally, and anally. Lucretia was afraid of Johnny; she was in no position to refuse his marriage proposal.

Rasheka's was a difficult Caesarean delivery with life-threatening complications. Lucretia hated Rasheka's father during the pregnancy; she had not wanted to conceive the baby but could not bear the thought of aborting it. Postpartum depression and another attempted suicide followed—this time Lucretia ingested drugs that Johnny had stolen from patients at the hospital.

As he had with David, Johnny enthusiastically and competently stepped in to parent Rasheka. Lucretia envied his domestic skills. He continued to manage the household without a hitch. Lucretia did not enjoy parenting when the children were young. It was about this time that she sought counseling and under that influence began resisting her dependence on Johnny as she had earlier resisted Pastor Baker. She was determined to empower her life by enhancing her self-esteem through independence and self-sufficiency. She became determined to find satisfying professional work and to master her domestic responsibilities—cooking, grocery shopping, budgeting, and child care. Later, after she left Johnny, she would enroll in classes designed to sharpen her parenting skills.

The abuse continued to escalate to unmanageable proportions. David witnessed his father hitting Lucretia on several occasions. Now all that kept Lucretia in the marriage was fear for the lives of her and her children. Whenever she attempted to leave, Johnny would take her keys or money and threaten to kill her, the children, or both. So she stayed. Lucretia spoke with Johnny's mother, who reasoned that as long as Johnny was bringing home the paycheck, Lucretia would just have to take the abuse. Lucretia sensed a total lack of support from both her own and Johnny's families.

GETTING OUT

In summer 1991 Lucretia and Johnny set out with the children to picnic at a local park. Johnny had been drinking, and Lucretia had become frightened by his erratic driving through the park grounds, so she admonished him to slow down or else to stop so that she could get out. With that, he pulled over and shoved her out, then returned twenty minutes later, demanding that she get back into the car. When she refused, he got out, hurled her to the ground, and choked her in the presence of passive bystanders. Then he forced her into the car and drove about half a mile to another area of the park, where he had left the children alone. She was outraged at his having abandoned them; they were only seven and two years old. At Johnny's insistence, he and Lucretia approached the children as though nothing were out of the ordinary. The children appeared a bit frightened and disoriented but were happy to see their mother. Lucretia put on a facade; as the children enjoyed their picnic, she cried inside.

Lucretia despised Johnny after the park incident. A month later she mustered up the courage to ask him for a divorce. He complied. However, that same evening he left home and returned around 3:00 A.M. to yank her out of bed, drag her into the next room, away from Rasheka, and threaten her. If she did not cancel her appointment with the attorney, he would kill her. Then he brought a large garbage bag and rope from the kitchen and proceeded to place the bag over her head. Lucretia begged for her life, then capitulated. At that point, Johnny left the room, went to bed, and passed out.

The next day Johnny got dressed for work and did not return home, which was not unusual for him. Seven days later Lucretia asked Charlezetta to keep her children while she checked herself into a psychiatric hospital in nearby St. Petersburg. During her three-and-a-half-week stay there, she underwent intensive therapy and was placed on antidepressant drugs. Johnny returned home during the first week of that hospitalization. Lucretia's therapist left phone messages informing him of Lucretia's whereabouts and inviting him to come in for joint counseling, but he never responded. At that point Lucretia decided to leave Johnny. She reflects:

I made the profound decision to get out of my ten-year abusive relationship while I was in the hospital. I realized I had been in a very sick relationship and didn't want to return. I wanted a better life for me and my kids. . . . I was afraid Johnny would kill me; I wanted a fresh start.

Charlezetta brought David and Rasheka to the hospital at Lucretia's discharge so that the three could be transported together to the Center Against Spouse Abuse (CASA) in St. Petersburg. During their twenty-three-day stay at CASA, Lucretia received generous support as she placed her life in perspective and prepared to move on. Her employer had been informed that out of fear of Johnny's reprisal, she would not be returning to work. For the same reason, the family could not go home.

So from CASA the family moved to Stepping Stones in October 1991, a transitional housing program in Largo, Florida. To qualify for Stepping Stones, Lucretia had to be a student or employed, so she enrolled in a business school to sharpen her secretarial skills and ultimately earned a diploma there. For six months during this transitional phase in Lucretia's life, she survived on food stamps and welfare. In September 1992, she entered the Partners in Self-Sufficiency Housing Program in Clearwater, Florida, where she intends to remain until her contract expires in a couple of years. The program sets membership guidelines and offers financial housing assistance based on a sliding-income scale. It helped Lucretia find and continues to help her pay for adequate housing for her and the children. It also serves as a liaison to the community resources critical to her journey toward self-sufficiency.

While at CASA, Lucretia initiated divorce procedures, but the process was prolonged for a year and a half while the court attempted to locate Johnny to serve him with the appropriate papers. To no avail, Lucretia hired a private investigator to track him down. Finally, Johnny responded to the published divorce notice. At the initial hearing he was awarded unsupervised visitation rights, but after two visits he never again came for the children. On that second visit he again asked Lucretia for a reconciliation. Her "no" was emphatic, as she recommended that he get on with his life. The divorce was made final in January 1993. That following Christmas Eve Johnny phoned from a drug rehabilitation center, weeping and apologizing and again seeking a reconciliation. He now stands in contempt of court for unpaid child support.

SEXUALITY RESOLVED

During her divorce proceedings, at age thirty-five, Lucretia again opted for celibacy as she grappled with issues of her sexual orientation, in an effort to develop a clear sexual identity. She had never experienced a satisfying sexual relationship with a man. Sex had been difficult with Johnny, which, in retrospect, she blames on the unconscious connection she made at the time with Dike's sexual abuse of her as a child. A year after this reestablished celibacy, Lucretia began relating to women sexually, but because she was uncomfortable with the label of lesbian, she came out as bisexual. Though men pursued her, she remained aloof from them during this brief "bisexual" period.

With participation in consciousness-raising group activities, Lucretia at last was able to free herself of her homophobic tendencies and embrace the lesbian identity. She contacted the local gay rights association to obtain information on gay support groups and meeting places and in December 1993 first patronized a gay bar. She felt at home there. Talking with women, dancing with women, being with women just felt better. Within a few months Lucretia met Sharon at a lesbian dance, and the two have gone on to forge Lucretia's first healthy relationship. Lucretia has come out to some friends and family, with mixed response. David grows continually more comfortable with the notion of his mother being a lesbian and has expressed gratitude for her honesty. Lucretia remains determined to avoid deceiving her children, as her mother did her regarding Lucretia's adoption.

REFLECTIONS

Life is satisfying and productive to Lucretia now. She is comfortable in her own skin. Recognizing threads of consistency among the various entrapments, captivities, and other demonic intrusions of her youth, she has been able to grab control and stop the counterproductive patterns. When asked to identify the most liberating forces of her journey, she names CASA, the shelter that took her in, nurtured her, then launched her on a trajectory to independence, self-sufficiency, and the dignity that accompanies them. And she is quick to acknowledge the critical contribution of her Stepping Stones counselor/advocate, Linda Darin, who mentored her through a feminist reconceptualization of herself and the world around her. Lucretia is especially proud of the likelihood her daughter will know that she does not have to stay in an abusive relationship and that her son will respect women.

CHAPTER THIRTEEN

Colette

One would never suspect from her current surroundings the tragedy of Colette's youth. There is a distinctively serene quality to her neighborhood, her home, and her demeanor. She and her musician/artistic painter husband live together, tucked away in a pleasant and tree fitted old neighborhood of Nashville, Tennessee. Visitors are greeted by a moderately friendly brown tabby cat, perched on the pillowed swing of their comfortably shaded, richly seasoned wood porch.

Colette, who volunteers at her local battered women's shelter, responded to my nationwide mailing to shelters. Our work together included a meeting at her home. That summer day with Colette, in her sunroom, marked a turning point in the development of this book. A series of incredible, tragic endings that may appear peripheral to her story of abuse and escape could not be minimized in her biography. To do so would be to violate the integrity of Colette's life and to remove her battering from its context. And that would be true for all the women who were trusting me to craft their life stories honestly. From Colette, I learned that this collection must be one of life stories rather than simply stories about abuse and getting out.

At forty-one Colette is well established as an energetic, creative, and productive citizen. She has worked successfully as a hair stylist, owning businesses in two states. The profit from the sale of her Nashville business has helped her and her husband launch a partnership managing and promoting his career. As a part-time endeavor she continues to receive invited clients in the privacy of her home-based hair salon.

Colette is pivotal to how I have come to think about biography and to how this project evolved. In her presence I sense a compassion and wisdom that both overwhelms and calms me.

Colette's French mother and American father met on a blind date in Germany in 1952, when he was serving as a corporal in the U.S. Army and she was a maid for the army officers' quarters. Both were twenty-five, and her mother had a five-year-old son, Charles, living in an orphanage. They quickly fell in love and married in Germany. Colette's father adopted Charlie, and they all came to live in the United States.

Colette was born a year later in Indianapolis, Indiana, in an rmy hospital. Her earliest memory of her mother is of her fixing Colette's hair in finger curls. The brushing would sometimes pull and hurt, but if Colette flinched or complained, her mother would hit her on the head with the brush. So Colette learned early on to hide her pain. Her mother would adorn her in pretty dresses and become angry if she failed to stay clean and perfect. Once, Colette asked if she could brush out her curls and wear her hair fluffy. The reply was no, the usual response to her daughter's requests. So Colette went ahead and did it anyway. Her mother was furious with the disobedience.

Her brother, Peter, was born five years after Colette in Tacoma, Washington, in an army hospital. Before that, the family had lived in Alaska for a year and a half. With Peter's birth, Colette's life revolved around keeping him safe and happy. Often she was spanked when Peter fell or hurt himself because she was supposed to be watching him. She was responsible for monitoring him in the baby pool and in the bathtub, as the two children always bathed together.

Colette remembers an incident where her mother ran out of diapers when Peter was naked on the changing table. Her mother instructed her to hold him in place while she went outdoors to get fresh diapers from the clothesline. Colette was terrified as Peter wiggled around precariously on the table, then sent a stream of urine high into the air, landing on Colette's head and face. She dutifully persisted with her grip on Peter and was crying when her mother returned to the scene. No appreciation was shown Colette for her stamina. Colette harbors no preschool memory of Charles or her father, who was a career military man and often away on army business.

Around the time Colette entered school, she had a problem with bed-wetting, for which her mother beat her and rubbed her face in the soiled sheets. Her mother was also disgusted by Colette's thumb sucking and as a remedy tied her hands behind her back. Other abuses included slapping, ear pulling, and whipping with a cat-o'-nine-tails (leather straps). Colette accepted this treatment as normal. She remains convinced that Peter, on the other hand, was adored by both parents.

Colette's childhood was spent isolated from any extended family: her mother's was unknown and her father's was estranged. She suspects that her father's childhood was unhappy. His father and despised oldest brother were alcoholics, and his mother was mean. Colette's mother did not socialize with other women; she dismissed them as gossips. When Colette had contact with other families, especially mother-daughter relationships, she noticed the differences but reasoned that her own mother was unusual because she was French. In reference to these early years, Colette reflects:

When I look at childhood pictures, I seem bland—the same sweet smile on my face all of the time and always with my arm around my little brother in a protective way.

And she expresses the elusiveness of her mother's love this way:

My birthdays were a big deal. My mother invited the neighborhood kids and she had a great outdoor party. I look at pictures of this and think she must have loved me.

Colette's father was transferred in 1963 to France, where she spent second through sixth grades. Colette remembers her mother being content during those years. She also recalls school being difficult. Not only was she shy but she was terrified of appearing stupid. Her grades were bad, and eventually she resorted to cheating. She was beaten when she brought home bad grades. It was in France that Charles, when he was seventeen and Colette about ten, molested Colette one night when their parents were out. He invited her to his room and began explaining how babies were made. She was uncomfortable but curious. He tried to penetrate her, first with his fingers then his penis. Colette cried in pain, and Charles stopped and comforted her. Then he fixed her a sandwich and instructed her not to tell anyone. Colette remembers thinking that she had failed Charles somehow. This never happened again, nor was it discussed.

The family was transferred back to the United States in 1967—to Fort Bragg, North Carolina. Colette's father retired halfway through her seventh grade, so they moved from army housing into a purchased camper trailer until the end of the school year, when they relocated, trailer in tow, from Fayetteville to Greeley, Colorado. These were the first in a long series of cramped or run-down trailer sojourns that Colette would endure in her young life. The family lived out of that trailer until summer's end, when Colette's parents succeeded in finding what her mother called their "dream house"—a four-bedroom, two-bath brick structure—for which they had been saving throughout their military career. So Colette entered her eighth grade in Greeley. Peter entered the fourth grade, their father became a hospital orderly, and their mother worked in the laundry room of a nursing home. Charles had joined the army after completing high school in France.

One day, upon returning home from school and entering the garage, Colette observed droplets of blood on the cement floor. With caution, she continued into the house, noticing more blood smeared along the washer and an odor reminiscent of Ben Gay. She called out, but no one answered. Then she followed the trail into the kitchen, where she was faced with pools, squirts, and smears of blood everywhere. Her father had discovered her mother half dead in the house and rushed her to the hospital, where she remained for fifteen days. She had severed both wrists down through the tendons and drunk a bottle of wintergreen muscle ointment. She was hospitalized and diagnosed as paranoid schizophrenic. Colette remembers:

My childhood ended that day. I was thirteen years old, and my brother Peter was nine years old. My brother Charlie was in Vietnam at this time.

After her mother's release, Colette became her caretaker: she bathed her, fixed her hair, shaved her legs. The woman was catatonic most of the time, except for the incessant murmur, "I want to die; I want to die." Later, Colette learned that during those days, and while in her father's care, her mother had attempted to drown herself in the lake and was saved by strangers. Also, she had threatened to throw herself under a truck on the highway. All knives and razors were hidden, and a lock was installed on her bedroom door. Colette missed school during this time, and her father missed work in order to care for Colette's mother. Eventually, the family committed her to a psychiatric facility in Denver, about eighty-five miles from home. They visited on weekends. She became progressively worse and remained heavily sedated. She hated it there and refused to eat. Her weight dropped to eighty-five pounds—a skeletal image at five feet two inches.

Children stared at Colette when she returned to school, and some who normally ignored her tried to befriend her in order to ask details of her mother's suicide attempt. Colette was repulsed by their curiosity. The family brought Colette's mother home again, and in March of 1968, at age forty-five, her final suicide attempt, through use of carbon monoxide poisoning, ended her life. Colette describes her feelings:

She was finally out of her misery. I was relieved more than grieved, as my whole relationship with my mother was more tormenting than nurturing. I mourned more for the mother I never had. . . . I felt really alone from then on.

A woman from human services came to the house to help for a while. After that, the three did the best they could. There were many TV dinners, pot pies, and Pop-Tarts. Colette's father still will not discuss her mother's mental illness, as though he is ashamed of it. Colette describes her father as bad-tempered and manipulative, always anxious to play the guilt card. In him, she sees an angry man with passive-aggressive tendencies. She states:

My father is very childlike and always has been. He's never been a daddy to me. I've been mother to him and my little brother.

Twenty-two days after the death of Colette's mother, they learned that Charles had been killed in Vietnam, blown up by a booby trap. Neither Colette's mother nor Charles knew of the other's death. Colette learned of Charles's death by noticing a photo of him in uniform in place of the one of her father that belonged beside her mother's wedding picture. When her father emerged from his bedroom all red-eyed and puffy, Colette asked if Charles had died. Painfully, he replied, "Yes," and walked off. Later, she gave the bad news to Peter, who just sat there sullenly in silence. Colette sensed her troubled life unraveling. It was after Charles's death that she learned that he had been a half brother and that as a teenager Charles had discovered his adoption by finding legal papers among his father's belongings. Colette was left unsettled by Charles's death:

the circumstances surrounding the molestation were now lost forever. She could never ask why. She grieved his loss, wished she could have known him better. Colette was traumatized by the quick succession of tragedies in her early childhood. She reflects:

After all this happened, I remember asking God for help. I guess I needed to make sense of all this. I needed strength to go on living, hope for the future. The rest of my eighth-grade and ninth-grade years were spent being wild. I had this new found freedom, since my mom had been very strict. I was sort of in charge of my life for the first time. My father, brother, and myself sort of went about our lives separately. We finished the school year and my dad went back to work. During summer vacation, my dad took us to Disneyland, thinking that would make up for the tragedies. We got to stay in nice hotels with swimming pools, eat in restaurants, etc., all of the things we never usually could afford. Later, my dad said we spent all the life insurance money on us and tried to blame us for his subsequent money problems.

After the Disneyland venture, Colette befriended a group of wild girls and began drinking, smoking, doing drugs, and being promiscuous with boys. She lost her virginity at fourteen. Sex wasn't that great; she endured it to please the boys.

Until Colette's father remarried, she and Peter were much on their own. Colette was in charge of household chores and mothering Peter. Because her wild streak had rendered her a liability, her father initially wanted to send her away to a girls' school but found it to be too expensive. Instead, he set out to find the children a new mother. He succeeded when Colette was fifteen and Peter ten. Two of Lorraine's four children were still living with her, but the reconstituted family was no *Brady Bunch*. Colette, her father, and Peter moved into Lorraine's house and were reminded of their intrusion daily. Colette hated all of them. She sensed that to Lorraine she was merely a "Cinderella," and Peter was teased and tormented by the daughter. Their father required Colette and Peter to call Lorraine Mother right away, although Lorraine's children barely spoke to Colette and Peter's father.

Colette's father and Lorraine fought constantly about the children or something petty. Finally, Colette left home at seventeen. She lived with various friends who were out on their own, sleeping on their couches and eating dry cereal. She missed a lot of school. Eventually, Lorraine located Colette and asked her to come home. But home was a continuation of the same old thing.

Her senior year was a marked improvement for Colette. She became spiritually active through the school organization Campus Life and Fellowship of Christian Athletes and entered a friendship network that influenced her life positively. She graduated with the bare minimum of required credits and was voted the "most unlikely to succeed." Convinced that she was stupid and had no future, Colette set her sights at maintaining her established work pattern of waitressing at the Pancake House, Dairy Queen, and the like.

THE ABUSIVE RELATIONSHIP

Colette was nearly eighteen when her friend Kyle invited her to move up to the mountains to waitress with her at a small restaurant for the summer. It was the perfect out from Colette's miserable home life, and her parents approved. Her father was always glad to be rid of her; he blamed her for some of the family tension, mainly because she clashed with her stepsister. The restaurant was isolated in the mountains, and Colette and Kyle lived in the upstairs quarters. A married couple owned and operated the business and lived with their eight-year-old son behind the establishment. Colette met Lanny that summer. She recalls her first impressions and the initial reeling in:

When I first met Lanny, I was repulsed by him. He was five years older than I was and had missing teeth, and the rest were rotting. His style was early construction worker, and he operated heavy equipment for a living. He was really confident about himself. He pursued me with a vengeance, always eating and drinking at the restaurant and playing pool with the rest of his construction crew, some of whom were his brothers. He always asked me to wait on his table, and he left me a five-dollar bill, which he folded into a bow tie for a tip. I was intrigued but still repulsed by his looks. He asked me out all the time and told me I was beautiful. Finally, I allowed him to take me out for dinner. I think he wore me down and I kind of felt sorry for him, but I can't explain why.

After this first date, Colette never regained her distance from Lanny. She knew he was not her type, yet he controlled her much as her father had—through guilt. She learned of his alienated family and mean and alcoholic father. And she noticed that Lanny drank too much. Colette became convinced that her becoming Lanny's girlfriend would make him so happy that he would stop drinking. She had the power to change him, and he would be eternally grateful. Eventually, they entered into a sexual relationship, and Colette capitulated every time. They frequented cheap hotels and had quickies in the car, which made her feel dirty and used.

Once during that summer Colette, Kyle, and two platonic male friends from their high school went out together to dinner and to a bar. When they returned to the restaurant, it was closed, but Lanny was outside, passed out drunk in his car. Colette woke him to find that he was angry that she had gone out with friends, and he accused her of having had sex with them. Colette details the scene:

I told him I wouldn't stand for this behavior and I didn't want to see him anymore. He then cried and said he had no reason to live anymore and he would drive his car off a cliff and I would read about it in the paper the next day. I took him seriously and agreed to continue to go with him. [Kyle], during all this time, couldn't believe I would put up with this behavior, but I told her I loved him and felt sorry for him, even though in my heart I knew I was in trouble from the start. Soon, as he put his sights on me, I couldn't get away. It was like I was under his power. The summer ended and Kyle went to college.

Colette agreed to move with Lanny to Grand Junction, Colorado, when his crew acquired a new construction job there. They lived together without her family knowing. Eventually she found work in Grand Junction, first busing tables, then at a state home for the mentally disabled. She worked in the infirmary and fed, diapered, and bathed the worst cases. It was a terrible experience; sometimes the patient died right there in her arms. She had frequent nightmares and became depressed but found consolation in the fact that she was providing a needed service. Colette had no friends or family contact during this period.

Lanny stayed out late drinking and playing pool on weekends. If Colette complained, he became obnoxious and called her a bitch. If she threatened to leave, he said he would shoot himself. The pattern was clear. When Colette withheld sex in anger, Lanny raped her. At times he would push her and intimidate her with looks. Eventually, Colette realized that Lanny was cheating on her. That was it for her; she moved out and shared a house with a nurse from work and some other young women.

Colette felt liberated now that Lanny was out of her life. But then he began to call and beg her to return, saying he loved her and that she meant everything in the world to him. He promised to quit drinking and cheating on her. He apologized profusely. Hoping he would give up, she told him she needed time to think. He continued harassing her: crying, begging, parking outside her house, and accusing her of sleeping around. He said, in fact, that some of her housemates were prostitutes and that she lived in a well-known whorehouse.

Colette did date during this time and enjoyed some nice men, but she always feared that Lanny would materialize to beat them up. He was violent with men, including his brothers, and participated in bar brawls, at least one involving guns. Eventually he slipped a marriage proposal into his persistent pleas and promises. When he had remained on the wagon for an impressive while, Colette agreed to marry him, mostly because she thought she should. She explains:

He continued trying to convince me to get back with him, calling me, bringing me flowers, telling me stories of his undying love for me. This time, he wanted to get married. He promised he would quit drinking, and he did real good for a while. I agreed to marry him, more out of thinking I had to, feeling like I wouldn't be able to ever get away from him. Part of me also wanted to believe his promises and maybe we could live happily ever after.

Colette was nineteen when she and Lanny married in a Lutheran church in her hometown of Greeley. Her father gave her away, and Kyle was her maid of honor. Lanny's family were all there from Grand Valley, Colorado. Colette recalls little about the wedding, except that she was sad and felt powerless, knowing in her heart that this was a big mistake. During the five-year marriage, the couple moved an average of around twice a year, following Lanny's construction work. They rented apartments, then eventually bought an eight-by-thirty-six-foot trailer that they pulled across Colorado, Wyoming, and Utah. Most of the time Colette remained unemployed, because they were always on the move.

A year into the marriage Colette became pregnant. Lanny was happy, but she was afraid, knowing this would complicate her ability to leave him if necessary. In her sixth month Lanny withdrew all support and affection and stayed out late in bars again. When Colette learned of his sexual involvement with one of the flag girls on his crew, she announced her departure. He retorted, "Not with my baby!"—her fear had been realized. When she threatened abortion, he grabbed her by the hair, threw her onto the bed, and began choking her. She fought him, finally digging her nails into his cheeks, leaving claw marks down his face as he withdrew.

Always after these fights Lanny would weep apologetically. Again he would plea his undying love and promise to stop. Colette always wanted to believe him and thought that perhaps she provoked the attacks by nagging and talking back. Maybe it was her fault. Sex was the usual way of making up; Colette was nauseous as Lanny climbed on top of her. Lanny minimized the abuse, saying, "Oh, I might have slapped you once." He claimed that Colette was overreacting. Sometimes she wondered herself.

Colette delivered Michelle in September 1974, at age twenty. She felt as though she were a child having a child. Lanny was working far away, so Colette stayed with his grandmother the month before the birth. His sister transported Colette sixty-five miles to the hospital and held her hand throughout the long, excruciatingly painful process of natural childbirth. Lanny showed up drunk at the hospital the next day. Colette recalls her embarrassment with the nurses' refusal to allow him to hold his infant daughter. Once again, Lanny had let her down at a vulnerable moment.

Colette resisted motherhood. Michelle would not nurse and was colicky her first four months. Colette and Michelle stayed with Lanny's grandmother while Lanny completed his Wyoming job, then the three settled in a trailer park in Salt Lake City. It was there that Colette learned of Lanny's continued infidelity; because he suspected venereal disease and thought Colette should be checked, he confessed to sexual activity in Wyoming. Colette was devastated; she sought advice from Lorraine, who had become her primary parental figure by default. Lorraine told her to forgive Lanny and give him another chance. In Lorraine's defense, Colette's family was unaware of Lanny's pattern of abuse and adultery. They had lost contact after the wedding; most of the time Colette had no phone. Colette did forgive Lanny, but she never forgot.

Colette became increasingly depressed and isolated. She elaborates on her pain at this juncture:

Life went on pretty much the same, him drinking at the bar after work, me doing a mediocre job, at best, of being a mother, feeling like such a failure in life. There were so many times I wished I was somebody else, like my friend Kyle who had loving parents and went to college, was an accomplished gymnast, and was a wonderful Christian girl. She was my only friend at this time. Our only contact was an occasional letter letting me know about her college life and boyfriends. She always included

Scripture from the Bible about how God loves me. I don't think I ever told her about the abuse. Her letters were a mainstay for me. It was nice to know someone I knew was so special and she cared about me.

Colette, Lanny, and Michelle moved several more times during the next two years. Family life remained pretty much the same. Colette learned to expect the drinking and abuse and attempted in various ways to keep it in check, including not complaining, fixing Lanny's favorite meals, and having his bath prepared when he returned home from work. Also, she never refused sex. Lanny brought home pornography and wanted her to look at it with him. He was good to Michelle but did not actively parent her; never did he watch, bathe, or diaper her. He was just proud that she was his offspring.

Back in Greeley, Colette's father and Lorraine's relationship had failed, and she was seeking a divorce. Colette did not blame Lorraine but worried how her father and Peter would survive on their own. It was hard. They stayed in different odd places, including a small trailer without heating or air-conditioning. Colette's father went from one odd job to another after his retirement from the army, in her mind never amounting to anything professionally. Peter washed dishes to support himself in high school, then went on to work his way through college. He never got into trouble. All this went unrecognized by their father. After her father's divorce, Colette took charge of holiday family gatherings, as well as such parental responsibilities as getting Peter a graduation gift from their father. Peter and their father visited Colette, Lanny, and Michelle at holiday times. Her father pointed out to Colette that Lanny earned a good living and that a woman's job is to keep her husband happy.

GETTING OUT

Colette left Lanny three times during their marriage. She remembers little about the first time—only that she left at 2:00 A.M. and drove about 350 miles toward Greeley before running out of gas alone and in the middle of nowhere.

The second time, however, is memorable. Peter had come to live with Colette, Lanny, and Michelle in Wyoming for the summer of 1977, to work for Lanny. One evening after work Lanny encouraged Peter to accompany him to the bar and play pool. While there Lanny attempted to get Peter drunk and involve him in a fight with another patron. Then he picked a fight with Peter, calling him a pussy. In anger, Peter left the bar, walked home, and told Colette of the incident. Colette was furious, as she had always been protective of Peter. It was dark, and the two were standing outside the trailer, with Michelle sleeping inside, when Lanny sneaked up from behind, drunk and surly, proclaiming Peter to be a liar and a baby. Peter yelled back, and Lanny punched him in the face, leaving blood spurting from his nose. Enraged, Colette leapt on Lanny and was thrown to the ground by her hair. Peter ran for the police. As Colette lay on the ground, Lanny entered the trailer and locked her out. She was terrified by his threat of never again allowing her to see Michelle. She could not rule out his hurting Michelle just to spite her. She beat on the door, begging him to let her in, then remembered that the keys were in the truck. Lanny rushed out at the sound of the ignition as Colette sped off for help. With heart pounding, she backed over Lanny's foot. He yelled and fell to the ground, so Colette stopped to help him. Even with the agonies of their relationship, she was horrified at the thought of having hurt him.

As it turned out, Lanny was not hurt after all. He had feigned the injury; his steel-toe boots had protected him. When Peter arrived with the police, Lanny sobered up on the spot and told them that Colette had attempted to run over him and that he had punched Peter in self-defense. Then he advised them that they were on private property and to leave because everything was fine. When Colette was asked to tell her story, Lanny glared at her, poking her chest and admonishing her to tell the truth. The police assured Colette that they would arrest Lanny if she wished to press charges. Instead, she wanted to leave safely with Michelle and Peter. They were off to Greeley that night.

Peter moved in with a friend, and Colette and Michelle stayed with Lorraine, who had eventually caught on to the dynamics of Colette and Lanny's relationship and wanted to help. Colette's father interpreted this decision as betrayal, but Colette and Michelle could not live with him because of the creepy man with whom he shared an apartment. He suggested that Lorraine's taking in Colette and Michelle was simply a ploy to get him back. On another occasion he remarked that Lorraine was helping Colette in order to spite him. Colette's father often demonstrated his inability to think past himself.

During her time with Lorraine Colette worked as a cocktail waitress. She remembers little about those days. She does remember that Lanny assured her that he had quit drinking and had learned his lesson. And she recalls promising herself that there would be only one more chance. If he started drinking again, she was out of there for good. In her heart she was certain this time. Colette describes her sense of desperation and her final honeymoon with Lanny:

I was disappointed in myself for going back to him. I felt no one would want to help me if I had to leave again. I think I knew the good behavior wouldn't last long, but I wanted to believe it would. Lanny was really wonderful for about three months. He was loving, home right after work, and we went on our first vacation this time.

Another problem had manifested itself during this marriage to Lanny: Colette became addicted to Percodan, the painkiller her physician was prescribing for her migraines. She recalls that when she took the first pill, she felt better than she had her entire life. So, of course, she wanted to take them every day. The drug helped her cope, but ultimately there was a downside. Her body required increasingly more drug to achieve the same effect, and she had a limited supply. Coming down off the substance produced irritability, severe stomach pains, and itching from head to toe. Once, when Michelle was whining and getting on Colette's nerves, Colette tossed her into the wall, screaming that she was the reason Colette had to stay in the abusive relationship. Colette was horrified with her own behavior, even though she knew it was chemically induced. She was able to wean herself from the drug several months after her final escape from Lanny.

Colette, Lanny, and Michelle left Wyoming for Colorado and settled into the tiny mountain town of Natarita. Eventually, Lanny began stopping at the bar after work for a game of pool, then for a beer. He reassured Colette that he would not get drunk. She decided to stay and not overreact over a few beers, as long as he didn't get drunk or violent. However, the incident that would propel Colette's final exit was on the horizon.

One evening Lanny returned home drunk and offered his apologies, which fell on deaf ears. When Colette refused to even look at him, he became belligerent. Four-and-a-half-year-old Michelle was in the bathtub; hearing Lanny hollering at her mother and calling her names, Michelle cried out, "Don't fight. Please don't fight." Lanny then told Michelle to "shut the fuck up." Colette was shocked to hear Lanny use such language with their daughter. At this point Lanny had not hit Colette, but she could see it coming. Then there was an unexpected knock at the door, and Lanny, who had sobered up on the spot, was summoned to a work-related emergency. The beating was aborted; Lanny was gone. Colette knew she must act quickly. In terror, she collected Michelle and some clothes and toys, and they ran for their lives.

A week prior to this episode, Colette had spotted an ad for alcoholism-related counseling and had called the hotline. At her counseling session, she had filled out a questionnaire and, from that, had been able to identify Lanny as an alcoholic. She had related her tale of drinking and abuse to the counselor and had asked if she should leave Lanny; she had needed the counselor's permission. When he had inquired as to why she had not left already, she had replied that Lanny's entire world would collapse. With that, the counselor had quipped, "So, you think you're God? You think you can make someone else's life happy?" She had replied, "No, I don't think I'm God; I think I'm nothing." He had told her that he had never met someone with such low self-esteem. They had parted with him clarifying that the decision was hers.

That meeting was a pivotal moment in Colette's exit process. Armed with this new perspective on alcoholism and abuse, she had been prepared to move forward. At the proper time she had confronted Lanny with a realistic appraisal of their marital problems and asked if they might seek counseling together. Lanny had denied the existence of marital problems but had told her she could go alone. The end was in sight. Colette's personal commitment to leave had been reinforced by Lanny's refusal to get help. So, after her terrifying flight with Michelle from the trailer, she stopped at a pay phone to call the local hotline. Because Natarita had no shelter, Colette was instructed to go to the Ray Motel on Main Street, where she and Michelle would be cared for by the owner, Dan Crane, and his wife, who took them in and hid their truck. It was the practice of the Cranes to provide emergency shelter to the needy of that community—a precursor to Project Debbie, a nationwide, growing, privately funded program created in 1991 by a hotel executive in Houston, Texas, which matches homeless women and their children with donated, unbooked hotel rooms.

Throughout the night Colette prayed and stared out of the window at Lanny's truck, which was parked at the bar across the street. She saw him leave the bar and then later, in the early morning, cruise the town in search of them. Tucked away out of sight in the motel room, Colette once again took stock of her situation. She recalls:

I prayed for God's help that night. I knew I needed supernatural strength to escape his power over me. I knew this had to be the final exit because I had been daydreaming and hoping that something bad would happen to him, like an accident at work, and he would die. Then we would be able to get insurance money and move away and not have to worry about money or Lanny harassing us. I didn't consider suicide because I didn't want Michelle to be left behind. All of these thoughts scared me to think I was thinking them.

The following morning a woman related to the hotline came for Colette and Michelle and, over breakfast, helped plan their escape. She arranged for police protection while Colette removed their belongings from the trailer and as they waited for Colette's father and Peter to take them away. This woman's caring gesture concluded Natarita's response to a battered woman on the run. The tiny community had mobilized a machine of donated services designed to enhance the safety and well-being of its members. This surely was community at its best. At the bank Colette discovered that Lanny had closed the account; she had eighty dollars to her name. Then came the final encounter with Lanny. He appeared at the trailer when Colette was packing up, and the police allowed him to enter and speak with her. He begged her to stay, then attempted to choke and rape her. The police intervened, but again, out of fear of retaliation, she would not press charges.

Colette's father and Peter arrived, and the four traveled, with U-Haul in tow, over the western slope, through the mountains, in a blizzard and with bald tires. Colette recalls the sense of combined freedom and terror that accompanied that ride. In Greeley, Colette and Michelle joined Colette's father and Peter in their run-down trailer. Colette took over the domestic responsibilities, and the men cared for Michelle while Colette worked at a Mexican restaurant and otherwise went out. A black-and-white framed and dusted photo displayed in Colette's home now, depicting a pigtailed little girl and her grandfather caught in a glance of mutual adoration, suggests that these were fairly happy times.

Despite his distance from her, Lanny began harassing Colette. He phoned her with news that he had spies reporting to him, that he knew that she was out "whoring around" and leaving Michelle unattended. He was headed to court to prove her an unfit mother. Once he showed up at her job and glared at her from the bar. Another time he picked Michelle up from her sitter's, then an hour and a half later dropped her off at the trailer before leaving town. With that, Colette had a restraining order issued. Because they were living far from each other, Lanny bothered Colette with his physical presence on weekends only. Colette eventually filed for divorce, and Lanny quit harassing her once he found a girlfriend. Colette struggled financially to buy a home for her and Michelle and to enroll in cosmetology school. Lanny's attempts to eschew child support payments failed.

HEARTBREAK

In her second year away from Lanny and seven months into beauty school, tragedy stuck again, this time harder than ever. Michelle was hit by a car one Sunday after church, as she played hide-and-seek with her friends. It is said that she was behind a telephone pole when a boy yelled, "I see you, Michelle," and she plunged into the path of a passing car. She never regained consciousness and died six hours later at age six. There are no words to describe the loss of a child, and no feeble attempts are offered here by Colette or me to detract from that reality.

Peter was sad but said little as usual. True to his nature, Colette's father expressed relief that he was not the one caring for Michelle at the time of the accident. Lanny and his family traveled to Greeley for the funeral. Colette remains grateful that there was not the subtlest suggestion of blame. Three years after Michelle's death Lanny appeared at Colette's doorstep, wanting her to accompany him to the gravesite. Colette declined. Both had remarried, and Lanny was now recently divorced. Colette believes Lanny was just checking on the possibility of her availability. He told her that he had never stopped loving her. Another time, he phoned her in an attempt to sell her an air purifier for her hair salon. And more recently, since her relocation to Nashville, Tennessee, he called to request a school photo for his wallet; the original had become ruined. Each time Colette saw or heard from Lanny, she trembled uncontrollably. The nightmare continues—that she is somehow back with him in a chamber of doom. The only merit to this dream is that Michelle is there. Colette gets to call back Michelle, but never in peace. Sometimes she believes that she had to lose a daughter to truly break free of her abuser.

REFLECTIONS

Looking back on her childhood and on her life with Lanny, Colette likens herself to a cat with nine lives. She says that those who know her now see her as a resourceful and self-assured woman. Even though seventeen years have passed since she left Lanny, the memory of the pain remains strong. She describes herself as a veteran of war. Colette realizes now that throughout the caretaker role that she assumed over and over again—with her mother, her father, Peter, Lanny, and Michelle—she never learned to care for herself. She acknowledges that she has had to teach herself to respect her own feelings and to ask and, if necessary, demand that her own needs be met. She still struggles with this, for it is difficult to avoid succumbing to familiar patterns.

Part VII

LEGACIES OF LOSS AND DEATH

CHAPTER FOURTEEN

Blanca

I met Blanca in my aerobic exercise class at the local tennis club. We were a small and rather intimate group of people who gathered several times a week to enjoy music, movement, and a bit of conversation. One day that conversation touched on Blanca's abusive former husband; one thing led to another, and soon Blanca and I were in her home, audiotaping her life story.

Blanca brings to this collection a glimpse of Puerto Rican poverty around the 1940s and witness to the plight of an ambitious Catholic immigrant family who struggled to upgrade their lives by moving to the United States and taking on factory work in New York City. Blanca's is the story of a lonely girl trapped in circumstances, including a deeply entrenched gender hierarchy, that ushered her into an abusive marriage. Her biography also alerts us to the dreadful personal toll exacted by United States's involvement in the Vietnam War.

Today Blanca is a resourceful and refreshingly direct woman who focuses her energies on her own ethical, moral, and intellectual development. At forty-seven she shares homes in Clearwater, Florida, and Bowling Green, Kentucky, with her fiancé and aspires to complete a college degree in interior decorating. Ultimately Blanca hopes to find challenging and satisfying work in Bowling Green.

The second of three children, Blanca was born in rural Puerto Rico to a family of simple means. Her father worked in the field cutting wood, and her mother took in sewing to help with the family's finances. Both parents were products of families similarly situated. Poverty was the rule in her parents' environment; no one knew anyone who had much more.

Both Blanca's parents came from large Catholic families. They met and married when her mother was in her teens. Her father, six years her mother's senior, used to pass by her mother's house every afternoon as she sewed handkerchiefs on the front porch. Eventually, he began to stop for conversation with her. When they married, they settled into a two-room house with a dirt floor, built for them by Blanca's father.

Blanca endured fragile health during infancy. After a couple of months, she failed to develop normally—to crawl, sit, stand, walk, or talk—and she lost her hair and refused to eat. Physicians were unable to diagnose her illness. They told her parents to give her anything her heart desired, for she could not survive much longer. But Blanca's parents never succumbed to such pessimism. They sought remedies everywhere and tried them all. Then Blanca's mother had a dream that directed her to the cure. In that dream she prepared and administered to her ailing baby a medicine derived from specific herbs growing nearby. So in both the dream and in reality, Blanca was strengthened and healed by this herbal regimen; her shiny black hair reappeared, and her cheeks pinkened. One day, as she sewed on the porch, Blanca's mother witnessed three-year-old Blanca pull herself up and walk along the wall—a precious moment to be relived endlessly within the family. Blanca was her parents' miracle child. Time and again her mother reminded her of that special status; she had been chosen to fulfill a mission yet undetermined. Blanca marvels at her parents' zeal and tenacity during that ordeal.

But the struggle did not end there. Within weeks of Blanca's wedding, tragedy would strike again, and this time the circumstances would alter the life trajectory of the family dramatically. They would forsake the familiarity of their world—the traditions of their kin and their very culture—to rescue their firstborn, and only son, from the clutches of a deadly virus. Blanca's brother, Eddie, one year her senior, was diagnosed with polio at age four, a condition considered untreatable in Puerto Rico at that time.

The parents immediately planned their strategy. Eddie would qualify for free medical treatment in the United States. First, the father would travel alone to New York in search of work. Then, when settled and financially able, he would send for Eddie and his mother and admit Eddie to the hospital for treatment. Blanca and her younger sister, Lucy, would remain behind in Puerto Rico, until the entire family could be reunited in New York.

The plan was implemented without a hitch. Blanca's father joined his brother, who years before had relocated his family to Brooklyn in search of work and a better life. Spurred by the passion to save Eddie, Blanca's father found work in a factory that produced women's handbags; there he would remain until retirement. His brother's apartment was crowded, so Blanca's father slept in his brother's car until he could get his own place. In the meantime, Eddie, Blanca, Lucy, and their mother waited in Puerto Rico. Blanca recalls how everyone missed her father and how her mother struggled with the three children, one quite ill. He sent letters and money, but still it was difficult.

A few months after he arrived in Brooklyn, Blanca's father had acquired a two-room apartment and had saved enough money to fly Blanca's mother and Eddie there. Eddie was placed in treatment right away. Now Blanca and Lucy awaited their turn, in the home of their maternal grandmother. Blanca remembers being without both parents and Eddie. Those were strained times for her and Lucy; they were so young, only five and four years old. But within a few months the two girls had boarded the airplane, escorted by their mother's brother, and shortly thereafter were back in the arms of their parents. Blanca smiles as she recalls that reunion and her new home:

Then we got together again with the family. I remember seeing my parents at the airport and saying, "At last we are together." We went to the apartment, and I remember at that time my mother's brother [who had delivered the girls to their parents] was staying in the same apartment [until he too could afford rent and to send to Puerto Rico for his parents and siblings so they could all have a better life]. So it was a big family staying in this apartment. I remember it would get so hot [in the summer] and so cold [in the winter]. And the bathtub was in the kitchen.

Eddie responded well to his polio treatment, and within a couple of years he had fully recovered. The price was dear, however. New York urban life would take its toll on this simple, rural, Catholic, close-knit, Spanish-speaking family. Blanca continues to contemplate the "what ifs" surrounding that decision, now four decades past, to leave the homeland.

Immediately upon arrival in New York, Blanca's mother took factory work as a seamstress; she would remain in a series of such jobs until retirement age. When the children were not with their parents or in school, they stayed with their father's mother, a woman of nasty temperament who lived nearby. Both there and at home, Blanca, as older daughter, assumed a domestic role, a role in which she was to remain. Now, at five, that meant monitoring Eddie and Lucy, keeping them safe, and taking responsibility for misdeeds and accidents. Later, by age ten, her responsibilities expanded to include cooking and cleaning after school. In time, Lucy helped. The house was expected to be spotless, and laundry was done by hand. Even after there was a washing machine, Blanca and Lucy were prohibited from using it. Their mother used it for herself and the two men; the girls continued to wash their own things by hand and to iron them.

Those days growing up in New York were focused primarily on a survival strategy that depended heavily on nuclear and extended family support. As a little girl Blanca was plagued with chronic ear infections and recalls her childless aunt from the Bronx coming to take her to the doctor once when she was very sick. And she remembers her parents growing distant from each other over those years, creating separate lives. Blanca never saw her father hit her mother but suspected that this occurred when the children were away. She sensed the doom surrounding her parents' relentless efforts to maintain some semblance of their traditional ways. And she and the others, each from his or her unique perspective, watched it all slip away.

When Blanca was about nine, the family moved next door into a larger apartment, one with a kitchen, living room, and two bedrooms. Her parents had a private room now, as did Blanca with Lucy. Eddie slept on the living room couch. Then, a couple of years later, around 1960, they moved again, this time to a larger apartment across town in a better neighborhood. Blanca reflects:

We moved to a bigger apartment, but we still had the same [sleeping arrangements]. The reason my parents moved to another was because the area we lived previous, it was changing. Our parents didn't want us to live there. So then we moved to a better side of town. And we still had a two-bedroom, living room, and kitchen. And my brother still slept in the living room, but, you know, he never seemed to mind. He never seemed to complain, "Oh no, we want our own beds." He never did that. We weren't spoiled like kids today.

From these adolescent days, Blanca remembers her parents' continued narrow focus on working and making money, and she recalls that they barely spoke to each other anymore. There was a clear double standard applied to Blanca and Lucy on the one hand and Eddie on the other. Blanca elaborates:

At that time I noticed a lot of changes started to occur in the family. My parents became very strict on my sister and I. And there was a limit to what we were allowed to do. For example, my brother was allowed to be in the Boy Scouts [and] go out to the YMCA. He could learn how to swim, go camping, and we were not allowed to do that. We weren't allowed to have friends come over or friends call us at the house. My brother's friends were allowed to come over. His friends were allowed to call. I guess that's what they call a man can do what a woman couldn't.

I remember once I wanted to be in the Girl Scouts so bad that I called the [telephone] operator asking information. And she must have gotten ahold of me, or I got ahold of her three or four times, because she said, "Can I speak with your parents?" because I wanted to be a Girl Scout. I didn't know how to go about it, so I called the operator.

Blanca realizes in retrospect that had the operator been able to catch her parents at home to speak to them about her wish to join the Girl Scouts, they would not have allowed her to join anyway.

Initially, all three children attended public school. Then, when Blanca entered fifth grade, their parents transferred them to a Catholic school that extended through junior high. Eddie graduated from that junior high and went on to complete public high school. The girls disliked the harshness of the nuns, so they were transferred to the public system as Blanca entered seventh grade. Neither graduated from high school.

School was difficult for Blanca. There she was required to speak English, but at home only Spanish was allowed. Communication was always limited at school. Though she and Lucy enjoyed learning and liked their teachers, their grades were never good. Their parents were unable to help with homework, and the girls were not allowed to call or meet with schoolmates. Eddie's grades were good because he studied with friends and got help at the YMCA and from priests at church. Blanca and Lucy were reared to be wives and mothers. In the early years they attended school only to conform to the law; they were allowed and perhaps encouraged to continue after that primarily to keep them out of mischief.

Because she was "sheltered" from peer friendships, family was an especially critical dimension of Blanca's life. She was close to both Eddie and Lucy, but during certain periods she and Lucy were inseparable. Blanca considers Lucy to have been the pretty one, with boys in constant pursuit. The two girls attended different high schools, Blanca preparing for cosmetology and Lucy for nursing. Blanca recalls the loneliness when the two separated for high school. They made separate friends and Lucy got into trouble a few times, requiring their mother to meet with her teachers. Blanca smoked cigarettes against her parents' wishes; that was the extent of her delinquency. Holidays were memorable, growing up in New York. Blanca's family would join her mother's kin in the Bronx for pleasant family gatherings.

Upon graduating from high school, Eddie was drafted into the army and ultimately sent to Vietnam. He had been contributing significantly to the family economy, so his absence required Blanca and Lucy to increase their employment at retail shops from part-time to full-time. That meant dropping out of high school. The family missed Eddie terribly when he left for Vietnam. His absence pulled Blanca and Lucy even closer but shrouded the household in a general loneliness. Blanca sensed her parents' pain and their fear when Eddie's letters arrived a bit late. When he returned a year later, Eddie was different—emaciated with malaria and entrenched in a world of prescription drugs and marijuana. Drugs had been dispensed to stimulate the soldiers, to sedate them, to dull the pain, and to minimize the side effects of the other drugs. Unable to shake his addictions and continue his education, Eddie reenlisted about two years later and again was deployed to Vietnam. This time, his "chopper" was shot down, and he remained "missing in action" for the six-month hospital stay that followed. The family survived in terror until Eddie's unexpected appearance on their doorstep, uniformed, with belongings tucked under his arms, and very thin.

THE ABUSIVE RELATIONSHIP

When Blanca was fifteen, in 1964, the family purchased a home in Brooklyn. At last Eddie had a bedroom.

Even in high school Blanca and Lucy were not allowed to date. The only boys with whom they spoke outside the school gates and workplace were Eddie's friends who visited the house. And those boys knew to keep their distance from Eddie's sisters. But all of this was of no consequence to Blanca; she recalls no interest in dating or in boys in general. Having witnessed the decline of her parents' loving relationship, she preferred to avoid that possibility. The split between her parents had become painfully apparent when Eddie was on his first Vietnam tour—her parents fell apart and were of no comfort to each other. They led independent lives; even their money was kept separate. Everything was still provided for the children but not in the context of the affection they had once known. Blanca did not want a marriage like that of her parents.

Three years after her parents bought the house in Brooklyn, a Puerto Rican family of four from the Bronx moved in across the street. The two families were of similar background and age and shared experiences relating to adjustment in the United States, and they quickly became friends. Their son, Louis, was a year older than Blanca and took a clear liking to her. Blanca was friendly toward Louie but not interested romantically. When he asked her for a date, she explained that she could not go unless he would ask her parents. He asked, they said yes, and so Blanca and Louie were off to spend the day at the Bronx Zoo. Blanca describes how her relationship with Louie began:

You gotta remember, since my parents were so strict against dating, I didn't even notice [Louie], and, you know, I can be honest with you, I wasn't looking forward to any relationship. I was looking forward to knowing who I was and getting what I wanted out of life before starting a relationship. . . .

He started taking a liking to me. He noticed me, since he lived across the street. He noticed me when I came home from work in the evening. He noticed when I got up in the morning to go to school. Coincidentally, he went to work the same time I went to school, and we got on the same subway. . . .

The reason my parents said it was okay [to date Louie] was because they knew his parents. They lived across the street, and they knew that I was not going to go with him to his house without them knowing it. I think that was one of the reasons they okayed it, because they could see a lot of what was going on.

Shortly thereafter, Louie was drafted and left for training in Texas. He and Blanca had become friends, so they corresponded by mail and spoke on the phone regularly. When he came home for Christmas, he had a diamond ring for her. They married the following summer, just before Louie departed for Vietnam and Eddie was returning from his first tour there.

Blanca had not spent time alone with Louie before the marriage; she had never gotten to know him well. He seemed kind, thoughtful, and considerate. She had learned of family problems, including his father's sexual molestation of Louie's sister, Alma, and Louie's suicide attempt, and felt pity for him. Blanca reflects on her decision to marry Louie:

I liked him, but I am honest with you, I don't know whether I loved him or not. I didn't know whether to believe him or not . . . so I told Louis, yeah, I felt something for him, but you know, I thought that's what I had to do. . . . I felt that I was of age already and that I was supposed to get married, have children, so I did.

While Louie was away that year, Blanca remained in her family home and kept her job at Bobby Ann's dress shop. When he returned, the two of them moved into his family home (still across the street from hers) with his parents and Alma, and Louie found steady work as an auto mechanic. Shortly thereafter his father died of cancer. Relationships quickly became strained in this new setting. Louie's mother was an obnoxious and meddling alcoholic, who seemed to resent Blanca's intrusion. So after eight months there, at Blanca's insistence, the couple established their own household in a three-room apartment nearby.

But independent living failed to improve Blanca and Louie's relationship appreciably. And they did not get away from Louie's family for long. About six months later Louie's mother joined them. She and Alma were in conflict over the mother's married boyfriend, and besides she clearly just wanted to be with Louie; he was her favorite child. So Blanca and Louie gave up the bedroom to her and slept on the couch.

Louie was economically controlling from the beginning. Blanca never knew how much money he made or how he spent it. He was responsible for paying the bills, and the bank accounts were his. She received a modest household allowance and felt free to ask for a little extra periodically. Never would she ask for much. The physical abuse commenced soon after the couple took up residence with his family. The first violent incident occurred in the aftermath of Blanca's miscarriage, and, in fact, she unwittingly precipitated it. Blanca was both upset and confused with the loss of this child. Both she and Louie had welcomed the pregnancy, and Blanca was well attached to the baby when she lost it. She recalls mourning the death alone; it was as though no one else viewed the fetus as a real child.

Additionally, Blanca realizes in retrospect, the miscarriage triggered a hormone imbalance that left her emotionally vulnerable, complete with mood swings. She knew she was not herself but failed to understand why. An argument erupted over Blanca's having spent time that day at the hospital with Eddie, who was still recovering from malaria. Out of frustration, Blanca slapped Louie; she was stunned when he reciprocated. Blanca never again struck Louie, but that single incident would be resurrected time and again throughout their relationship as justification for Louie's assaults on Blanca.

Blanca is convinced that Vietnam changed Louie. She had seen what it had done to Eddie; Louie's transformation was a replay. He emerged from the experience listless, unfocused, without direction, and hooked on alcohol and drugs. Additionally, Louie came back mean. He saw no purpose in the war, resented having been forced to go, and was bitter over how he had been treated there. Angry and with a sense of entitlement, he returned home self-centered, uncaring, and controlling. There was no recovery. Blanca acknowledges that Louie had always displayed that macho temperament so typical of Latin American men. But she says that this in itself rather benign trait combined with the demons of Vietnam to produce a regrettable distortion of the man she once knew.

By the time the couple had moved into their own apartment, Louie's rage was way out of control, and the violence had escalated from slaps to shoves and punches. And now, because they were in their own place, it expanded to include fists through walls and flying plants and pottery. No longer were incidents restricted to the context of arguments; they were coming from seemingly nowhere. The house was not just right, or the meal did not suit his taste. Within a couple of months of the move, Blanca became pregnant again, and again they were both pleased with the prospects of parenthood. About four months into the pregnancy Louie struck Blanca publicly for the first time—it was on a beach in the presence of his family. Apparently a man was eyeing Blanca as she sunbathed in her swimsuit. Louie approached the stranger, hollering, "Hey, what are you looking at!" The man responded quite simply that he thought Blanca was pretty. Blanca chastised Louie for his inappropriate behavior toward the stranger. If he did not want men looking at her, he should stay near her rather than sitting several yards away, playing dominoes with his family. Louie slapped her on the spot. The argument carried over into their home that evening, with Blanca on the offensive, until Louie apologized for his jealousy and promised to restrain himself in the future.

With the arrival of Derick in December of 1969, their domestic life took a turn for the better. Louie's mother's boyfriend defected, so she returned to her own home and Alma, leaving Blanca, Louie, and Derick to begin life anew in privacy. For a year a tranquillity settled over Blanca and Louie, not because they had established an improved rapport but because Blanca, now unemployed, was devoting herself to the baby. She simply put Louie and his moods and outbursts on the back burner. Quite telling of the climate of their relationship and the household during that period is a brief exchange between them at Derick's homecoming. Observing Blanca's involvement with the baby, Louie queried, "Just who do you love more, me or the baby?"—to which Blanca quipped, "The baby!"

A year brought noticeable change in Louie. He began spending his off-work time in bars with friends and drinking heavily. And there was thinly veiled evidence of women in his life. After outbursts with Blanca, he would stay weeks at a time with his mother—though he was always careful to get Blanca's allowance to her. The abuse intensified and the words became harsher. When he arrived home late for dinner and Blanca resisted warming over his food, he was quick to remind her that her purpose was to serve him. She recalls one incident following a violent episode:

My mother [and brother] came to see me the following day, and I didn't even come out of the room [because] I was afraid if my brother saw [my black eye], he would kill him. So I just said to tell them I am sick.

Blanca began to speak of leaving Louie, but he let her know that she was going nowhere, now that she had the baby and was without education, job, or car. Besides, no one could love her as he did, not her father or even her mother. And what man would want her with a baby?

Just fifteen months after Derick's arrival, Blanca, now twenty-four, became pregnant with Cynthia. Though she remained ambivalent about bringing children into her marriage, she was pleased to have a little girl this time. Cynthia's arrival brought much joy, but it also introduced a couple of new elements of tension into an already troubled family. After the age of two, she remained medically fragile because of a ruptured appendix that nearly took her life. That near-fatal experience, coupled with Cynthia's resultant frail health, meant that even fewer of Blanca's resources were available to Louie. He seemed to resent Cynthia for that, but there was perhaps another reason why he remained aloof from her. Since learning of Alma's sexual abuse at the hands of their father, Blanca had emphasized early on that there would be none of that if they were to have a daughter. Louie seemed to walk on eggshells around Cynthia.

Following Cynthia's brush with death, Blanca became pregnant again. She could not bring another child into that family such as it was, so suggested an abortion; Louie concurred and transported her to the clinic. After the procedure, he dropped her at home and went off to socialize with friends. With time Blanca became deeply embittered toward Louie for allowing that abortion, feeling that he should have used that pregnancy as an incentive to alter his life to accommodate another baby and the family as a whole. He knew the decision to abort had its source in his abuse of Blanca. He was the one who had always wanted a family; now she was having to endure the abortion. If he really loved her, he would have put a stop to it.

GETTING OUT

When Cynthia was a year old, Blanca initiated her marital exit process with an economic scheme. During one of the times when Louie was off staying with his mother, Blanca reported him as having abandoned her, and for the next eighteen months collected welfare payments and stashed them under the carpet. To that she added withholdings from her household allowance from Louie. She planned to take the children and leave when she had enough money.

Louie had not wanted Blanca to work outside the home since the dress shop closed, leaving her unemployed soon after he returned from Vietnam. But then, about five years into apartment life, he wanted a house for the family. In order to accumulate money, he moved them back into his mother's house with the understanding that Blanca would get a job. By this time Alma also lived there with her husband and baby. The plan was that Blanca and Alma would work full-time staggered hours and care for one another's children. Everyone would profit financially. Blanca clerked at the Robert Hall department store. The family's welfare payments were discontinued at this point.

As with the first time Blanca had attempted to live with Louie's family, the arrangement did not work out. It was a brutal seven months. Blanca's family was relegated to basement quarters, and

Alma failed to do her share. Blanca did the household cleaning, cooking, and laundry, and she came home to find the children unfed and Cynthia in dirty diapers while Alma was sleeping or caring for her own baby. The last straw was an incident where, in one of his rages, Louie hit Derick. Blanca describes that turning point:

My little boy had a bowl of grapes, and he went to walk by Louis, and Louis had a cut on his foot, and my little boy tripped over it. He was in such pain, and he reached and hit my little boy very hard. And my little boy just fell on the floor, and he had scrapes all over the place, and that ticked me off. I told him how I felt, and I said, "Why are you so stupid, you know, to leave your feet in the middle of the living room if you know it's not feeling well. . . . What do you expect—everybody to step aside because you're stupid not to see a rock and bump into it? You don't hit my son like that." And I grabbed both of my kids and I went to the basement. And he beat me in his mother's house. That's when I decided there ain't nothing.

The next day Blanca quit her job, collected the children, and took a cab to Lucy's apartment in Brooklyn. The following morning Louie and his mother came to retrieve them. They challenged Blanca's ability to leave Louie—until Blanca produced the money from her secret hoard. In the meantime Blanca and Lucy had hatched a plan to take their children to Florida and to buy a house there with Blanca's money. From photos, Blanca had always thought Florida was beautiful.

Louie persuaded Blanca that if only he could go with them to Florida, their problems would be over. He acknowledged that his family was a major impediment to their marriage, and that they particularly needed to escape his mother. He offered to forsake his lucrative longtime job of managing an auto repair business.

Blanca accepted Louie's offer to start anew. They traveled to New Port Richie, Florida, and contracted to have a new home built. Then they returned to Brooklyn until it was completed. For those six months the family stayed in Eddie's two-room apartment, while Eddie lived temporarily with his parents. In April 1974 Blanca, Louie, and the children headed for Florida, followed by Lucy and her small son. A year later Lucy reunited with her son's father, and they got a place of their own in nearby Largo. In 1983 Lucy met an untimely death there as a victim of cervical cancer.

The first two or three years in their New Port Richie home were the high point of Blanca and Louie's marriage. Louie found employment as an auto mechanic, and Blanca managed the household. There was no drinking, no abuse—there were no other women. For the first time Blanca could relax with her children. She recalls pleasant walks with them. There was now more time to indulge Cynthia, who grew progressively weaker from her ruptured appendix. Also, for the first time in her marriage, Blanca made friends—in the neighborhood and at Kingdom Hall (a religious organization), where she attended Bible study classes.

But this all came to a halt when Louie's family relocated to be with him and settled only a town away. Gradually, life regressed. Louie began spending his time with his family; then came the drinking, abuse, and women. It all gushed back: the sense of betrayal and entrapment, as well as all the anxieties and fears that accompany battering. Then came the devastating blow. In October 1977, at age six, Cynthia died quite suddenly of complications from the ruptured appendix. It was not altogether unexpected, but death is never really expected either. Derick lost his childhood that day, at only eight years old.

Four months later, having had precious little time to grieve, Blanca became pregnant—a condition she faced with great ambivalence. Timmy nearly died once during the pregnancy and again at delivery. Blanca welcomed him enthusiastically after all and felt his survival was a blessing. Derick and Timmy took to each other immediately; Derick was and would remain protective of his little brother. And Timmy looked to Derick for direction. Later that month, suffocating in debts from Cynthia's medical treatment and burial, Blanca sold their home and relocated the family to a less expensive house. By this time Louie had become a peripheral household figure—he was with his mother much of the time.

In 1985, when Derick was thirteen and Timmy was five, Louie struck Blanca for the last time. Beatings were frequent now—about every two weeks. This incident was different because it elicited a visible visceral response from Derick, who stormed out of the room, clenching his fist in rage. Before this, Derick had shown little if any emotion; he would routinely escort Timmy into the bedroom to shield him from the violent episodes. Now he was old enough to know what it all meant. Blanca refused to allow her sons to live in this abusive reality.

It was time to leave Louie, and Blanca knew she could not support the children—she had no advanced education, money, job, or even car. They were safe and content in their home; she would not tamper with that stability. Louie and the boys all got along; Louie was good to them, and the boys were now old enough to survive without her on a daily basis. Blanca describes that parting scene:

Before I left we sat down and I told them that I had to do what I had to do. Things were getting out of hand, and I didn't want [Derick] to have to see his father abuse me, and he understood. They both understood. We always kept our relationship open and we always talked. I always expressed my feelings to them. They didn't say anything. I walked out the door. I left a few minutes before Louie got home. But I never left the kids; I left Louie.

And, in fact, for the first few months, Blanca commuted daily after work from Tampa (ninety minutes away) to make sure that they had all they needed and to spend evenings with them. Blanca walked out that summer afternoon with her suitcase and never moved back to the house. By arrangement, a friend transported her to the home of her cousin in Tampa. This was a long-anticipated and carefully planned exit. Blanca had simply been waiting for the proper time. She instructed the boys to explain to Louie why she had left and why he should not attempt to reverse her decision.

Upon Blanca's departure, Louie shaped up immediately. He became a sober, responsible father, and his mother moved into the house to help care for the boys. Blanca's visits were well received by all, even after Louie remarried. She struggled to keep her relationship with him on an even keel.

Upon arriving in Tampa, Blanca purchased a 1970 Dodge and procured sales work in a Clearwater department store. She was awarded an uncontested divorce in six months. She had taken nothing from the house and was required to pay no child support for joint custody. After a year she got her own apartment in Clearwater. Two years after she left and immediately following Louie's divorce from his second wife, he phoned Blanca seeking a reconciliation. She declined. It was a civil exchange.

REFLECTIONS

Blanca has no regrets. Her relationships with Derick and Timmy have remained close and mutually rewarding.

In Blanca's case, the gender of her children strongly affected the circumstances of her exit from abuse. Never would she have allowed a daughter to live with Louie without Blanca being there too; her image of Louie's father sexually molesting his own daughter was too compelling. Blanca's original escape agenda, conceived eight years into the marriage, when Cynthia was a year old, involved stashing money away, then leaving with the children. Buying the house with Louie and Cynthia's death profoundly altered her exit trajectory. Consolidating her stash with Louie's finances to purchase the house dashed her chances of getting away with the children because she was unwilling to compromise their standard of living. Having only sons allowed Blanca to spare her children a childhood of witnessing woman abuse without jeopardizing their life chances. They could thrive in a reasonably healthy and safe environment, with the benefit of two actively involved parents who lived apart. Blanca believes that she made the best choice from among her options. She stands by that choice and remains appreciative of Louie for upholding his part of their parental responsibility.

CHAPTER FIFTEEN

Judy

I shall not soon forget the scene surrounding Judy's approach to me about participating in this book project. She was a particularly enthusiastic, outspoken, and uninhibited front-row student in my Introduction to Sociology course. One day she came up after class to suggest the possibility. Clearly that approach required every smidgen of courage that Judy could muster. She was uncharacteristically nervous and reticent about discussing the abusive relationship in her past.

When I invited her to accompany me to my office to talk about it, she resisted, saying that probably her story would not qualify, and so I would not be interested. I coaxed her to walk with me as far as the lobby, but she would not continue on into the corridor that led to my office. So there we stood amidst the crowd of mostly strangers as they scurried and darted about between classes. Judy's eyes swelled and watered as she told me that her story probably was not what I wanted because her abuser was now dead. As she spoke, she became progressively disturbed; by now the tearful scene was being noticed. Still Judy would not move on into my office. I pressed her about the death. She painfully explained that soon after she had severed ties with her husband, he hanged himself in their home where she was sure to find him. Astounded, I proclaimed outrage at the lengths to which a batterer will go to exert control over a woman. How dare he extend his campaign of abuse from beyond the grave!

In his death he could still reduce her—in public, moreover—to a quivering shell of a woman. On the spot Judy visibly transformed: her shoulders straightened, her eyes dried, composure settled over her. For more than three years she had remained convinced that this death was her fault; now she knew it was not. It was that easy. We agreed to meet later to commence work on her biography. Then, as the crowd in the lobby broke, Judy hurried on to her next class. We went on without a hitch to produce her remarkable story.

Today Judy focuses her energies on rebuilding her life and those of her two young daughters. Now in her mid thirties and having worked as a secretary and office manager for eighteen years, she has taken steps to improve their life chances by enrolling in the university's graphic design program. Her long-range plan is to open her own advertising and printing business. With the support of Social Security benefits, a small stipend from her husband's retirement plan, and her mother's help with childcare, Judy is able to maintain a comfortable lifestyle for her family while attending school fulltime.

Judy comes from a rural south, central Kentucky background. She lived with her parents and her two sisters, seven and eleven years her senior. She remembers that as the youngest child, her sisters picked on her constantly as only siblings can. Judy's family, from what she recalls, got along fairly well—that is, when everyone conformed to the oppressive discipline system. While home represented closeness and caring, it demanded strict conformity to traditional gender roles. Judy remembers one incident at age sixteen. She had been doing well in high school, and her teachers strongly encouraged her going on to college. However, her parents refused to even discuss it. She had to beg and pay her sister to provide transportation to her SATs.

Because of the age differences between Judy and her sisters, she often felt as though she were an only child. The chronic tension and jealousy between the two of them and Judy left her with the sense that she was not really one of them—that she was on the outside looking in. When she was around seven, one sister locked her in the school bathroom, refusing to release her until she sang some stupid song for her and her girlfriend.

Judy was ill much of her young life and, as a result, was restricted in physical activity. Hepatitis A, rheumatic fever, and asthma contributed to her childhood isolation. Judy says, as a consequence of that isolation, she "grew up more in love with books and daydreams than did most kids." She remembers being something of a handful for her parents, seemingly always in trouble and questioning everything. She recalls attempting to run away from home at around five years old over someone's being abrupt with her. And she incessantly challenged her parents' authority. Judy's flagrant nonconformity would bring her parents right to the edge.

Judy was fairly popular during her elementary school years, changing best friends every other day, and loved the whole learning process. Teachers always encouraged her. When she was around nine, her father changed occupations, from that of a small grocery store owner to that of an ordained Baptist minister. Judy recalls how that dramatically altered her life:

Our home environment became even more strict and straitlaced. I always felt like my actions were constantly being monitored by everyone. Basically, to please my father and mother, I became the perfect "preacher's kid." I played the piano at church, sang with the choir, got good grades, and pretty much tried to become something I really wasn't. . . . I remember feeling frustrated at never having a Sunday to call my own—do what I wanted to do rather than spend it at someone else's house after church services.

Upon entering high school, Judy was uncomfortable with herself both physically and emotionally. She was totally unprepared for puberty. Her bustline developed early, so in some ways, at first, she felt like a freak. Because her mother was uneasy with the subject, she avoided discussing Judy's maturation and sexuality with her. And both sisters had married and left home, so were of no help. It took time for Judy to realize that she was a normally developing girl. Her recognition during her high school years that her family was somewhat economically disadvantaged added yet another source of tension at that typically awkward stage. She felt a bit inferior because of it.

During those days Judy maintained several casual and a few close friendships. School was both fun and interesting—at least as far as the classes went. Though her interest in boys surfaced long before that, she was forbidden to date until age sixteen. She had always had boyfriends in the lower and middle grades, but with physical maturation that all changed. Judy simply was not as comfortable with boys in high school and wound up being rather introverted. Her body had matured ahead of her emotions. She suffered a kind of self-consciousness common to adolescent girls: the sensation that everyone was noticing the ways her body was changing—and that they were staring at her. She dared not show interest in boys; after all, the church matrons were watching for her to act on her budding sexuality. There would be no reputation of being "that kind of girl"! Most boys were just friends. Judy dated very little before high school graduation.

By mid-adolescence, Judy had become painfully aware of the hypocrisy associated with her fundamentalist religious setting; the backbiting, malicious gossiping, and power-playing left her unsettled and angry. There were always petty problems with the congregation, but one incident relating specifically to her father marks a critical juncture in her life. Judy reflects:

My father was a very jolly, outgoing kind of person, and he truly loved his congregation. There was a couple in his church who were having marital problems. I remember my father counseling them hour after hour. It seemed he was called out in the middle of the night a few times, and for a few months, daily phone calls could be counted on. He was always there for them, no matter what time of the day or night they called. He eventually helped them reconcile. Shortly after this, rumors started to arise about my father's sanity: forgetfulness and strange and inappropriate behavior. I will never forget my father's face when he was told who had started those rumors—the very couple he had spent so much time and heartbreak over. He forgave them, even though they never apologized or even acted remorseful. I was never able to; it seemed like all of the time and concern that he had given them was just a joke. After that ordeal, I seemed to take a perverse kind of pleasure in doing everything a preacher's kid was *not* supposed to do.

Looking back now, I think I felt that if the so-called religious congregation wanted something to talk about, I would give them something to talk about. I failed to understand my father being able to forgive and forget. I wanted him to get angry and fight back. I guess this was my first real experience with hypocrisy, and I was outraged by it. But I'm not really sure if I was outraged at the church congregation or by my father.

Judy loved her family; however, she always felt different, and sometimes estranged, from them. She viewed the world differently from the way they did. They perceived life as black and white, while she saw shades of gray. They viewed her independence and self-reliance as odd and eccentric, while she viewed her family as compliant, inert, and without passion.

STRIKING OUT, MOVING ON

To support her new and rather wild lifestyle, Judy got a part-time clerical job after school with a mining company. Her relationship with her parents deteriorated rapidly. She came and went at will; they knew virtually nothing of her friends or whereabouts. She began drinking and doing drugs heavily at the close of her high-school career. Judy's parents did not understand what had happened to their perfect child, and, to tell the truth, neither did she. There was not much that Judy didn't experiment with and attempt to do in those days. Looking back now, she remains unable to explain that behavior. Perhaps it was a combination of hormones and personality clashes. She still wonders.

At seventeen, upon graduation from high school, Judy continued working, now fulltime, with the same mining company, and accumulated some money. On her eighteenth birthday she quit that job and informed her parents that she would be moving to California. She packed up her car and drove alone to Diamond Bar, in southern California. Immediately, she sought work from the local employment agency and, with her first job interview, was hired by Sears to fill a position in their purchasing department. Judy remained there for three years and proceeded to live in the fast lane. Parties, alcohol, men, and drugs were her life in California. What she did not do was sleep, worry, or tax her intellect. The family did not hear from her at one point for nearly six months. Judy learned quickly that one cannot trust everyone and that a person can rely on only oneself. Those days of hard knocks, independence, and self-reliance prepared Judy well for what was to come later in her life. Both parents suffered strokes while she was away—a grim reminder of their mortality. She found herself realizing that they were not nearly as stupid as she had once thought. And she came to understand that what they had done for her throughout her life was rooted in love and the desire to protect her—normal parental behavior.

After four years in California Judy wanted to return to Kentucky to be closer to her parents. At twenty-two, she settled in the Bowling Green area, about twenty-five miles from where she had grown up, and secured a fairly prestigious secretarial job in a hospital. Having developed an outgoing disposition during her California stint, she got to know a lot of people very quickly and was always surrounded by a large group of partying friends. Relationships were tentative during this time, except for one involving a man to whom she somehow found herself engaged. The engagement disintegrated after about nine months, when his job relocated him to another state. Judy suspects that no love was lost there.

Judy was around twenty-six when she met her husband-to-be, Randy, and had reached a point in her life of thinking seriously about settling down and having children. Up till then she had been a party person who dated a lot of men, many of whom took advantage of her sexually or financially. In retrospect Judy believes that she was seeking reassurance of her desirability to men. At that time she believed that having a boyfriend was synonymous with beauty and worth—no matter what you had to do to keep the boyfriend. There had been no physical abuse in any of those relationships, however.

Randy was about a year younger than Judy and seemed to be a nice, warm kind of person. Before Randy, she had picked older, more emotionally distant men. Judy met Randy while celebrating the birthday of a girlfriend in a local bar. He was a surveyor with the Kentucky Department of Transportation, employed in Paducah but on brief assignment in Bowling Green. They talked for hours that night and seemed to have much in common, including the love of music, dancing, and sports. Judy learned that Randy's family consisted of his parents, two brothers, and two sisters, and that all of his siblings were married. His father worked as a plant supervisor in Paducah, and his mother was an elementary school cafeteria manager. Randy spoke affectionately of them all. He made Judy laugh and seemed to be impressed with her independence. He joked about how poorly he had done in high school, stating that he had been bored and simply uninterested. His main pastime now was jogging. When the evening was over, the two exchanged telephone numbers and addresses. Randy was to return to Paducah the next day. Judy remembers:

He sent me several cards over the next several weeks from Paducah and phoned frequently. He always made me feel very special and wanted. We carried on a long-distance relationship for about nine months—getting together when we could and calling all of the time. I later learned that he had been in a divorce process when we met that continued through our long-distance courtship.

About this time Judy was beginning to feel restless with her job and was considering transferring to Florida. Randy became distressed with the prospect of their separating and proceeded to talk Judy out of that and into moving to Paducah instead. So she quit her job and relocated to be with Randy. Almost immediately she found a similar hospital job in Paducah. During Randy's separation and divorce he had returned to his parents' home. With Judy's arrival they moved into an apartment together. At first life with Randy was fun.

Looking back now, Judy sees much that she refused to recognize then. Randy believed that he should be allowed unlimited freedom in the relationship and that Judy was to be the sit-at-home type and never question his whereabouts. This double standard irritated Judy. When she did question Randy, arguments, sometimes intense in nature, ensued. Judy believed it common courtesy to call if you were going to be late. Randy was undependable about time; he was never where he was supposed to be. He would disappear for hours at a time, and she would be unable to get a straight answer on where he had been. Randy thought Judy was prying when she thought she was simply showing concern. But, as long as she didn't push it, they got along fairly well. At this point there was no physical abuse. After their arguments Randy would apologize profusely and go out of his way to make up to Judy. He would bring her gifts, flowers, or surprise her with something unusual.

About nine months of living together found Judy and Randy discussing marriage. Randy backed out of their first wedding date, stating that he was not ready. But he flew into a rage and subsequently lapsed into deep depression when she suggested splitting up. They did marry on the second planned date—July 25, 1987. Judy became pregnant with their first child very quickly. Things immediately went downhill. Judy elaborates:

At first he was not happy with the pregnancy, and he demonstrated such with verbal abuse, but soon he realized that my condition could be employed as a way of controlling me. Randy seemed to always want me to be under his thumb. He hated the fact that I was independent and would not ask him to take care of anything. Yet if I did ask for help, he seemed almost gloating about it. He was very fond of telling me that I had better be grateful that he stayed with me; after all, who else would want a pregnant woman. During this time, his dislike of my voicing my opinions became apparent. If I mentioned women's rights in a supportive way, I was told that I was crazy and I didn't know what I was talking about. Many ugly and unpleasant arguments ensued.

Randy criticized me constantly about weight gain (I wound up gaining about twenty pounds during my pregnancy) and how I acted (I suffered from acute morning sickness and was hospitalized for dehydration, so I didn't feel peppy). My friends from work were very concerned about me and my pregnancy. My obstetrician became concerned since I lost about ten pounds in my second trimester because of

Randy's constant supervision (there were constant comments on any-thing and everything I ate, sarcasm became commonplace with him, and he accompanied me to the grocery store so he could monitor what I bought). I never told my family about any of this. The few times Randy was around my family, he was the perfect son-in-law—always very lov-ing and indulgent.

The first episode of real physical violence occurred when Judy was about five months pregnant, in December 1987. Randy had gone to a work-related holiday party. She was not allowed to go since she was not "looking good enough." He returned home drunk and disorderly, ranted about the pregnancy, calling her stupid, fat, and ugly. Judy recalls this as the first time she truly feared Randy. He was out of control. When she spoke up, he hit her for the first time with his fist. Judy responded with anger—big mistake. That's when he went wild, shoving her around, knocking her up against walls, slapping her, and hitting her with his fists. The final blow was one to her stomach. Believing that he might have done some real damage, Randy immediately began to cry and beg forgiveness. Fortunately, the blow did not seem to harm the baby. But when Judy went into premature labor about a month later, she wondered if Randy's vio-lence may have triggered it. Bed rest was required for a couple of weeks, and eventually Judy returned to work, but now part-time. Crista was born two weeks early. Randy swore that he would never again hurt Judy, that Crista and she were the only important things in his life. And for a while things eased up. In reality, though, Judy sensed that it was just a matter of time before he would explode again. She recalls flinching every time he raised his hand or even if he came very close to her. After that first beating incident, Judy was unable to respond to Randy sexually; consequently she was called a cold bitch. Sex became an issue of bitter contention between them.

Though the relationship was filled with anger and consterna-tion, there were no violent scenes again for about a year. Randy badgered Judy to lose the weight she had gained during pregnancy. Their going out always culminated in an argument over why she could not look as good as someone else, why she did not dress a certain way. Sometimes it would be verbal abuse, and other times it would be a slap, always ending in tears and recriminations. Randy always said that he didn't know why he behaved this way, but that he loved Judy and would try to do better.

Day-to-day life with Randy was stressful; Judy lived in constant fear. She could never predict his mood and, as a result, became moody and difficult herself. He had lived in Paducah all his life and seemed to know everyone in town. They could not walk down the mall without being stopped innumerable times by his friends. Everyone seemed to like Randy so much that it still seems hard for Judy to reconcile the two different sides of him. She remembers feeling that no one would believe her if she were to divulge his abuse. Everyone viewed Randy as a wonderful, sweet, easygoing kind of guy—and to everyone else, he was just that.

Randy seemed to delight in fathering Crista and expressed determination in being better at it than his own father had been. Randy was a good father; Crista worshiped him. He always took her with him, and he loved playing with her. The only problem regarding Crista related to discipline. Judy was always made out to be the bad guy, while Randy left her undisciplined.

Randy's father always had been critical of him, and his mother had attempted to compensate for that by giving Randy money. Judy recalls Randy changing a tire at his parents' house and his father standing over him yelling that he couldn't do anything right. When Randy came inside the house, his sisters and brothers seemed to view the incident as a big joke. They continually put Randy down and viewed him as the sweet but stupid little brother. Randy never spoke out against his siblings. He never defended himself.

Randy hated his job. He was subordinate to several men, and, from what Judy could determine, they ridiculed him constantly. He was always seeking other work but never seemed to find that job that would pay him lots of money for doing little or nothing. Nearly every day when Randy returned home from work, he would immediately collapse in the recliner. He was exhausted, even though his job was not physically demanding. Judy surmises that the stress of just being there drained him.

GETTING OUT

When Judy became pregnant with their second child, approximately two years after Crista's birth, things declined rapidly. Financially, Judy and Randy were always in a mess because of Randy's mismanagement of funds. He refused to listen to her financial advice, even though she dealt with finances every day at work. He was not happy with this pregnancy, and Judy heard a lot about her trapping him and tying him down. This pregnancy was a repeat of the first. One morning, when Judy was about six months along, she woke up ill. Randy refused to take her to the doctor because she was "just wanting sympathy." When Judy threatened to call an ambulance, Randy reluctantly took her to the emergency room, where she was diagnosed with spinal meningitis. He visited her only once in the hospital and refused to let her speak with Crista. When Judy phoned, Randy would say Crista was asleep or outside playing—anything but let her speak with her daughter.

After Lisa's arrival, the marriage took a distinct nosedive. Randy came to the hospital twice after Lisa's birth. He brought Crista once to see her new sister and then returned two days later to bring Judy home. As the family became acclimated to its new member, Randy spent less time with Lisa than he had, and still did, with Crista. Crista was still his pride and joy. Judy believes Randy did love Lisa, but that his now established bond with Crista overpowered those sentiments.

The worst and deciding incident that promoted Judy's exit from her relationship with Randy occurred shortly after Lisa's birth. Judy describes it this way:

I began a new job with a government agency that had rejected his employment application. This seemed to deeply affect Randy. One day he disappeared for hours and returned home drunk. He began criticizing everything; the lunch dishes weren't washed and put away (I was busy with the children), and then it escalated into screaming at me for trapping him in a cold nothing-of-a-marriage. I was rocking Lisa when I suddenly found myself projected out of the rocker and slammed against a wall, with him screaming at me to listen to him. As I tried to protect the baby, he proceeded to let loose with his fist on my back, shoulders, and arms. I screamed for him to stop or he would hurt the baby. He replied that he didn't care; my protests seemed only to accelerate his anger. I finally worked my way around to the kitchen and pulled a knife on him, still holding Lisa in my arms. This caused him to back up and weigh his options, I guess. It gave me enough of a reprieve that I got the baby back to her crib and got her away from the violence. I put down the knife thinking that he had lost his steam, but I unfortunately was very wrong. I was kicked, shoved around, and hit repeatedly. Finally, he seemed to pass out on the couch, and I gathered up the kids and went to his parents. That was the only place I felt I could go. When I reached Randy's parents, they were shocked at first and then told me that I shouldn't nag at Randy so much. Basically, I was told that I deserved this kind of treatment. However, they did take me in and protect me and the children until he sobered up.

Randy came over the next day, and his parents took the children with them so Randy and Judy could talk. He was once again apologetic but blamed the alcohol. He claimed to not remember a lot of what happened. Judy realized then that she could count on no help or support from his family. She remembers looking at Randy and feeling that she didn't know this man anymore. She was unsure at that point that she ever had known him. But she was certain of one thing: somehow, some way, she was going to escape this mess. Up to that point she had believed that she deserved this kind of treatment: that there was something wrong with her, that it was all her fault. Perhaps it was the intensity of this last incident that changed her mind; no one could deserve to live under such tyranny.

The family returned home together, but Judy never felt so isolated and alone in her life as she did that day and for the remainder of her marriage. She confided in no one about the incident or the abuse in general. She was too ashamed and embarrassed and was confused about her feelings.

Randy was arrested about a month later on charges of trafficking in cocaine. This was Judy's first awareness of his involvement in drugs. It reinforced her determination to get out. She was terrified with the thought of him possibly taking Crista with him on a drug transaction. When Judy told Randy of her intention to leave, he cried and pulled all of the old guilt strings—she was kicking him when he was down. He stated that the kids and Judy were all that was worth living for and that he would not survive this bout with the law if they did not stay with him. Still today, Judy regrets agreeing to see Randy through his legal battles; once again he had reeled her in with guilt. But he was well aware that Judy and the children were all but gone from his life and were destined to move out at the resolution of his legal problems associated with the cocaine charges. This occurred in July 1991; Judy was thirty-two years old, Crista was three, and Lisa was six months.

That November Judy's father, who had been seriously ill with uncontrollable diabetes and depression, committed suicide. Her mother was asleep in the house with her father when he shot himself. This incident, of course, was especially traumatic for Judy's mother. Judy had spoken with her father a few days before he died and had realized something was seriously wrong, but she was unaware of the depth of his depression. He had not allowed Judy's mother to inform Judy of the critical nature of his illness. Judy's sisters were and remain angry with their father about his death, but Judy never felt anger, only incredible sadness. For most of Judy's life, her father was a funny, outgoing, warm individual, and she believes that when the depression set in, he simply was overwhelmed. Her father's death was difficult for everyone, but her mother had been so dependent upon him that she still finds it difficult to adjust. Randy provided Judy with very little support during this traumatic period. He refused to speak of the suicide and barely even showed up for the funeral. As a final reconciliation attempt, Randy and Judy saw a church counselor during this time, but observing Randy weave his tale of deception only angered Judy. Randy could not be honest even in that situation.

At Christmas 1991, a few weeks after Judy's father's suicide, her mother came to Paducah to spend the holidays with Judy, Randy, and the children. It was then that she came to realize that things were not right between Randy and Judy. At first she questioned why Judy was so cold to Randy. Judy responded simply that she had serious doubts about the survival of the marriage. It was not until four years later that she told her mother of the abuse; her sisters still do not know.

Judy and Randy hardly spoke after her father's funeral. It was all over but the moving out. Judy describes the painful realization of that fact:

I had already left Randy. Even though we still shared the same house, we were no longer together. . . . I no longer feared Randy. He knew I no longer feared him, and he did not understand it. I felt nothing toward him most of the time. But there were times when I looked at him, alternating pity with hate. The thought of his touch nauseated me. It was rather strange, after years of my self-confidence being slowly picked apart and destroyed by this man, I realized that I could leave him. I would catch myself staring at him sometimes and know that I was going to leave him. The constant wear and tear on my emotions had left me feeling nothing for quite a while, so when the feeling started coming back, it was pretty painful.

REFLECTIONS AND AFTERMATH

Judy realizes now and did then that she had to leave Randy as much for her children as for herself. She shudders to contemplate what might have developed with the children and Randy once the children got past the "cute, dependent" stage. She is convinced that it would have been a short step from beating and degrading her to his starting in on the children, once they got older. It was difficult for Judy to accept the fact that she was not responsible for Randy's actions. She had believed all along that she was the source of her and Randy's marital problems. She preferred to accept the blame, perhaps because it is easier to attempt to change oneself rather than one's spouse. Finally, Judy realized that she was responsible for only her behavior. Now she accepts blame only for tolerating the abuse. She regrets having married Randy. She had been not so much in love with him as with the idea of being married and having children.

Randy sensed Judy's withdrawal and was desperate to reverse it. He reverted to gift giving and calling home during the day just to chat. She recognized his agenda, however, and refused to reenter the trap. Randy knew that Judy was determined to move out with the children. They never actually discussed that possibility, but Judy refused to plan a future with Randy. She was strong and confident for the first time in years and was looking forward to a future without Randy. She knew it would be a struggle with two children, but she also realized it would be one that she could manage.

On January 11, 1992, Randy was awaiting sentencing on the drug charges, now less than a week away, when the unthinkable happened. Judy tells it this way:

A few days after our youngest child's first birthday, Randy left home one morning, after telling me how much he loved me but I was impossible to live with. When he returned home a couple of hours later, he went directly to our garage and hung himself. I found him about 45 minutes later.

Randy got her best and last. Because he had taken his own life, Judy was left with the ultimate burden of guilt—and this happened just after she had managed to free herself of the chronic guilt associated with a six-year battering relationship. With this single final violent act of control, Randy robbed Judy of the possibility of true freedom from his abuse. Even now he brutalizes her with that death image. A masterfully planned and executed act of terrorism altered the landscape of her life forever. He simply refused to let her get away from him.

Here is Judy's appraisal of her progress on her journey to freedom and health, as well as her message to those women still in captivity:

I feel great pity for him now. I believe any woman who was strong and independent would have threatened him and his self-esteem. Personally, I am glad that all of the upheavals and chaos are out of my life, but I regret that it ended the way it did. There are days still that he controls my actions as surely as if he were here—self-doubt, lack of confidence, and unresolved anger, to name a few. But those days are becoming less frequent.

The only message I have for someone in an abusive relationship is to try to hang on to a little bit of her self-worth. Try to remember that you are an important person in your own right and worthy of having a relationship that is healthy. I would say that to lose faith in one's self or to have that taken away from you is devastating. Try to retain that and do what you have to do in regards to your current relationship, whatever that might be.

CHAPTER SIXTEEN

Freda

Freda responded to my national call to battered women's shelters. She attends weekly group meetings at Finex House, a women's shelter in Boston. Because Freda stays in homeless shelters and is, therefore, hard to track, I asked the director of Finex House, Chris Womendez, to work with Freda and me In coordinating phone calls and my visit. It worked like a charm. I visited Freda for a couple of days in the winter. Her infant daughter, Natalie, was ill at the time, so much of my getting to know Freda and audiotaping her was in the context of caring for Natalie. We taped in the sitting room at the church-supported homeless shelter for mothers with children where Freda and Natalie were living. Natalie happily observed, drank from a bottle, and napped as we talked. When I became hungry, the shelter cook offered me lunch. One day we three bused from the suburbs in to Boston Children's Hospital to get Natalie to a doctor. Most of what I learned from Freda came as we rode buses, took walks, and sat in hospital waiting rooms. In the frigid temperatures we were all bundled warmly, Natalie harnessed comfortably to her mother's chest as we moved from place to place. Freda preferred the front harness to the back harness because it let Natalie feel her mother's heartbeat. One evening Freda and Natalie joined me and my criminologist friends at a concert and dance sponsored by the American Society of Criminology, whose annual meeting I was attending at the time. We all took turns cuddling Natalie so that Freda could get out there and dance too. It was a charmed evening.

Freda's story introduces us to an underworld of poverty, racism, sexism, physical disability, disease, homelessness, interpersonal abuse, and societal neglect—a brutal place where a competent mother can be denied her children for a simple lack of money, where children can be yanked from their caring mothers and siblings to be sexually abused in foster care. Freda lives in a place where most of us wouldn't be caught dead.

Freda is a refreshingly lucid, direct, and articulate mother of five who, at age thirty, struggles daily to reclaim custody of her four oldest children and to secure safe housing for all of them.

Freda knows little of her parents' beginnings. They met in the military somewhere in the South in the 1950s, then somehow a decade later reconnected in Boston, Massachusetts, where Freda was born. Her mother was the unwanted product of a Toledo, Ohio, teenage union and had been adopted and reared as an only child by a kind, middle-aged Santa Barbara, California, couple. In young adulthood, she traced her Ohio kin and, in fact, ultimately relocated to and died in Ohio. She had married once or twice and had three children when, at age thirty, she took up with Freda's father in Boston; he was more than two decades her senior.

Freda's father came from Mobile, Alabama, and at some point migrated to Boston with his mother, wife, and four children. Eventually he divorced and sent back to Alabama for his longtime soulmate, Ruth, who would remain with him in Boston until his death at seventy-nine. His mother, who worked as a domestic until age eighty-five, lived with them till she died—when Freda was seventeen. Freda's father was a career army man and a World War II veteran; after retirement he joined the Coast Guard. Freda's mother was White; her father was Black.

Freda's parents never married, and shared residence only those few times that her mother was in transition and in need of temporary housing. Her father always shared his house with his mother, Ruth, and whichever of his children happened to be there. Her mother worked steadily as a head secretary and rented comfortable apartments for herself and her children. Freda and her maternal siblings always had enough of the things money can buy.

For the first nine years of her life, Freda lived in Boston, alternating between the homes of her parents. When she was living with her mother, she was often placed in custody of baby-sitters and older siblings. At her father's house she was mostly with her grand-mother, who even in death remains her spiritual stronghold. Per-haps the best way to introduce Freda and her early years is through her own voice. Freda describes her homecoming as a newborn:

Well, this is interesting. I'm in a big house; it's real huge. It looks like giants might live here. Who the heck is Mommy calling? Well, this is nice—I've friends named Brenda, Eugene, and Ouida [pronounced Weedah]. Wait a minute: Mom says these are my sisters and brother. They look cute. Brenda [age fourteen] is huge, dark, muscular, and she's wearing a green shirt and brown pants. Eugene [nearly eight] is tall, slender, pink, and he's wearing all black; his pants are shiny. Ouida [seven] is wearing a white T-shirt and dark blue pants. She has a lot of freckles; she's pink-skinned too and slightly chunky. Brenda and Eugene have black hair; Ouida's hair is a blondish and brown black mixture. Mommy looks nice too. She's a pink woman—real fat, short, has black brown and blonde mixed hair—and she's wearing a black flower print dress too. I'm having fun in my new home.

But Freda's world of joy collapsed at age three, a critical year that introduced abuse and chronic illness into her life. Her best memories of childhood relate to her grandmother and her worst to her mother. Her father remained a distant figure; he was abusive but not cruel as was her mother. Here are snapshots highlighting that digression to a world less safe, less caring, less free:

I'm three years old. I wish I were still having fun like I used to, but I'm not. Today I was left at a mean, fat, Black lady's home. She hates me. I can tell. She locked me in a closet with no food, water, light, or com-fort. I'm hungry and stinky. I keep crying, but my tears fall on deaf ears and a very cold heart. (Time passes.)

About a month has passed now, and I've not only been strapped in a high chair and locked in a closet by my baby-sitter, but I have also been beaten by this mean woman. (Time passes.)

I don't know what day it is today, but I almost died. My mother strapped me in the high chair and started cooking dinner. Oops, she forgot something. She asks Brenda to watch me while she goes to the corner store, and to turn off the food in five minutes. Ouida is at a sleepover and Eugene is asleep in his room. Brenda decides to sneak off to see her boyfriend. Before she leaves, she tells Eugene to watch me. Eugene isn't fully awake and doesn't understand what she tells him. He sleeps a few minutes more, then gets up and goes out to find his friends to play football. He leaves me by myself trapped in the high chair in the kitchen. Thank heavens he couldn't find them. He comes back home and my father pulls up at the same time. Daddy is here to pick me up so I can spend time with him and Grandma. Eugene and Daddy come upstairs. They smell smoke. They think the Jamaicans on the second floor are cooking again, but they're wrong. Eugene opens the front door and smoke rushes out. They hear me crying. They find me in the kitchen surrounded by fire. They grab a couple of blankets and start to beat the flames out. Dad turns the stove off. They check to see if anybody else is around. Nobody. So then Mom comes in, and she and Dad get into a fight over leaving me home alone. He beats her and dares her to call the police. He yells at her that she shouldn't have left Brenda in charge of me because Brenda is boy crazy and irresponsible. That was their only fight I'd ever seen. He tells her as he's leaving with me to straighten up her fucking act or he'll kick her ass again. He takes me to see my grandma for the entire summer.

In August, a month before my fourth birthday, my mother says she wants me to come home. One week later, while she's ironing her work clothes, I start crying. I'm strapped in the high chair next to Mom. I'm hungry. I keep crying and telling her to the best of my ability that I'm hungry, I wanna eat, I want food. She gets angry and yells at me to shut up. I keep crying. In a fit of rage she says, "You wanna eat?! Fine, eat this, baby!" and proceeds to bend me over and burn me on my back with the iron. I cry more and louder. How could she be so mean to me? I never did get breakfast, but I was taken to the emergency room at Children's Hospital. They asked what happened, and she claimed I was playing near the iron when it fell on my back. What did I do to deserve this cruel, hateful act? She never once regretted it. Not for even one second. I was only three years old when all this terror started happening to me.

A week or two later, I go to the hospital but don't know why. They keep me for a week to run some tests. Finally, as I'm going home, my parents are told I've arthritis, bronchitis, and epilepsy and that an anxiety attack had set off all three. They explain there's no cure for any of the problems, but, with medication, they can be controlled. This was the start of a long history of going in and out of hospitals and receiving tons of medication. I took every pill imaginable up till the age of eleven: Dilantin, phenobarbital, codeine, uppers, downers, legal and illegal drugs, red pills, yellow pills, green and blue pills, white pills, star pills, moon pills, round pills, long pills, short pills, big pills and little pills, and every other size and shape possible to think of.

Beginning at age three, Freda lived more with her grandmother than her mother, and by seven she stayed mostly with her grandmother. Her disabilities prevented her from walking, running, and playing until age nine, and her attendance at school was infrequent and sporadic during those early years. Her teachers misunderstood her epilepsy, and she was usually removed from school abruptly by two months into the academic year. That meant staying home with her grandmother. The two became best friends over time; they did everything together and could talk about everything. Freda's grandmother sewed her dresses, and they shopped together and frequented their favorite restaurants. Today Freda remains spiritually connected to her grandmother, who structured her moral life and mentored her. Freda's most treasured memories are of moments shared with her grandmother.

When Freda was five, her sister Linda was born. Linda cried a lot, and Freda resented almost everything about her. Some of Freda's best times with her mother were in conjunction with Linda's father, however. He was a boxer and took the family to the beach and nice restaurants. And he bought Freda's mother a pink Cadillac. There were some happy times in there. But mostly Freda remembers her mother for her drunkenness and cruelty. She was mean-spirited and regularly beat all her children except Linda, the pampered sweetheart. She threw Eugene out of the house permanently when he was around age fourteen.

In 1975 Freda's mother relocated herself, Ouida, Freda, and Linda to her birthplace, Toledo, to be near her birth family and to rejoin her oldest daughter, Brenda. They all stayed with Brenda and her family until Freda's mother secured a job and an apartment. By this time Freda had outgrown much of her early illness. She was nine years old and enrolled in the third grade. She loved school and for the first time was able to run and play with friends. These Toledo days were marred by two destructive apartment fires, one resulting from Freda's mother's careless cooking and the other from a faulty coal-burning stove. Also, Freda missed her grandmother terribly. After a year or two, for some unknown reason, Freda's mother moved everyone back to Boston, where they stayed for a few months in Freda's father's house.

Then they returned to Ohio to stay once again with Brenda, who was now living in Youngstown with her children and new husband, Gus. For Freda, this year in Youngstown was devastating—for months she was continually raped by Gus. Freda spoke out, but her cries fell on deaf ears. Her mother and Brenda would hear nothing of it. Freda was relieved when they found a place of their own away from Gus. But the horrors were not over yet. On one occasion she was molested while visiting a girlfriend; the friend's uncle cornered her in the bedroom but was interrupted by another of Freda's friends who happened by. Hearing of this incident, Freda's mother had her checked at the hospital. Tests indicated that Freda was two months pregnant with twins. Freda explains:

My mother had a talk with the doctors and they gave me an abortion on the spot. It was so horrifying. Both babies looked like space alien creatures from the movie *Aliens*, starring Sigourney Weaver. I've always regretted everything that happened when I was twelve.

In the context of this sexual abuse and Freda's abortion, Freda's mother's alcoholism was progressively debilitating her; she was never without her glass of gin, and her brutality intensified with time.

Again, for some unknown reason, the family was disrupted. Freda and Linda were returned to Boston to live with their fathers while their mother remained in Ohio. Then, four days after her thirteenth birthday and having just entered sixth grade, Freda's grandmother informed her after school that her mother had died. Freda expresses her ambivalence:

I said, "Well, that's the way life goes." After a while, I went into the bedroom and jumped for joy, but then a few hours later I actually cried myself to sleep because something in me said this is nothing to be happy over. I don't even know how she died. I mean, I tried to convince her to stop drinking for years, and something inside said that she really didn't deserve to die that way. I had this interesting dream where she was wearing this white dress and these big white wings, and she comes and she says, "I'm all right, honey—I've been forgiven." She said, "Don't worry about me; you will be okay. I will always be near you." I'm like, yeah, right, okay! So I don't know what's going on here. This nice-looking angel is supposed to be my mother? She floats up into the air, and that's all they ever wrote. I'm like, yeah, right; I know that woman ain't in no damn heaven.

Freda continued living in her father's house beyond high school graduation, until she was twenty-seven. Junior high and high school days were her best: she was active in choir, chorus, and several sports. Friends and family occupied her, including her older fraternal siblings and their children, many of whom were near her age. She avoided boys, alcohol, and illicit drugs and remains free of any substance abuse. Her beloved grandmother's wise and gentle hand anchored her and ushered her through adolescence without a hitch. Then at seventeen Freda lost her grandmother to "old age." She is conspicuously silent on the matter—when pressed, says she just went on. But life deteriorated after that. It was as though she and her father had lost all common ground; they argued incessantly. Freda has yet to regain that sense of well-being kindled by the presence of her grandmother.

THE ABUSIVE RELATIONSHIP

Freda was twenty-two, living with her father and Ruth, and seeking employment. Since graduating from high school at nineteen, she had worked intermittently and would continue to do so until the birth of her first child. She met Larry early one morning while leaving the hospital after having been treated for a fever. He was near the bus stop. It was love at first sight for Freda. For an entire year she had dreamed of falling in love with a stranger, and Larry was her dream come true. Larry was nearly twenty-seven, dependent on general relief, unemployed, and homeless; he stayed at a local homeless shelter. From the beginning his life chances were severely compromised by his family circumstances. Of French-Creole and Blackfoot Indian descent, he was the twelfth of sixteen children born to a woman entrenched in poverty and openly abused by her husband. He recalls the regularity with which the older boys jumped in to rescue his mother from the beatings. Larry dropped out of high school to help support his siblings and ultimately digressed to a world of substance abuse and unemployment. For the most part his siblings champion lives of drugs, prostitution, and incarceration.

For a month or so Freda and Larry simply enjoyed one another's company. They went to the park, took long walks, and frequented the aquarium and museums. Then Freda introduced Larry to her father and soon thereafter requested that he be allowed to move into the house. Freda's father complied, with the condition that Larry get a job and pay rent. Now the household was expanded to include Freda, her father, Ruth, Blue the dog, and Larry, who had a room of his own.

In the months that followed, another side of Larry surfaced. The first incident occurred within two months and involved the accusation of infidelity. Here is Freda's account:

He started talking about I was having an affair with Dieter Lambaur next door. I said he'd lost his mind and he slapped me. I shoved a piece of cake in his face and we began to fight. I punched him; he punched me. I kicked him; he kicked me. We went back and forth until he wrestled me to the ground and kicked me in the ribs. I got up after I caught my breath and called the police. He was escorted to the bus stop.

Larry stayed away from home several weeks, then approached Freda apologetically, promising that it would never happen again if she were to take him back. She loved him and much between them was still good, so she took the chance.

Despite Freda's protest, Larry's drinking intensified, and the abuse resumed. Soon a major confrontation resulted in Freda injuring Larry. Freda recalls:

I told him to leave me alone because I was fixing dinner. He kept trying to egg me on into a fight. He said I was having an affair with a White boy. I said, "Go watch TV so you can keep fantasizing." He told me, "Bitch, don't you ever insult me by telling me what the fuck to do." I told him to either get out of the kitchen or there'd be a problem. He said, yeah, the problem would be for my fucking ass. He tried to get into a wrestling match with me, but I turned my back on him and went on cutting vegetables. When he tried to hurt me, I decided to pretend that I was going to kill myself. When he approached me, instead of hurting myself, I sliced the palm of his hand with the big meat knife. He punched me in the ribs, then went to see Dr. Emma.

For the next several months Larry's abuse was limited to verbal attacks. A couple of months after the cutting incident, in February 1988, he began skipping work and moping around the house, so Freda's father evicted him. He returned to shelter life, where he remains to this day, with no significant impact on his and Freda's relationship. That same month Freda discovered she was pregnant.

Larry was particularly kind and loving to Freda during this and the pregnancies that followed. She describes him as a "Dr. Jekyll/Mr. Hyde." Most of the time he was sweet, reserved, interesting, fun-loving, and romantic. He charmed and pampered her, and she enjoyed pampering him in return. He would put her "on a pedestal as tall as the Empire State Building" and she would "feel so special." But then there were the yelling, criticism, and moodiness. And there were the periodic episodes of rage that always included name-calling—slut, bitch, witch, lesbian whore—and nearly always focused on Freda's imaginary White lovers. Once in a while these episodes culminated in physical violence. Freda continued to hope that Larry would stop hurting her, as promised; she wondered if the guy with whom she originally fell in love would ever resurface—but he never did.

The next physical attack occurred seven months into the pregnancy, this time accompanied by a death threat. Clearly the abuse was escalating. Freda claims to have won that fight—by kicking Larry with her work boots hard and repeatedly in the groin, ribs, and legs. She fled her home, in fear for her safety, to stay with Boston relatives, behavior that would become a pattern throughout this abusive relationship. Freda returned home two weeks later. Larry stayed away for a while.

Larry was present at Nathaniel's birth in October to cut the umbilical cord. But shortly thereafter he again accused and threatened Freda. She reflects:

When the doctors left the room for a minute, Larry said he was going to kick my ass later because he had proof now that I'd been seeing a White boy. He asked who was Nathaniel's father, who was the White boy. He thought Nathaniel was a White boy's baby because he thought Black children automatically came out brown-skinned. I explained all babies come out prunish- or pink-colored unless both parents are dark brown. He asked the doctors if I was right and they all said I was.

When Freda returned home with Nathaniel two days later, flowers and candy awaited her. Larry had sent them by messenger because Freda's father forbade him to come around the house. Near Christmas he gave her $250 for baby clothes. That was the only financial support she would ever get from Larry for Nathaniel and their three subsequent children.

Larry's abuse first intersected with the criminal justice system when Nathaniel was five months old. Late one night Larry sneaked into the house high and drunk to taunt Freda. Ultimately, the entire family was drawn into the resulting violent episode: Freda suffered a "fat lip" and bruises; her father got a "black eye" and was knocked down; Nathaniel was slapped in the face; Ruth was shoved into the bathroom; and Blue was hit on the head. Freda called the police, and Larry was arrested. She and her father filed a formal complaint later on that morning. Larry spent a month in jail and another seven on probation. The first of a series of yearlong restraining orders against Larry was granted. Freda would continually renew them, then call the police only when Larry arrived in his "Mr. Hyde" mode. Three or four times a year he would be arrested and detained for several hours.

Freda's life circumstances remained constant, and over the next two years she had two more sons by Larry: Richard and Keith. She had wanted two children, a girl and a boy, and was willing to continue trying for that girl. She loved her sons and was able to care for and support them with the help of her father and AFDC. Larry took some interest in the children: he stopped by to see them two or three times a week and, once in a while, took the family out. He remained obsessed with Freda's sexual activity, checking to see if her bed was unmade and becoming uneasy if the house was too clean—as if in anticipation of company. It was during this time that the abuse went public—shouting matches initiated by Larry at department stores and bus stops and on street corners—and continued to escalate. Freda kept it all to herself to the extent possible; she attempted to cover her bruises with makeup and sometimes unseasonably concealing clothing. Larry continued to be the worst—and the best—part of Freda's life.

GETTING OUT

When Nathaniel was a year old, Freda knew that Larry would never change and that ultimately she would have to get out of her relationship with him. Hope had diminished. He would promise to get treatment and stop drinking but then would not or could not follow through. Freda's energies were consumed with keeping her growing family in check; that included caring for her now elderly father and scrambling around to maintain the quickly deteriorating house that with time would be condemned, leaving her homeless. Years would pass before she would muster up the resources necessary to make the break. Also, there would have to be a precipitating incident—and that was still over the horizon. For now, it was simply easier to endure it all for another day than to orchestrate such dramatic change. Furthermore, once, when Freda was carrying Keith, Larry threatened, "If I can't have you, nobody will." She knew that, for now anyway, he would not let her just slip away.

In January 1991, when Keith was a month old, Freda and her father took him to the hospital with a cold and temperature of 104.9. Tests indicated that Keith was infected with the HIV virus. Freda, Larry, and the other two boys were tested and retested soon thereafter: Freda and Larry tested HIV positive, but the boys' test results were negative. It was later that Freda learned that since Richard's birth Larry had had several affairs and had in fact fathered two other children. At the same time, he had used street drugs intravenously. In the midst of this testing, Freda became pregnant again, and in January 1992 she delivered her and Larry's daughter, Nitanju, who at first tested HIV positive. Today only Freda and Larry carry the virus; the four children now test HIV negative.

Just prior to Nitanju's birth, in November 1991, the house was condemned and its residents rendered homeless. Freda's father was in a hospital at the time and was later transferred to a nursing home, where he eventually died. Ruth found an apartment, and Freda placed Richard and Keith with her paternal sister Sally while she and Nathaniel lived with Linda. A few weeks later Freda and all three boys were in Linda's home. Then, in 1992, after Nitanju arrived, everyone lived with Ouida for two months, until with the help of welfare, they relocated to first one hotel, then another. In June Freda acquired a subsidized-housing voucher and found an apartment in nearby Brockton.

Freda's homelessness and resulting transience reinforced her efforts to escape Larry. He stalked and taunted her, but she remained elusive as she moved from place to place. He would find her now and then, and she endured three life-threatening altercations that required outside intervention during that time (one while still in the hospital bed after having delivered Nitanju). Overall, however, Larry lost momentum in his campaign to control Freda. Though his desperation was apparent in the escalation of his violence, she was winning ground. She joined forces with an otherwise devastating set of circumstances in her attempt to achieve freedom from abuse. There was a restraining order in effect as usual, but now Freda called the police every time Larry threatened her. Larry had no legal access to the children, and Freda stopped granting visitation. It was all but over between them. She was nearly out.

In September tragedy struck again. Freda had grown to trust and respect Yvonne Montero, her longtime caseworker, as the two formed a partnership in the struggle to keep Freda's family together, housed, safe, and healthy. Then, after Nitanju's arrival, Ms. Montero was replaced by someone far less competent and compassionate—and a racist. This caseworker monitored Freda closely as she was shuffled from place to place, always threatening to take her children away from her. On one occasion she appeared on Freda's doorstep, flanked by two police officers in search of Larry. An exchange between Freda and one of the officers culminated in these words:

Bitch, don't come fuckin' screamin' at me just because you can't take care of your fuckin' bastardy nigga' children. I'll take your fuckin' kids 'cause I know I can do it. You want us to take the kids now, Miss Pachas?

When Freda left the Brockton apartment to return to Linda's home because her racist landlord was harassing her and Larry had found her yet again, this new social worker ordered the children taken from Freda and placed in foster care. She showed up at Linda's home unannounced and accompanied by five male police officers. While the others were collecting the children, a White officer unsuccessfully tried to rape her. Freda remembers:

He grabbed me, wrestled me down to the ground, fought me, pulled my underwear off, started feeling between my legs, saying, "You know you want it, bitch." And when I started yelling rape, he said, "Why don't you get some class, bitch." You know, and I'm like, "Excuse me; you're the one who tried to take my underwear off!"

Freda avoided the rape, but when it was over, her children were gone. Still today, she can list from memory the "reasons" provided by the Boston Municipal Court System:

My children had bad hygiene;
my children had poor nutrition;
I didn't love my children;
my children were subjected to drug abuse;
my children were subjected to domestic violence;
my children lived in a filthy environment;
my children had insufficient medical care;
my children had poor education;
my son Richard didn't get timely care for a burn on his leg; and
my children were homeless.

Her service plan for renewed custody included the requirement that she occupy safe, permanent housing. But without the public assistance allowed by the custody of her children (AFDC), Freda was unequipped to secure such housing. Especially considering her health circumstances, she was and remains unable to earn enough income to support the family.

It is more than three years later, and Freda's children remain in foster care. Technically, she is allowed one hour of visitation per child per week at the offices of the Department of Social Services. But in reality, she gets much less. At the hands of the state, the children have suffered many different kinds of physical abuse. This mother's pain resonates through her voice:

My daughter was molested in the foster homes. I could not believe it— they would take an eight-month-old baby and actually do such things to this child. She showed up at one visit with the most disgusting diaper rash I have ever seen. There were puss and blood and sores between her legs. It looked like someone had taken a damn clothes iron and pressed it between her legs. She had welts. I have never seen anything so disgusting in my whole damn life! I tried to get something done about that, but nothing was done. I tried to get something done about the fact that the kids were being beaten, but there was nothing done about that. I kept complaining about the diaper rashes every week I came to visit. It just went on and on endlessly.

Since the children were taken, Freda has occupied five homeless shelters, two battered women's shelters, and one apartment and currently resides in her second transitional shelter (where residents must be in compliance with an official housing plan).

The loss of the children provided the death blow to Freda's abusive relationship with their father. From her perspective, the two no longer shared any common ground. Larry would not and never had joined Freda's struggles for family unity. He had nothing to contribute to her now transformed life, which was bent on reclaiming the children. From his perspective, there was no longer a need to control her. She was under control: the combination of the HIV contamination and the loss of children had devastated her. He could rest assured that her wings were clipped. Since September 1992 Freda's and Larry's interaction has been limited to brief cordial exchanges when they meet in public by chance.

Freda's recent unplanned pregnancy has resurrected Larry's agenda of reinstating his dominance over her. Word of his stalking and death threats filter back to her. Natalie is now three months old, and Larry has yet to find Freda, who surmises that he learned of the pregnancy by word of mouth and resents her continued sexual activity (her partner, Natalie's father, tested HIV positive years before she met him). She was not under Larry's control after all.

Natalie's birth has introduced new hope for bringing the family together once more. Her AFDC stipend will allow Freda to secure a subsidized apartment. With that housing assured, she can regain custody of the other four children. Then, with the subsidies she will get for those children, she plans to be able to survive.

REFLECTIONS

Freda views her life as heavily textured with racism and government ineptitude. Her job, as she sees it, is to learn the survival skills to get her through. Larry is a victim of many of the same forces, and in that sense she feels akin to him. He was wrong to hurt her, but in the larger scheme of things, she sees him primarily as a victim.

A Message for Battered Women

Things are improving for battered women. Awareness, attitudes, and laws all around us are changing to protect and benefit them and their children, and there are more resources than ever before, including educational materials, shelters, hotlines, organizations, and agencies. Since the airing of *The Burning Bed*, a true story about a Michigan housewife who resorted to killing her abuser in self-defense, introduced television viewers to battering in 1984, cases and stories have come to light in shocking numbers. People are becoming aware of the widespread nature of domestic violence against women, its devastating effect on women, men, children, and families, and the tragic consequences of turning away.

The highly publicized 1996 brutal slaying of the battered Nicole Brown Simpson did much to advance the cause for battered women. Blow-by-blow accounts of a battering relationship dominated the media for eighteen months, teaching the American public how to identify violent battering and demonstrating that batterers can be successful, handsome, gifted men—even heroes—and that even women who appear to have ample means of escape through money, intelligence, family, and friends can remain trapped in controlling and violent relationships. We as a nation have become much smarter about battering and, as a result, much less tolerant of it. And that lowered threshold of tolerance is producing a safer world for women.

Laws dealing with domestic violence against women have been springing up at an accelerated pace for two decades now (Berry 1998, 141–191). Women have come a long way since the days when they could legally be beaten by their husbands as long as they used a stick no larger in diameter than their thumb—hence, "the rule of thumb" (Dobash and Dobash 1979:56–57). Most states now have special laws setting criminal penalties for domestic physical abuse. One of the most important changes to come about as states have modified or enacted laws that specifically address domestic violence is the exception to the usual requirement that a police officer must witness a misdemeanor in action in order to make an arrest. In all states an arresting officer responding to a domestic violence call need now have only probable cause to believe that a crime has been committed, and seeing a woman's injuries will generally suffice for the officer to have such probable cause. Also, by statute or policy, most law enforcement officers are required or strongly encouraged to arrest an abuser rather than try to mediate the "dispute" or require the abuser to leave temporarily. Historically, some insurance companies have denied health, life, and disability insurance to battered women, characterizing physical abuse as a "preexisting condition" or on the ground that abuse is a "lifestyle choice"—like smoking or skydiving. Now many states have passed or introduced legislation prohibiting insurance companies from discriminating against abuse victims. Stalking is a frequent problem for women who have left a violent relationship. Until 1990 no state recognized stalking as a separate crime. Today all states have enacted stalking laws, although most of those laws are far from adequate in the protection that they provide stalking victims.

In 1984 the U.S. government issued its first official statement denouncing domestic abuse as a serious crime when Congress passed the Family Violence Prevention and Services Act into federal law. That act and its companion, the Victims of Crime Act, wor together to provide federal funds to help states and local communities develop and support shelters, coordinate research efforts, conduct training, compensate victims, and continue related activities.

President Clinton reaffirmed federal-level commitment to the safety of women in their homes when he signed the Violence Against Women Act as part of the Violent Crime Control and Law Enforcement Act of 1994. The Violence Against Women Act authorizes 1.2 billion dollars over five years for criminal justice programs and social services to aid battered women and sexual assault victims. That act also established a new civil rights claim for women who are victims of crimes motivated by gender. It states that such crimes violate a woman's civil rights; this means a woman can sue the perpetrator who violates this law for compensatory, punitive, and other damages. In 1996 Clinton established the first Violence Against Women Office in the Justice Department to coordinate the various federal efforts in support of the Violence Against Women Act.

THE DOMESTIC VIOLENCE HOTLINE

Clearly, today is a better time than a hundred years ago, or even twenty years ago, for a woman to leave a batterer. Understanding and help are available for the asking. If you or someone you care about needs help or just a sympathetic ear, there are plenty of resources out there. Perhaps the most important resource is a single phone number. A nationwide twenty-four-hour toll-free domestic violence hotline was established by the Violence Against Women Act and put into operation on February 21, 1996. This hotline can be used in two ways. First, it can be used as a comprehensive general resource. That means that if you are considering or even just pondering leaving an abuser and your needs are not immediate, you may call the hotline simply to test your thoughts on someone with knowledge and experience in the area. Operators are trained to listen, to provide counseling, and to offer information about how to begin seeking help and support in your particular community. They have lists of local, regional, and state-level, as well as nationwide, organizations and services that exist to help battered women, most of which operate free of charge. Second, the hotline may be used in a crisis. If the situation is urgent, the hotline operator stands ready to offer emergency counseling, to refer you to emergency services and shelters in your community, and to assist battered women and those who want to help them in reporting abuse to authorities.

The National Domestic Violence Hotline numbers are:

1–800–799-SAFE (7233)
and
1–800–787–3224 (TDD) (for the hearing impaired)

These numbers provide help to all callers, including those who do not speak English.

In addition to calling the hotline, there are many other ways to learn more about battering and to help to prepare for a safe exit from abuse. I suggest that you begin your journey to freedom by consulting two particularly helpful resource books designed specifically to advise battered women: Marian Betancourt's *What to Do When Love Turns Violent: A Practical Resource for Women in Abusive Relationships* (1997) and Dawn Bradley Berry's *The Domestic Violence Sourcebook* (1998). These books will equip you with the basics of what you need to know in order to escape abuse safely and with your rightful belongings. They even include sections about how to begin building a life without violence once you are free. Never underestimate the importance of educating yourself for a long slippery battle to liberate yourself and your children from the firm clutches of a controller.

Betancourt (1997) will take your hand and stay with you through every twist and turn of the seemingly endless process of fits, starts, and reversals so characteristic of the journey out. She will instruct you about how to work with police, lawyers, and other elements of the criminal justice system. Of particular importance is her detailed advice about obtaining a protective order with "teeth." Betancourt prepares her readers for trips to the doctor's office and the emergency room, and advises them on getting proper medical treatment and on how they can obtain and preserve medical information that will strengthen their legal case against their batterer.

Betancourt also provides detailed instructions for designing various types of personalized safety plans. She emphasizes the need for safety plans for home, for work, and for children at school. Long-term safety plans are as important as immediate ones. Just think of Sharon's and Blanca's well-developed and successfully executed long-term plans to escape safely.

In addition, Betancourt takes special care to prepare her readers for divorce court. I concur with her advice to battered women to make every effort to avoid joint custody. A controller cannot be trusted to carry out that kind of an agreement, which is dependent upon the goodwill and cooperation of two people of equal power.

If breaking free from your abuser involves divorce, I recommend a third book, Karen Winner's *Divorced from Justice: The Abuse of Women and Children by Divorce Lawyers and Judges* (1996). This feminist New York City investigative reporter and former policy analyst will inform you of the misogyny, corruption, and incompetence that lie at the heart of the U.S. family court system and put you on the offensive as you prepare to battle for divorce, child custody, and property.

These books by Betancourt, Berry, and Winner are filled not only with seasoned knowledge, wisdom, and advice but also with a gold mine of resource listings. Here is an outline of those listings:

Marian Betancourt, *What to Do When Love Turns Violent*—

Appendix A: What's Available in Your Community: A State-by-State Guide to Resources

Appendix B: National Domestic Violence Organizations and Other Services (includes special listings related to the needs of the elderly, minorities and immigrants, and children)

Appendix C: Books and Videos About Domestic Violence (includes special listings for ethnic women, women of color, and children)

Dawn Bradley Berry, *The Domestic Violence Sourcebook*—

Resources and Suggested Readings (includes special listings about battered women of color and violence in gay and lesbian relationships)

National Organizations (annotated)

State Coalitions

Local Programs (this is a paragraph instructing how to use a telephone book to locate the various kinds of local resources)

Internet Websites

Other Sources of Information, Referrals, and Help

Karen Winner, *Divorced from Justice*—

Appendix 1: Addresses and Telephone Numbers of Lawyer Disciplinary Agencies, Lawyer Funds for Client Protection, and Judicial Commissions

Appendix 2: Organizations and Resource Numbers (annotated, and includes special sections on self-help organizations for women, legal organizations, battered women's services, and an invitation to visit Karen Winner on the Internet for more information on women, children, and consumers dealing with the inner workings of the U.S. courts)

Published lists of resources are generally outdated by the time they appear in print, but remember that the National Domestic Violence Hotline can update you on many of these listings, especially those pertaining directly to domestic violence.

Battered women typically maintain a precarious balance between fear and hope. When the fear finally overcomes the hope, a battered woman wants to leave. Then she must weigh the comparative risks of staying and leaving. If the man is violent, she must consider the possibility of serious injury to herself and others. The battered woman herself is the best judge of her abuser's potential for harm because she has lived by his signals and patterns. She can predict the context, timing, and intensity of his explosions. Listen to your inner voice. You know when you are safe and when you are not. You know if you can manage to get out safely now or if a long-term safety plan will have to do. You may be the recipient of much advice, some solicited and some not, but never forget that you know more about this man, yourself, and your children than anyone. Fear serves an important purpose in guiding us to safety (De Becker 1997). Do not ignore it.

Evidence tells us that if your partner is a batterer and shows no signs of changing, reasoning with him and trying to help him change is a losing proposition. It is draining, probably futile, and possibly dangerous. When that becomes clear to you, it is time to turn the focus away from him and toward yourself and your children. We all have fundamental rights: "The right to speak your mind. The right to privacy, choices, some free time, some money of your own, friends, work, bodily integrity, freedom from fear, treatment with respect and dignity" (NiCarthy 1997, 42). The women whose lifestories grace the pages of this book found ways to reclaim those rights. Many of them told their stories in hopes that you and other women held captive by the men in their lives will gain from their accounts of their losses and find strength and inspiration in their courage and tenacity.

References

Acker, Joan. 1989. "Making Gender Visible." In *Feminism and Sociological Theory*, edited by Ruth A. Wallace. Thousand Oaks, CA.: Sage.

Bachman, Ronet. 1992. *Death and Violence on the Reservation: Homicide, Family Violence, and Suicide in American Indian Populations.* New York: Auburn House.

Bachman, Ronet and Linda E. Saltzman. 1995. *Violence Against Women: Estimates from the Redesigned Survey* (NCJ–154348). Washington, DC: U.S. Bureau of Justice Statistics. August.

Bernard, Jessie. 1972. "Marriage: Hers and His." *Ms.* December: 46–49, 110–111.

Berry, Dawn Bradley. 1998. *The Domestic Violence Sourcebook.* Los Angeles: Lowell House.

Betancourt, Marian. 1997. *What to Do When Love Turns Violent: A Practical Resource for Women in Abusive Relationships.* New York: Harper Perennial.

Brantenberg, Gerd. 1985. *Egalia's Daughters: A Satire of the Sexes.* Seattle: Seal.

Campbell, Jacqueline C. and Daniel J. Sheridan. 1989. "Emergency Nursing Interventions with Battered Women." *Journal of Emergency Nursing* 15: 12–17.

Castiglia, Christopher. 1996. *Bound and Determined: Captivity, Culture-Crossing, and White Womanhood from Mary Rowlandson to Patty Hearst.* Chicago: University of Chicago Press.

Clifford, James. 1986. "Introduction: Partial Truths." Pp. 1–26 in *Writing*

Culture: The Poetics and Politics of Ethnography, edited by James Clifford and George E. Marcus. Berkeley: University of California Press.

Davies, Jill, Eleanor Lyon, and Diane Monti-Catania. 1998. *Safety Planning with Battered Women*. Thousand Oaks, CA: Sage.

De Becker, Gavin. 1997. *The Gift of Fear: Survival Signals That Protect Us from Violence*. Boston: Little, Brown.

Dobash, R. Emerson and Russell P. Dobash. 1979. *Violence Against Wives*. New York: Free Press.

Dobash, Russell P., R. Emerson Dobash, Margo Wilson, and Martin Daly. 1992. "The Myth of Sexual Symmetry in Marital Violence." *Social Problems* 39 (1): 71–91.

Dobash, Russell, Rebecca Dobash, Kate Cavanagh, and Ruth Lewis. 1998. "Separate and Intersecting Realities: A Comparison of Men's and Women's Accounts of Violence Against Women." *Violence Against Women* 4 (4): 382–414.

Dutton, Mary Ann. 1992. *Empowering and Healing the Battered Woman: A Model for Assessment and Intervention*. New York: Springer.

Ferraro, Kathleen J. and John M. Johnson. 1983. "How Women Experience Battering: The Process of Victimization." *Social Problems* 30 (3): 325–339.

Gerth, H. H. and C. Wright Mills, eds. and translators. 1946. *From Max Weber: Essays in Sociology*. New York: Oxford University Press.

Goetting, Ann. 1995. "Fictions of the Self." Pp. 3–19 in *Individual Voices, Collective Visions: Fifty Years of Women in Sociology*, edited by Ann Goetting and Sarah Fenstermaker. Philadelphia: Temple University Press.

——. 1996. "Ecofeminism Found: One Woman's Journey to Liberation." Pp. 174–179 in *Private Sociology: Unsparing Reflections, Uncommon Gains*, edited by Arthur B. Shostak. Dix Hills, NY: General Hall.

Graham, Dee L. R., Edna Rawlings, and Nelly Rimini. 1988. "Surviving of Terror: Battered Women, Hostages, and the Stockholm Syndrome." Pp. 217–233 in *Feminist Perspectives on Wife Abuse*, edited by Kersti Yllö and Michele Bograd. Thousand Oaks, CA: Sage.

Greenfield, Lawrence A., Michael R. Rand, Diane Craven, Patsy A. Klaus, Craig A. Perkins, Cheryl Ringel, Greg Warchol, Cathy Maston, and James Alan Fox. 1998. *Violence by Intimates: Analysis of Data on Crimes by Current or Former Spouses, Boyfriends, and Girlfriends* (NCJ–167237). Washington, DC: U.S. Bureau of Justice Statistics. March.

Gusdorf, Georges. 1980. "Conditions and Limits of Autobiography." Pp. 28–48 in *Autobiography: Essays Theoretical and Critical*, edited and translated by James Olney. Princeton, NJ: Princeton University Press.

Hendrickson, Roberta M. 1996. "Victims and Survivors: Native American Women Writers, Violence Against Women, and Child Abuse." *Studies in American Indian Literatures* 8 (1): 13–24.

Horton, Annie L. and Barry L. Johnson. 1993. "Profile and Strategies of Women Who Have Ended Abuse." *Families in Society: The Journal of Contemporary Human Services* 74 (8): 481–492.

Kirkwood, Catherine. 1993. *Leaving Abusive Partners*. Thousand Oaks, CA: Sage.

Kohli, Martin. 1981. "Biography: Account, Text, Method." Pp. 61–75 in *Biography and Society: The Life History Approach in the Social Sciences*, edited by Daniel Bertaux. Thousand Oaks, CA: Sage.

Kurz, Demie. 1996. "Separation, Divorce, and Woman Abuse." *Violence Against Women* 2 (1):63–81.

Lorber, Judith. 1994. *Paradoxes of Gender*. New Haven, CT: Yale University Press.

Marx, Linda. 1997. "Room Service: A Hotel Executive Turns Extra Rooms Into a Refuge for Women Running from Abuse." *Hope: Humanity Making a Difference* July/August: 14–17.

Mercy, James A. and Linda E. Saltzman. 1989. "Fatal Violence Among Spouses in the United States, 1976–1985." *American Journal of Public Health* 79: 595–599.

Mills, C. Wright. 1959. *The Sociological Imagination*. New York: Oxford University Press.

Moss, Vicki A., Carol Rogers Pitula, Jacquelyn C. Campbell, and Lois Halstead. 1997. "The Experience of Terminating an Abusive Relationship from an Anglo and African American Perspective: A Qualitative Descriptive Study." *Issues in Mental Health Nursing* 18: 433–454.

Mousseau, Marlin and Karen Artichoker. 1993. *Domestic Violence Is Not Lakota/Dakota Tradition*. Sisseton, SD: South Dakota Coalition Against Domestic Violence and Sexual Assault. To obtain free copy, call 1–800–572–9196, or write P.O. Box 141, Pierre, SD 57501.

NiCarthy, Ginny. 1997. *Getting Free: You Can End Abuse and Take Back Your Life*. Seattle: Seal Press.

Okun, Lewis. 1986. *Woman Abuse: Facts Replacing Myths*. Albany: State University of New York Press.

——. 1988. "Termination or Resumption of Cohabitation in Woman Battering Relationships: A Statistical Study." Pp. 107–119 in *Coping with Family Violence: Research and Policy Perspectives*, edited by Gerald T. Hotaling, David Finkelhor, John T. Kirkpatrick, and Murray A. Straus. Thousand Oaks, CA: Sage.

Pfeufer Kahn, Robbie. 1995. "Interviewing the Midwife's Apprentice: The Question of Voice in Writing a Cultural Ethnography of Patriarchy." Paper presented at annual meetings of the American Sociological Association, Washington, DC.

Riessman, Catherine Kohler. 1993. *Narrative Analysis*. Thousand Oaks, CA: Sage.

Salts, Connie J. 1979. "Divorce Process: Integration of Theory." *Journal of Divorce* 2 (3): 233–240.

Straton, J. C. 1994. "The Myth of the 'Battered Husband Syndrome,' " *Masculinities* 2: 79–82.

Straus, Murray A. 1977–78. "Wife-Beating: How Common and Why?" *Victimology* 2: 443–458.

——. 1986. "Medical Care Costs of Intrafamily Assault and Homicide." *Bulletin of the New York Academy of Medicine* 62: 556–561.

——. 1993. "Physical Assaults by Wives: A Major Social Problem." Pp. 67–87 in *Current Controversies on Family Violence*, edited by Richard J. Gelles and Donileen R. Loseke. Thousand Oaks, CA: Sage.

Straus, Murray A. and Richard J. Gelles. 1990. "How Violent Are American Families? Estimates from the National Family Violence Resurvey and Other Studies." Pp. 95–112 in *Physical Violence in Families: Risk Factors and Adaptations to Violence in 8,145 Families*, edited by Murray A. Straus and Richard J. Gelles with Christine Smith. New Brunswick, NJ: Transaction.

Strube, Michael J. and Linda S. Barbour. 1984. "Factors Related to the Decision to Leave an Abusive Relationship." *Journal of Marriage and the Family* 46 (4): 837–844.

Szinovacz, Maximiliane E. 1983. "Using Couple Data as a Methodological Tool: The Case of Marital Violence." *Journal of Marriage and the Family* 45: 633–644.

Tannen, Deborah. 1990. *You Just Don't Understand*. New York: William Morrow.

Tompkins, Jane. 1989. "Me and My Shadow." Pp. 169–78 in *Gender and Theory: Dialogues on Feminist Criticism*, edited by Linda Kauffman. Oxford: Basil Blackwell.

U.S. Department of Labor, Bureau of Labor Statistics. 1996. *Usual Weekly Earnings of Wage and Salary Workers: Fourth Quarter 1995*, Table 6. February 15.

Walker, Lenore E. 1979. *The Battered Woman*. New York: Harper and Row.

White, Evelyn C. 1995. *Chain Chain Change: For Black Women in Abusive Relationships*. Seattle: Seal.

Wilson, Margo and Martin Daly. 1993. "Spousal Homicide Risk and Estrangement." *Violence and Victims* 8: 3–16.

Winner, Karen. 1996. *Divorced from Justice: The Abuse of Women and Children by Divorce Lawyers and Judges*. New York: Regan Books.

Wiseman, Reva S. 1975. "Crisis Theory: The Process of Divorce." *Social Casework* 56 (4): 205–212.

Zambrano, Myra M. 1985. *Mejor Sola Que Mal Acompanada: Para la Mujer Golpeada/For the Latina in an Abusive Relationship*. Seattle: Seal.

——. 1994. *No Mas! Guia Para la Mujer Golpeada*. Seattle: Seal.